Office Productivity Pack

Laurie Ulrich

201 West 103rd Street, Indianapolis, Indiana 46290

Office Productivity Pack

International Standard Book Number: 0-7897-1727-1

Library of Congress Catalog Number: 98-85291

Printed in the United States of America

First Printing: September 1998

00 99 98   4 3 2 1

Trademarks

EXECUTIVE EDITOR
Angie Wethington

ACQUISITIONS EDITOR
Stephanie J. McComb

DEVELOPMENT EDITORS
Lorna Gentry
John Gosney

MANAGING EDITOR
Thomas F. Hayes

PROJECT EDITOR
Lori Lyons

COPY EDITOR
Julie McNamee

INDEXER
C.J. East

TECHNICAL EDITOR
Bill Bruns

SOFTWARE DEVELOPMENT SPECIALIST
Andrea Duvall

PRODUCTION TEAM
Lynne Miles-Morillo
Cheryl Lynch
Megan Wade

Contents at a Glance

Table of Contents

Dedication

When Macmillan approached me about writing *Office Productivity Pack*, they asked me to submit an idea for a book that would be a true companion for the Office user. In coming up with my ideas for the book, I thought of my students—the 6000+ people I've trained to use computers since 1992. As I wrote this book, I remembered the secretaries and CEOs, the working moms and senior citizens, the wide spectrum of people I've met in my life as an instructor. My students have been a source of ideas and inspiration—they've shown me what works, what doesn't, and what keeps people interested. I dedicate this book to them.

About the Author

Laurie Ulrich has been writing computer books for Macmillan/Que for the past two years and is the author of *Using Word 97, Using PowerPoint 97, Que's Office Companion with CD-ROM,* and the upcoming *Special Edition Using Excel 2000* and *The Complete Idiot's Guide to Running Your Small Office.* In addition to writing, Laurie teaches computer classes and writes training materials for universities and corporate training centers in the Pennsylvania, New Jersey, and the New York area, and has been doing so since 1992. She also runs her own firm, Limehat & Company, Inc., specializing in technical documentation, multimedia presentations, and Web page development. She can be reached at `Limehat@aol.com` and welcomes your comments and questions.

Acknowledgments

Writing my acknowledgments is no easy task. I feel like the poor guy on the stage at the Oscars, trying to remember everyone who helped with his movie—I'm afraid I'll leave someone out. At least in this venue, the music won't start and no supermodel will hustle me off the stage!

Everyone at Macmillan has been great to work with. I am grateful to Stephanie McComb for contacting me about this book. I'm glad I've had the chance to work with her and to write a book that I hope comes close to her vision for this project. Thanks also to Lorna Gentry, who started as my Development Editor, and then moved to a new position (I did *not* drive her to it!), and to John Gosney, who took up where she left off. On the rare occasions that I saw any dreaded colored text in my chapters, the suggestions were succinct, insightful, and improved the book. Thanks also to Bill Bruns, my Technical Editor, for a very thorough yet practical job. We (the readers and I) must also acknowledge Andrea Duvall for her tireless search for the best software to put on the CD—it's a great selection. Thanks also to Patrick Blattner, for the contributions he made to the CD.

I must thank my friends and family who are always understanding about my not being available when deadlines are approaching, who don't get upset when they hear me typing while we talk on the phone, and who excitedly await the release of my books. They put up a good front, anyway!

Thanks, finally, to Jasper for sleeping on my desk and pushing my papers on the floor, and to Robert for love, encouragement, and never doing the dishes.

Tell Us What You Think!

As the reader of this book, *you* are our most important critic and commentator. We value your opinion and want to know what we're doing right, what we could do better, what areas you'd like to see us publish in, and any other words of wisdom you're willing to pass our way.

As the Executive Editor for the General Desktop Applications team at Macmillan Computer Publishing, I welcome your comments. You can fax, email, or write me directly to let me know what you did or didn't like about this book—as well as what we can do to make our books stronger.

Please note that I cannot help you with technical problems related to the topic of this book, and that due to the high volume of mail I receive, I might not be able to reply to every message.

When you write, please be sure to include this book's title and author as well as your name and phone or fax number. I will carefully review your comments and share them with the author and editors who worked on the book.

Fax: 317-581-4663

E-mail: office@mcp.com

Mail: Angie Wethington
        General Desktop Applications
        Macmillan Computer Publishing
        201 West 103rd Street
        Indianapolis, IN 46290 USA

Introduction

If you've spent much time in bookstores or online looking for technical documentation on Windows applications, you have noticed that there are stacks of books on Microsoft Office, and most of them cover the same topics. What differentiates this book from the rest? Its accuracy, ease of use, and the attention to detail that the author, editors, and publishers give each book. This book is unique in that it wasn't designed to cover every feature and every command you'll encounter in your use of Microsoft Office. What sets this book apart from other Office books is the goal the author had in writing it.

My goal in writing this book was to provide you, the reader, with a book that could replace or supplement that Office expert that everyone wishes worked down the hall. In most offices, this person doesn't exist. If the person exists, they may explain things too quickly or not have the time to help you. This book, on the other hand, can be read and reread at your leisure, and will always be there when you need it. By including a really great CD with the book, full of templates, clip art, sound and animation files, and programs that will enhance your use of Office, this book is an unmatched resource.

In writing this book, I have used the successful techniques, analogies, and examples that have served me well the better part of this decade, teaching people to use Microsoft Office. As for the best-selling suite of business applications, the vast majority of the training I've done since the early nineties has been on Microsoft Office. I wanted to share the program features that my students found most useful—the ones that resulted in a student exclaiming "So *that's* how you do that!" When a particular feature creates excitement in the classroom, I know that skill I've just shared will make someone's job easier and their efforts more productive.

I hope that I've succeeded in my goal, and that you'll enjoy this book and its accompanying CD.

Who Should Use This Book?

Que's *Office Productivity Pack* is intended for any user who's familiar with the basics of the Office applications. Most people don't use all of the applications in whichever edition of Office that they have (Professional, Standard, Small Business, Home). The applications you do use, we assume you use fairly often and are comfortable with their basic features.

That's not to say this book isn't for Office beginners—many new users have to get up-to-speed on a seemingly advanced or esoteric feature quickly. This book is written for anyone needing to master a tool quickly and simply.

If you see yourself anywhere in this list, this *Office Productivity Pack* is for you:

- You already know one of the Microsoft Office applications and want to increase your knowledge of it and begin using the other applications.
- You recently began using Microsoft Office and must master a complex feature quickly.
- You've used older versions of Office and need to know how to use familiar features in a more recent release.
- You know how to use most or all of the Office applications on their own, but wish you knew how to use them together.

This list covers just about anyone, except for someone completely new to computers in general or new to Windows. If this sounds like you, you might try a book designed for a more basic user, on general computer topics or Windows specifically, such as *Easy Windows 98*.

How This Book Is Organized

This book is divided into five major parts, plus four helpful Appendixes. The book approaches the use and mastering of Office in a logical and linear fashion, by covering the following topics:

- Part I: Working with Office Applications—The Common Elements
- Part II: Getting Your Word's Worth
- Part III: Picking Up the Pace with Excel
- Part IV: Making a Statement with PowerPoint
- Part V: Fast and Flexible Database Management with Access
- Appendix A: Mouse Power
- Appendix B: Keyboard Shortcuts
- Appendix C: Getting the Help You Need
- Appendix D: What's on the CD

Part I is devoted to the features that are common to all the core Office applications—Word, Excel, PowerPoint, and Access. Most of the covered features apply only to the first three programs, as Access has fewer things in common with them. From opening a new file to saving it, to sharing files via email and the Web, to using OLE (Object Linking and Embedding) to link documents from any and all Office applications, this part enables you to share both your skills and your work across the applications.

Part II covers the most popular word processing program on the planet and takes you into features that many seasoned users don't know about or take full advantage of. Using, editing, and creating style to format text is just the beginning, followed by the use of tables, perhaps the most powerful (and often neglected) feature in Word. You'll find out how to handle long documents, to use Word's templates and build your own, and to use Word's automatic features to correct and build documents with quick and simple commands. The last section of this part tells you how to customize Word by adding and customizing toolbars and work with Word's Options to set new defaults that work the way you need to work.

Part III shows you how to get more done and get it done faster with Excel. Although you may know how to enter your data and perform simple calculations, the chapters in this section of the book show you quick and easy techniques for getting things done. Learn to use the keyboard's navigation keys to speed your data entry, and how to name your cells and ranges for even faster access in the future. Learn to make your spreadsheets look as professional or exciting as the audience and topic require, and how to make charts that convert your complex (and possibly dull) data into easily understood pictures. The last chapter, "Working with Excel Data," shows you how to use Excel as a database program—storing, sorting, and filtering thousands of records simply and quickly.

Part IV takes the casual PowerPoint user and turns him or her into a power user. From techniques for building a slide show in just minutes to the creation of charts and the use of clip art and drawing tools, this section of the book enhances your slide presentations more than you thought possible. Again, we've saved the best for last—the last chapter in this section, "Creating Dynamic Multimedia Effects," shows you how to create a narrated or self-running slide show complete with sound and animation.

Part V is only for users of the Professional Edition of Microsoft Office, as it covers Access, Microsoft's database management tool. Whereas Excel can handle list databases, this program enables you to build many tables of data and link them through creative and powerful queries and reports. This part of the book takes you from the beginning ("Building a Database") through the basic skills ("Editing and Reviewing Your Data") to the real power tools in Chapter 21, "Querying a Database." Part V of the book enables a new Access user to master the basic as well as the powerful tools of this seemingly complex program.

The Appendixes in this book give you extra information about using your mouse to open powerful shortcut menus, getting work done faster with keyboard shortcuts, and accessing Help files when you're not sure what to do or how to do it. Appendix D gives you a comprehensive list of what you'll find on the CD that comes with the book.

Conventions Used in This Book

This book was designed for users who utilize the mouse (with the left mouse button dominant) but also covers the use of the keyboard to activate menus, select commands, and use dialog boxes. The *hot keys*, those letters you see underlines in menus and dialog boxes, are underlined in the text. This makes it easier to take the procedures in the book and apply them to the software.

Whenever there is an icon that achieves the same goal as a menu command or keyboard shortcut, it appears in the left margin, alongside the procedure to which it relates, as shown below:

 Choose File, New or Press Ctrl + N to create a new document.

In this procedure you notice the underlined menu and command names. To use the underlined menu name, press your Alt key and this underlined letter. After you're inside the menu, press the underlined letter.

The figures throughout this book were created on the author's computer. My computer is set up with standard appearance and monitor settings. If your screen is slightly different, this will be due to your Control Panel's display settings for color, font size, and screen resolution.

Throughout the text, the following elements are used to alert you to quick alternatives, background information, and things to look out for:

TIP Look for this element to show you faster ways to do things that are being explained in the text. For example, Press Ctrl+A to select your entire Word document.

NOTE If there's anything that the author knows from experience or some behind-the-scenes information that will help you use a particular feature, you'll find it in a Note. For example, you can use your ruler to adjust your margins while in Page Layout view. Drag the gray section of the ruler inward to increase your margins, outward to decrease them. Your top and bottom margins can also be adjusted, dragging the gray area up to decrease, down to increase.

CAUTION

Cautions warn you of potential problems you'll encounter if you're not careful to avoid certain situations or when seemingly friendly commands are not executed in a specific way. For example, be very careful using Replace All in the Find and Replace dialog box. You can accidentally change text you didn't intend to if you haven't made use of the Match Case and/or Find whole words only options.

If another section of the book contains additional or related information on a given topic, you'll find it in the form of a reference:

▶ **See** "Using the Internet and World Wide Web" **p. 28**

You'll also find Internet references in the book, pointing you toward Web sites that contain helpful information, files, or programs that will enhance your use of a related feature. These references appear in Note format:

ON THE WEB

http://www.wavplace.com   If you need more sound files that we've provided on the CD, check this site for hundreds of sounds from TV, movies, cartoons, and other sources. They even take requests. Files at this site are in .WAV format and can be downloaded for free.

Working with Office Applications—
The Common Elements

Getting Started

Creating a New File

Taking the first step in any project is probably the most difficult. Depending on your comfort level with whatever the project might be, getting started can feel like a "leap of faith." Taking this leap, however, is made easier in Microsoft Office applications. Each time you start one of the Office programs, you are given a blank file—a document in Word, a spreadsheet in Excel, a slide in PowerPoint, or a table in Access.

Understanding the Blank Document

Just how blank is a blank document? Not very. Although it contains no text or numbers, the blank document contains many settings that have been built-in to allow you to get started with little or no preparation.

In a blank Word document, your margins are set to standards appropriate for a business letter. Your text is left justified, and your tabs are set at every half-inch. Your font is set to Times New Roman, and the font size is 10 points. Your seemingly blank Excel workbook is also based on a blank template, one that determines the size of your text and numbers, automatically left-aligns text, and right-aligns numbers. Hundreds of *default* settings enable you to jump in and start typing.

How is this achieved? Your blank document is based on a *template*, a foundation that enables you to concern yourself primarily with content, and worry about tweaking the document layout later.

Accessing the blank templates for any Office application is simple:

- In Word, just start the program. Word opens, giving you a blank document. Your cursor is blinking at you, awaiting your text. You can also choose New Office Document from your Start menu, and double-click Blank Document from the General tab (see Figure 1.1).

- Excel also gives you a blank workbook as soon as you open the program. If you prefer to use the Start menu, choose New Office Document, and double-click the Blank Workbook icon in the General tab.

- To begin with a blank presentation in PowerPoint, choose New Office Document from the Start menu, and double-click the Blank Presentation icon. If you start the PowerPoint application first, you can choose Blank Presentation from the starting dialog box.

- Starting a new database in Access is made easy by double-clicking the Blank Database icon in the General tab, which is also found by choosing New Office Document from the Start menu. If you begin by opening the Access application, you can choose Blank Database from the starting dialog box.

After you open your application and begin typing, you can always start a second blank document by clicking the New button on the toolbar. This gives you a new document, based on the Blank template.

FIG. 1.1
Choose from the icons in the General tab to open a blank document.

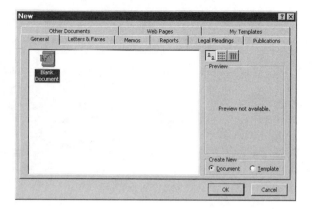

 In Office applications, the menu command File, New and the New File toolbar button don't work in exactly the same way. If you choose File, New, the New dialog box opens and you must select the Blank template (or other template) from the dialog box. If you click the toolbar button, a blank document opens with no questions asked.

These blank templates will meet your needs for most documents you'll create with Office—basic letters, standard spreadsheets, generic presentations, and typical databases. To meet more specific needs, however, Microsoft Office provides many other templates that may contain text, formatting, graphics, or preset fields to assist you in the creation of special documents.

Getting a Jump Start with Office Templates

The templates that Office provides for you are designed to make your life easier. Rather than worrying about how to construct an invoice, a resume, a business plan, or an inventory database, you can use these task-specific templates to lay a foundation that eliminates much of the design phase. Again, the goal is for you to be able to jump in and start typing.

Using Installed Templates

You can choose your template in one of two ways:

- Choose New Office Document from the Start menu. The New Office Document dialog box opens, offering several tabs that organize the installed templates by application categories (see Figure 1.2).
- Open the application itself, and choose File, New. The New dialog box opens, offering templates (organized in several category tabs) specific to the open application.

▶ **See** *"Harnessing the Power of Templates,"* **p. 91**

FIG. 1.2

From within the program, the New dialog box offers templates specific to your application.

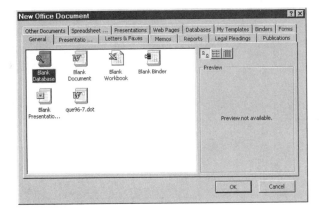

Accessing Templates from the Companion CD

The companion CD that accompanies this book is filled with useful items to enhance your use of Microsoft Office. We have included an impressive array of templates for use in Word and Excel, and you can find them in a folder named Templates.

After you've opened the CD and browsed to this folder location, you can copy the templates to your Templates folder, or use them from the CD each time you need them. To copy them to your hard drive in the Templates folder, follow these steps:

1. Place the CD in your CD-ROM drive. The CD activates automatically, displaying its contents in a window on your screen.

2. Double-click the folder called Templates.

3. Choose View, List.

4. Press and hold the Ctrl key while you click each of the templates that you want to copy to your hard drive.

5. When you've selected the desired group, release the Ctrl key, and choose Edit, Copy (or press Ctrl+C) to copy the files to the Clipboard.

6. Open My Computer or Windows Explorer.

7. Open the Program Files folder on your hard drive, then double-click the Microsoft Office (or MSoffice) subfolder to display its contents.

8. In the Microsoft Office subfolder, double-click the Templates subfolder.

9. Choose Edit, Paste, or press Ctrl+V.

 Don't hesitate to categorize your new templates by making a new folder (under Templates) for your new templates, or by placing them in one or more of the existing subfolders under Templates. If you store them by topic, program, or type, it will make them easier to find in the future.

Opening an Existing File

After you've created, saved, and closed a file, you may need to reopen it, especially if you need to do some editing or reuse the document. Windows and Microsoft Office make the process of opening a file easy—you can view and select from a list of recently used files or search for files that you created in the more distant past.

Accessing Most Recently Used Files

Each of the Microsoft Office applications offers a list of Most Recently Used Files at the foot of the File menu (see Figure 1.3). By default, the list will show the last four files you created or opened, and saved. To select one of these files, click it in the menu list as you would any other command.

FIG. 1.3

Select your file from a convenient list of Most Recently Used Files, found on the File menu in all Office applications.

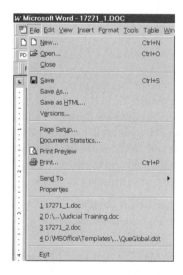

 To choose from a list of the last 15 files you used in any of your applications, choose Documents from the Start menu.

If you find that you'd like to see more than four of your Most Recently Used files when you open the File menu, follow these steps in Word, Excel, or PowerPoint:

1. Choose Tools, Options.
2. Click the General tab if it isn't already on top (see Figure 1.4).
3. Enter the number of Recently Used Files you'd like to see displayed in the File menu. The maximum is nine.
4. Click OK to confirm your change and close the dialog box.

FIG. 1.4

Increase or decrease the number of Most Recently Used Files displayed in your Word, Excel, or PowerPoint File menus.

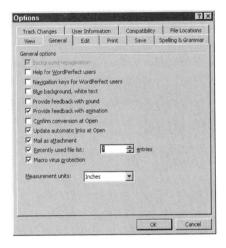

Searching for Files

As often happens, we forget the names and/or location of our files. Sometimes we didn't choose an illustrative name when we saved the file in the first place or we didn't choose a logical folder in which to save it. Even if you did make good choices when you saved the file, it can still get lost. What to do? Use the file search tools available from your Office applications' Open dialog box (see Figure 1.5). With these tools you can use the name, type of file, sample text, date of last modification, or any combination thereof to search for your file in the directory displayed in the Look In listbox. Use the search criteria as follows:

- *File Name.* Enter one or more letters in the filename as you remember it. If the letters are at the beginning of the filename, make that clear by using the * wildcard, as in "Let*" for all documents that start with the letters Let.

- *Files of Type.* Choose an extension to refine your search to specific file types. The list of types varies depending on the application you're in. If you're in Word, for example, the file types are for word processing and text files.

- *Text or Property.* Enter a word or phrase that you know is in the document. Office searches the files in your selected folder for that text.

- *Last Modified.* Click the drop arrow to see a list of time frames such as anytime, today, last week, or last month.

To use your Office application search tools, follow these steps:

1. Choose File, Open from the menu bar.

2. At the bottom of the Open dialog box, enter information in one or more of the search criteria boxes.

3. Click Find Now. The results of the search (if any) will appear in the large white box on the left of the dialog box.

FIG. 1.5
Use the search tools in your Office applications' Open dialog box. Enter what you know about the file's name, location, content, or date modified.

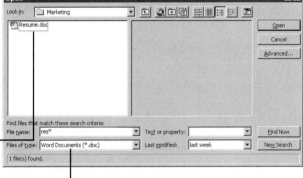

File meeting search criteria

Portion of name with wildcard

4. If your search doesn't work, click New Search and enter new criteria. Click Find Now again to search with the new parameters.

5. If your lost file is among the search results, double-click it or click it once and click the Open button.

N O T E   If your search didn't work and you have no idea what to do next, you can try the Advanced search feature. Click the Advanced button in the Open dialog box. This box assumes you've chosen a file type, and then allows you to search among your files' properties—comments, version numbers, author names, and so forth. You can also extend the area searched by choosing a folder and clicking the Search Subfolders check box. This will search, for example, My Documents and all the folders within it.

Working with the Window Menu

Just like you can have several applications open at once, you can have many documents open simultaneously in any Office application. Normally, you have multiple files open so you can switch between them for the purpose of comparison, cutting or copying content between them, or so you can juggle several unrelated documents in one session.

Whatever your reason for having more than one file open at a time, the Window menu makes it easy to switch between them or view them simultaneously.

To switch between open files, open the Window menu and choose the file that you want to activate. An active file appears on top of all other open files.

Your simultaneous viewing options vary for each Office application:

■ In Word and PowerPoint, choose Window, Arrange All. Each open document will appear in its own window, with no overlapping windows. This is referred to as Tiling.

■ Excel gives you more flexibility for simultaneous viewing. Choose Window, Arrange. The Arrange Windows dialog box opens, from which you can select various tiling options (see Figure 1.6). You can also choose to Cascade the open files, but this is the least effective method for viewing several files at once.

FIG. 1.6

Choose from several options for viewing your open Excel files.

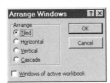

■ Access gives you some of the flexibility you have in Excel, but the options are available directly from the Window menu. Choose Window, Tile Horizontally, Tile Vertically, or Cascade.

CAUTION

It's important to note that the same files that appear on your Most Recently Used File list can also be in your Window menu, as currently open files. Be careful to check your Window menu before potentially reopening a file that's in your Most Recently Used list in the File menu. If you receive a message that tells you that you must open the file as Read Only, this tells you that you're attempting to open a file twice.

CHAPTER 2

Printing and Saving Your Work

Creating Printed Output

One of the most rewarding parts of the creation process is the tangible evidence of your efforts—holding the product of your labors in your hand, and then distributing it to others. Although many documents are never printed because their creators prefer to send them via email or by fax modem, many documents require hard copy.

The Microsoft Office Print dialog box is virtually identical across the suite. Although each application has specific needs that its printing process must accommodate, you'll find that the basic procedures remain constant whether you're working in Word, Excel, PowerPoint, or Access. Figure 2.1 shows the Print dialog box in Word.

FIG. 2.1
Choose your printer, range of pages, and the number of copies you'd like printed in the Print dialog box.

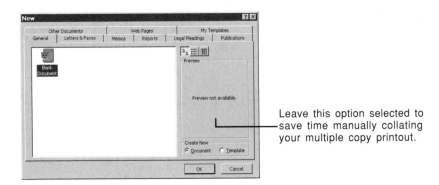

Leave this option selected to save time manually collating your multiple copy printout.

The printing options you can rely on finding in each of the Office applications are as follows:

- *Select a printer.* The Print dialog box shows you the currently selected printer. Click the listbox to see other printers to which you may be attached over your company's network.
- *Determine your range of pages.* Whether slides in PowerPoint or pages in Word, Excel, or Access, this feature lets you choose specific pages, ranges of pages, or combinations thereof.
- *Choose the number of copies.* The default is one, and you can increment that number as high as you'd like. It's a good idea, however, to set it no higher than the capacity of your printer's tray, unless you want to stand by the printer and keep feeding it with more paper!

CAUTION
Don't assume that the Print button on the toolbar and the File, Print command perform in exactly the same way. Clicking the toolbar button will result in a one-copy printout of your entire document, no questions asked. If you need to alter your print settings in any way, issue the Print command from the File menu.

Understanding Printing Options

In most cases, your printing options revolve around the specific needs of the application. In PowerPoint, for example, your printing options are rather extensive—you have a variety of ways to print your slides, and the print feature must offer them all, enabling the user to extensively customize their printed output (see Figure 2.2).

FIG. 2.2

PowerPoint's Print dialog box enables you to choose the type of slide output you require. The remaining options are the same as the other Office applications.

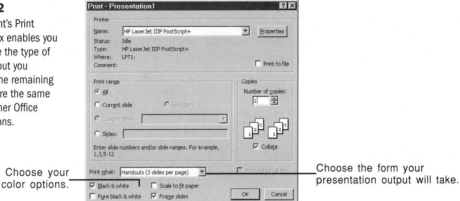

Choose your color options.

Choose the form your presentation output will take.

N O T E   Word offers you an Options button in the Print dialog box that gives you access to settings for printing in draft mode (no graphics or fancy fonts), choosing which tray your paper will be drawn from on the printer (based on your installed printer's features), and whether your print jobs will be processed in the background or not.

Word, Excel, and Access documents require that most of their customization be done before the print job is even started. Adding headers and footers, for example, or determining how much data will fit on a page, will be performed prior to invoking the Print command.

Preparing to Customize Your Print Job

Before you print your document, be it a letter in Word, a spreadsheet in Excel, a series of slides in PowerPoint, or a report in Access, you should take a look at the potential print job onscreen by performing a Print Preview. This serves two purposes—you save paper by not printing out something that doesn't look the way you wanted it to, and it gives you a chance to make changes to the document's overall layout. Many times, as you're working on a document, you're too close to it to see the "big picture" and see how it will look on the page.

Longer documents—those exceeding two printed pages—require special consideration. Some things to consider:

- How will the document be printed? Will your document be single-sided or will you want content on both sides of the paper?

■ Will the placement of items on the pages affect the reader's understanding of the content? In Excel, for example, having a stray column on page 3 can make it hard to follow the flow of information in the worksheet on pages 1 and 2.

■ Is there extra information that you need to print along with the document? If you added comments to your letter, spreadsheet, or slides, you can print them as an addendum to your document's printout.

Printing Two-Sided Pages

To print two-sided documents, you must work with the Odd and Even Pages print feature. The capability to print odd or even pages is only available in Word. If you want to print your Word document on both sides of the paper, you use the Print option to print just the odd and then just the even numbered pages. To do this, follow these steps:

1. With the document you intend to print open, choose File, Print.

2. In the Print box, choose Odd Pages (see Figure 2.3).

N O T E   If your printer is capable of duplex printing (printing on both sides of the paper in one process), you needn't use the Odd Pages or Even Pages feature.

FIG. 2.3

To print on both sides of the paper, print the odd pages first, and then print the even pages on the other side.

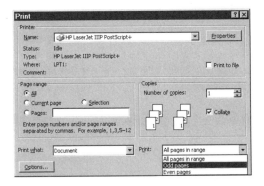

3. In the Page Range section, make sure All is selected.

4. Set your number of copies, and click OK. The odd numbered pages from your document will print.

5. Remove these pages from your printer, and place them back in the printer's tray, positioned as your printer requires it for printing now on the back of these sheets.

CAUTION

Beware of paper jams when using this technique with some printers. Many times, on the first pass through the printer, the paper becomes curled (from the heat inside the printer). When this curled paper goes back through, it can get stuck, or two or more pages can be fed through at once. Either problem can cause the matching of odd and even pages to be thrown off, and the job must be restarted from the beginning.

6. Re-open the Print dialog box by choosing File, Print.

7. In the Print box, select Even Pages.

8. Again, All must be selected in the Page Range section.

9. Click OK. The odd numbered pages will now print with the even numbered pages on their reverse.

N O T E If you aren't sure which way to insert your odd pages so the even pages will print right side up, try this trick: Take a blank sheet of paper, and draw an arrow, pointing in the direction of the printer, and put the sheet in the printer tray, arrow on top and pointing toward the printer. Print something. By comparing the arrow to the printing on the sheet, you can determine the proper way to insert your paper.

Part

I

Ch

2

CAUTION

If you're printing multiple copies of an even pages or odd pages print job, be sure the Collate option is on during both the odd and even page print jobs. This will save you from having to worry about page order when you send the pages back through the printer for the other side to be printed.

Scaling a Print Job to Fit

Excel offers you the capability to reduce the size of the content to be printed so you don't end up with stray rows and columns on subsequent pages in your printout.

Excel's print feature offers two options for adjusting the scale of your printed document:

- Use the Adjust To option to change the percentage of original (100%) size. To make your printout half as large, change the percentage to 50%.

- Choose the Fit To option by selecting the number of pages tall and wide you want your printout to be. If your printout is currently leaving a stray row on an extra page, decrease the tall setting; if a column or two is spilling over to an extra page, reduce the number of pages wide.

To take advantage of the Scaling feature, follow these steps:

1. With your Excel worksheet open, choose File, Page Setup.

2. Click the Page tab (see Figure 2.4).

3. In the Scaling section, use the Adjust To or the Fit To options to control the size of your printout.

4. After making your adjustments, click the Print Preview button to see how your changes have affected your printout.

5. If the desired effect has been achieved, click Print. This opens the Print dialog box.

6. Click OK to print your document.

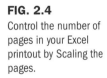

FIG. 2.4

Control the number of pages in your Excel printout by Scaling the pages.

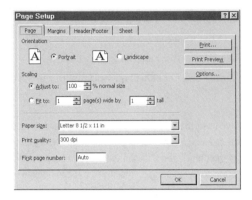

N O T E   By default, Excel breaks your spreadsheet into pages by working down, and then across. If you want to adjust this so your page breaks occur naturally across the columns and then down the rows, choose File, Page Setup, and go to the Sheet tab. In the Page Order section, click the Over then Down option. Click OK to close the dialog box.

Printing Properties, Comments, and Other Additional Information

Of all the Office applications, Word gives you the most options for printing additional information such as your document's properties, style list, comments, and so forth. Excel allows you to print your spreadsheet comments along with your printout, and PowerPoint will print your comments with no questions asked, requiring an action on your part in order to *not* print them.

To print additional information about your Word document, follow these steps:

1. With your document open, choose File, Print.

2. In the Print What section (see Figure 2.5), choose from the list of additional items such as comments, properties, styles, and AutoText entries.

N O T E   The Print What feature allows you to choose only one from the list. If you want to print more than one extra item, such as Comments and Properties, choose Tools, Options and click the Print tab. In the Include with Document section, select the items you want included with your document printout. You can make selections in this dialog box in addition to those chosen through the Print dialog box.

3. Click OK to print your document with the selected item as an additional page at the end of your document printout.

Creating a document for others to use? Print the AutoText entries and styles for them so they know what supporting tools were used in the document's creation.

Excel enables you to print your spreadsheet comments. Spreadsheet comments are the parenthetical information items you attach to specific cells or ranges of cells within your worksheet.

FIG. 2.5

Choose to print extra items such as comments, properties, or AutoText entries along with your document. This can be helpful to you in recalling how your document was constructed.

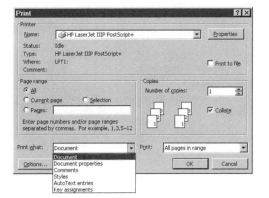

To print these comments with your worksheet, follow these steps:

1. Open the workbook containing the sheet you want to print, and choose File, Page Setup.
2. Click the Sheet tab (see Figure 2.6).

FIG. 2.6

You can add valuable information to your Excel printout by including cell comments. To print comments you must change the Comments setting from the default, (None).

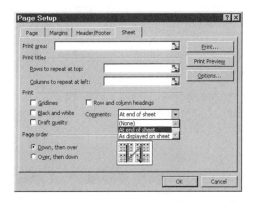

3. In the Print section, use the Comments listbox to determine where in your printout to include the comments. You can print them with the cells to which they refer, or at the end of the printout.
4. Click OK to close the dialog box. You can also click the Print button to go directly to the Print dialog box.

If you've added comments to your PowerPoint presentation (they'll appear as text boxes on the face of your slides), you will see them on any printouts of your slides unless you delete them. As comments are generally added to facilitate team development of your slide presentation (containing text such as "Shouldn't we have a chart here?"), you'll want to remove them before you print your slide transparencies or run the slide show onscreen. Figure 2.7 shows a PowerPoint slide that contains a comment.

▶ **See** "Drawing Shapes, Lines, and Text Boxes," **p. 228**
▶ **See** "Building a Document with AutoText," **p. 116**

FIG. 2.7
Comments can be
added to PowerPoint
slides to remind you to
add elements or make
important changes.
These comments should
be deleted before
printing or showing
slides to your audience.

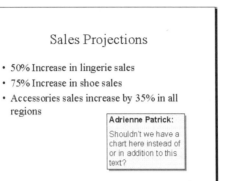

Saving Your Work

Even veteran computer users seem to forget to save their work. Without a doubt, the most valuable advice I can give you is to save early and often. As soon as you've done more than you'd want to redo in the event of a software or system crash, power outage, or other mishap, you should save your work. This goes for all the Office applications, no matter what you're working on. Even if you don't intend to keep a document after you've printed it or sent it on to someone, you should still save it periodically so you don't lose it while you're still creating it. You can always delete the file later.

The process of saving doesn't vary between applications in the Microsoft Office suite—whether it's the first time you're saving the file or you're changing the filename to protect a new version, the techniques are always the same. Figure 2.8 shows the Save As dialog box in Excel.

FIG. 2.8
The Save As dialog box
looks the same in all
Office applications. Rely
on this consistency, and
perform this essential
step frequently!

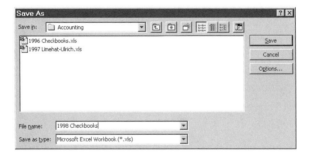

Saving for the First Time

A first-time save is important—it gives you the chance to give your file a name and choose a location to save it. Microsoft gives you quite a few methods of initiating a first-time save:

■ Choose File, Save from the menu. Because it's a first-time save, the Save As dialog box opens, asking you to name your file and choose a location for it.

- Choose File, Save As. Because the Save command gives you the same dialog box, this may seem like a redundant command. Making this choice, however, can become a good habit—you're less likely to replace a file that you intended to rename if you use this technique religiously when saving.

- Press Ctrl+S. This is a global keyboard shortcut that works in just about any Windows application. If it's a first-time save, the Save As dialog box opens. If you've already saved the file, the saved version of the file will be updated to include your latest changes.

 - Click the Save button on the toolbar. This works just like the File, Save and Ctrl+S commands.

Part
I

Ch
2

Naming Files

Choosing a name for your file can have a significant impact on your ability to find and use your file in the future. Choosing a name that's easy to recall and that clearly indicates the content of the file is your best bet. Some other things to keep in mind:

- *Keep names short.* Short names are easier to work with whether you're working with DOS users (who can't see the full filename if it exceeds eight characters) or all of your coworkers/friends are using Windows 95.

- *Keep names relevant.* Don't call the report on first quarter sales Report. Call it 1stQReport or something similar that indicates *which* report it is.

- *Don't type the extension.* Let the program do that for you. Because Windows uses the extension to link the file with its native application, your accidentally typing **dox** (instead of doc) for the file extension could make it difficult to open your files from within Explorer or My Computer.

Creating and Naming Folders

Perhaps even more than your choice of a name for your file, your choice of where you save it can directly affect your ability to find the file in the future. Just like a file cabinet in your office, if you have one or two large folders with lots of files in them, looking through them all to find one file in particular can be a headache. To avoid this situation, create many smaller folders that clearly categorize your files. You don't need to be in Explorer or My Computer to do this:

1. With the file you want to save open and active, choose File, Save, or initiate a first-time save in your method of choice.

2. Move to the folder in which you want to save the file. Your system will probably default to My Documents, or to the last folder you used in this session with the open application. Figure 2.9 shows the Save As dialog box.

3. To create a new subfolder to categorize your file appropriately, click the Create New Folder button.

4. In the New Folder dialog box, type the folder name. Like filenames, folder names can be up to 255 characters, but are better kept short.

FIG. 2.9
When saving a file for the first time or saving it with a new name, you can use the Create New Folder button to add a folder for the file you're about to save.

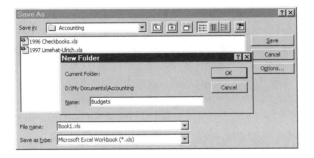

CAUTION

When naming files, do not use the following punctuation: / \ | , . ? * . These symbols would be interpreted as meaningful by the operating system, and you will be told that your file- or folder name is invalid.

5. Click OK. Your new folder appears in the large box that shows the contents of the Save In folder.

6. Double-click the new folder, moving it to the Save In box.

7. Name your file if necessary, and click OK.

Updating Your Work

As you continue to work on your saved file in any Microsoft Office application, you can use any of the following methods to save your latest changes:

- Choose File, Save from the menu. Because the file has already been saved, the Save As dialog box will not open.

- Click the Save button on the toolbar.

- Press Ctrl+S.

Using the keyboard or toolbar methods (and committing them to memory) will make it faster and easier to perform frequent saves as you work. Anything you can do to encourage yourself to save often will increase your productivity and save you a lot of repeated effort.

Using Save As

When you want to change the name of your file, save a new version of your currently saved file, or save your file to a new location, you can choose File, Save As. There is no keyboard or toolbar equivalent for this function.

N O T E   Word gives you more tools for saving versions of files. If you're working on a document and want to save it at each phase of its development, click the Save Version button in the Save As dialog box. Enter a comment about the version you're saving, such as "First Edit" or "Final Proof", and click OK. To see these versions (and a history of your document's development), choose File, Versions.

Working with File Types

Microsoft Office applications have default file types, visually indicated by the filename extensions:

- Word files have a .doc extension.
- Excel files have an .xls extension.
- PowerPoint files have a .ppt extension.
- Access databases have an .mdb extension.

Part

I

Ch

2

You should accept these default extensions in most cases. The only exceptions are when you're creating a template in Word, Excel, or PowerPoint, or when you're saving to an older version of the application for another user. You can also save to other program's file formats, such as WordPerfect, Lotus, dBASE, or FoxPro.

To save your file in another format, follow these steps:

1. Choose File, Save As. This can be done on a first-time save or on a previously saved file.

2. In the Save As dialog box, click the Save as Type listbox and choose your format (see Figure 2.10).

FIG. 2.10
If you're not accepting the default format, choose another one from the Save as Type listbox.

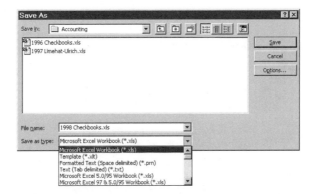

3. Enter a filename if necessary, and click OK.

If you're sharing a Word file with another user and you don't know which word processor he or she has, save your Word file in .rtf (Rich Text) format. This will save your formatting and graphic content along with the text, and is a universally acceptable format for Windows and DOS-based computers.

▶ **See** "Creating Your Own Templates," **p. 96**

Protecting Your Files with Passwords

Perhaps you're on a network and each user has a protected folder or drive into which he or she can save their work, knowing that it will not be available to other users. In that situation, however, the network manager (and anyone who may know your login and password) *can* view the files in that folder or drive.

If you're using Office on a standalone PC, you have no such capability to protect folders or drives—and the files on them—from prying eyes. You can, however, protect your individual Word and Excel documents by applying a password for opening and/or editing them. To create this extra level of security, follow these steps:

1. Choose File, Save As.

2. Click the Options button. If you're saving a Word file, the Save dialog box opens, offering several options (see Figure 2.11). If you're using Excel, the Save Options dialog box opens (see Figure 2.12).

FIG. 2.11

The open password will keep other users from seeing the file; the modify password will protect the file from being saved with changes. Enter a password for either or both options.

FIG. 2.12

Excel's Save Options dialog box contains fewer saving-related options. Enter passwords for the type of security you need.

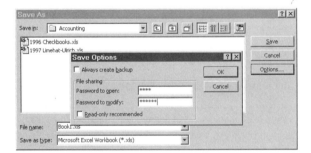

3. In the File Sharing section of the dialog box, type a password in one or both of the text boxes.

4. Click the OK button. A Confirm Password dialog box opens for your open password (see Figure 2.13).

FIG. 2.13

To make sure you didn't make a mistake the first time you typed it, the Confirm Password dialog box requires you to reenter your password.

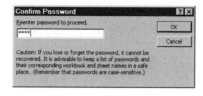

Part

I

Ch

2

5. Reenter your password, and click OK.

6. If you also set a modify password, a second Confirm Password dialog box will open, requiring reentry of that password as well. Reenter the password, and click OK.

7. If you need to enter a filename for your file or select a folder in which to save it, do so, and then click OK to save the file.

CAUTION

Don't forget your password! There is no way to open or modify the file without it, and you can't retrieve it if you forget it. Make sure it's something you can't forget, or find a discreet place to write it down.

CHAPTER 3

Reaching Out to Coworkers and Customers

In this chapter

Sharing Files

One of the primary motivations for creating a document is to share information. By writing a letter, creating a spreadsheet, or designing a presentation, you express the desire to put your thoughts and supporting data into a digestible format for others to see. Some databases can be created purely for personal use, but most computerized creations are meant to be shared.

Microsoft Office gives you many ways in which to share your documents:

- *Printing.* As soon as you've printed your document, you can distribute one or many copies to interested parties.
- *Saving to a network drive.* If you save your file to a public-access drive on your company's network, other users can get to it for viewing or saving to their own local drives for future use.
- *Sending files via fax.* Through your computer's fax modem, you can send a document to another person's computer or fax machine.
- *Sending via email.* Attach your file to an email message and send it to one or many people, all over the world.
- *Turn your document into a Web page.* By saving your file as HTML, you make it postable to the World Wide Web. This feature is available only in Office 97.
- *Link your document to the Web or other documents.* By inserting a hyperlink to your file on either a Web page or another document on your network, you give other people the ability to access it with a single click. This feature is available only in Office 97.

Choose one or more of these methods to distribute your creations—your choice will depend on how far and wide you want to share the document.

Sending Files

The most direct methods of sending your file to another user is to choose File, Send To. A submenu appears (see Figure 3.1), offering the following choices:

- *Mail Recipient.* If you're using Microsoft Exchange (or another email program that is set up to work with Office), you can create a message and attach the file to it. This command is available in Word, Excel, and PowerPoint.
- *Routing Recipient.* You can route a document, accompanied by a routing slip, to one or more people in your Exchange address book. Each person who receives a routed document passes it along, by choosing File, Send To, Next Routing Recipient. You'll find this command in all applications except Access.
- *Exchange Folder.* Choose from any of the installed or user-created folders in Exchange as the home for your document. This command appears in Word, Excel, and PowerPoint, but not Access.
- *Fax Recipient.* This starts the Fax Wizard, which takes you through the process of creating a cover sheet and faxing a document to a selected user. You'll find this command in Word only.

FIG. 3.1

Available in Word, Excel, and PowerPoint, the Send To command enables you to direct your open document to one or more other users.

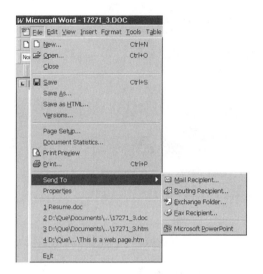

Part

I

Ch

3

TIP If you use the File, Send To command in Word, you can send your document to PowerPoint, creating a presentation outline from the document's text. Conversely, PowerPoint files can be sent to Word, creating an outline from a presentation.

Creating Hyperlinks to Office Application Files

Another way to share a file is to create a link to it within another file. Imagine that you're sending a report (created in Word) to your boss. You are citing an Excel spreadsheet in your report, and you'd rather not waste space with copying and pasting the entire spreadsheet into your document. Inserting a hyperlink instead enables your boss, while viewing the report document onscreen, to click the link and open the supporting data in your Excel spreadsheet. He or she can then read the spreadsheet and when finished, close it, returning to the report document. The process of inserting a hyperlink in any Office document is simple:

1. In the document that will contain the link, position the insertion point where you want the link to appear and choose Insert, Hyperlink. The Insert Hyperlink dialog box opens, offering you the ability to type in or browse to the path and filename to which you want the link to point.

2. Insert a path and filename, or an actual Web site URL in the Link to File or URL text box (see Figure 3.2).

   If you don't know the exact path and filename, click Browse. Locate the folder and file, and click Open to insert the path and filename in your document. It will appear wherever your cursor was when you started the insertion process.

3. Click OK to close the Insert Hyperlink dialog box and create your link. Your link text appears in color, with an underline.

FIG. 3.2
The Insert Hyperlink command enables you to add a link to a particular file right inside your document, making access to supporting information a simple click for the reader.

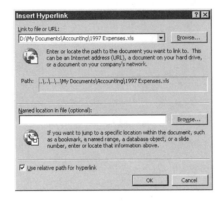

N O T E   In addition to file links, you can also create a link to a specific bookmark within the same or a different document, a named range in an Excel spreadsheet, or a slide in a PowerPoint presentation. In the Named Location of File box, type or Browse to the specific location, and a link to that place will be inserted in your open document.

To use your links, merely point to them with the mouse (it will turn to a pointing hand), and click.

 If your linked file is on a network, make sure it is in a folder to which other users have access. If your link is in a protected folder, they won't be able to open the linked file.

CAUTION
Don't rename or move a hyperlinked file from its original location without reestablishing the link. To reestablish a link, highlight it and repeat the link insertion procedure.

Using the Internet and World Wide Web

By its very nature, the Internet gives you the ability to share your documents with the entire world. Whether you choose to email your document to someone or post it as a Web page (or *on* a Web page), your document takes on global proportions!

Word, Excel, and PowerPoint give you the ability to save your documents as HTML, which converts them to a format digestible by the Web. You can also bring the Web to your local documents by adding Web hyperlinks to them.

Saving Files as HTML

HTML stands for *Hypertext Markup Language*, a programming language for creating and formatting Web pages. By adding the capability to save your Word, Excel, and PowerPoint documents as HTML, Microsoft has eliminated the immediate need for you to learn HTML.

TIP Although learning HTML isn't essential for creating Web pages with Microsoft Office, you might find a rudimentary knowledge of it to be useful if you want to edit your Web page through any other program, such as your Web browser. Try *HTML Web Publishing 6-in-1*, by Todd Stauffer, an excellent book from Que.

Although the capability to save an Excel or PowerPoint file as HTML is available, this process makes the most sense in Word. It isn't terribly productive to try to turn a spreadsheet, no matter how fancy the fonts and shading, into a Web page. If you want people who visit your site to be able to see a particular spreadsheet, you can create a link on the page to that specific spreadsheet. PowerPoint presentations can be placed on a Web site for an Internet slideshow, but turning the slides themselves into Web pages doesn't make much sense.

To save your Word document as HTML, follow these steps:

1. Choose File, Save as HTML.
2. Choose a folder and enter a name for your file, as in any Save As procedure.
3. Click Save.
4. A prompt may appear, telling you that some of your formatting may be lost if you continue. This will happen if you have applied formats that aren't compatible with HTML. Click Yes to continue.
5. Your document, saved in HTML format, changes to Online Layout view, and new tools appear onscreen to assist you in further development of your Web page. Figure 3.3 shows a file, saved as HTML, in Online Layout view.

Part

I

Ch

3

FIG. 3.3
Online Layout view
gives you a set of tools
for formatting and
viewing your Web-page-
in-progress.

New formatting tools—

Graphic as hyperlink
(see mouse pointer)

Hyperlink text—

Web page
design tools—

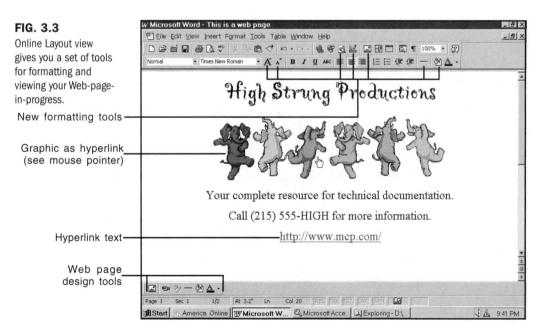

You can use Online Layout view to work on any document, even those not saved as HTML. Choose View, Online Layout, or click the Online Layout View button on the View toolbar (lower-left corner of Word window).

N O T E Your document saved as HTML doesn't have the typical .doc extension. Rather, it has an .htm extension, telling Windows that it is an HTML file. If you attempt to open the .htm file from within Explorer or My Computer, Windows looks for an HTML program to open the file. If you want to edit the file in Word, use Word's File, Open command to open the document.

After you've saved your file as HTML, you can insert graphics, choose a document background, and insert video and sound files to enhance the document. These commands are all available from the Online Layout toolbar, shown earlier in Figure 3.3. Continue to save your work with typical File, Save or Ctrl+S commands as you work.

▶ **See** "Inserting Graphics from the companion CD," **p. 60** for more information on inserting objects into your Word documents.

Inserting Hyperlinks to Web Pages

You can add hyperlinks that point to Web sites to your Word, Excel, PowerPoint, and Access files. The process is much like the previously discussed method of inserting hyperlinks that point to other documents. In Word, Excel, and PowerPoint, follow these steps:

1. With the insertion point placed where you want the link to be, choose Insert, Hyperlink.

 If you want to turn existing text or a graphic into a hyperlink, select it before choosing Insert, Hyperlink. Whatever link you establish will be triggered by the selected item.

2. In the Insert Hyperlink dialog box, type or Browse to the URL (Web address) to which you want to link. The URL will appear in the Link to File or URL text box.

CAUTION

If you choose to Browse for a URL, you'll find that you can only get to any Web addresses that you've saved in a Favorites or Bookmarks folder (depending on your Web browsing software) on your system. If the link is to a site you haven't saved to your local drive, you must type it into the Link to File or URL text box manually. Be sure to check the accuracy of the address before posting the HTML document to the Web.

 Can't remember the exact URL? Start your Web browser, and connect to the Web. Go to the site you want your link to point to, and copy the URL (listed on the toolbar) to the Clipboard (Ctrl+C). Return to the Insert Hyperlink dialog box, and Paste (Ctrl+V) the URL into the Link to File or URL text box.

3. Click OK to close the Insert Hyperlink dialog box.

If your hyperlink was added as a new object to your document (instead of turning existing text or graphics into a link), the hyperlink text appears in color, with an underline. You can move any hyperlink (text or graphic) within your document/Web page, by using Edit, Cut and Edit, Paste, or by using Edit, Copy and Edit, Paste if you want to duplicate the link elsewhere in this or another document.

 TIP The Clipboard's keyboard shortcuts are a lot faster to use, and fairly easy to remember: Ctrl+X (Cut), Ctrl+C (Copy), and Ctrl+V (Paste). These particular keys were chosen because of their proximity to one another, making them easy to invoke with one hand.

ON THE WEB

http://www.dopportunities.com/attract/animation/ Check this Web site for categories of animated gifs (.gif format graphic files) to use in your documents. Select the animated gif and then insert a hyperlink to a file or Web site.

Enhancing Your Web Pages with Files from the CD

The CD that comes with this book contains many sounds, video clips, graphics, and backgrounds. The clip art images are great choices to serve as hyperlinks in your Web pages, as shown previously in Figure 3.3. Users will find pictures more fun to look at than text, so using them as your link objects or purely for visual interest is a good idea.

To access these Web site-enhancing graphics as well as the sound files (.wav format), animated .gifs, and video clips (.avi format) on the companion CD, follow these steps:

1. Insert the companion CD. The CD automatically opens. (If the CD doesn't activate automatically, go to Explorer or My Computer and choose your CD-ROM drive.)

2. From the CD's contents, choose the folder that contains the type of file that you want to insert, such as \clipart, \animgifs, \photos, or \sounds, each found in the root directory of your CD-ROM.

3. Scroll through the files in the appropriate folder, and double-click the one you want to insert in your Web page.

4. Repeat steps 3 and 4 for inserting additional objects.

5. Close the CD window in My Computer or exit/minimize the Explorer window, and remove the CD from the drive.

You can choose to copy the graphics, sounds, and video files to your computer. You can place them in the Microsoft Clip Gallery, or save them to any folder or folders you choose.

To save your CD files to the Microsoft Clip Gallery, follow these steps:

1. With the companion CD in your CD-ROM drive, open Word (you can also do this through Excel or PowerPoint, but we'll use Word for this procedure).

Part

I

Ch

3

2. In a blank document (you'll be closing it later without saving), choose Insert, Picture, Clip Art. The Microsoft Clip Gallery opens (see Figure 3.4).

3. Click the appropriate tab for the type of file(s) you will be adding from the CD.

FIG. 3.4

Open the Microsoft Clip Gallery to add CD files to your gallery of clip art, sounds, and video objects. You can then use them in any Office document without having to open the CD each time.

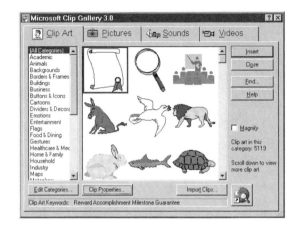

4. Click the Import Clips button. The Add Video (or Clip art, or Sound) to Clip Gallery dialog box opens (see Figure 3.5).

5. Navigate to your CD-ROM drive and to the appropriate folder on the CD.

FIG. 3.5

Open the CD and find the folder containing the file you want to import into the Clip Gallery.

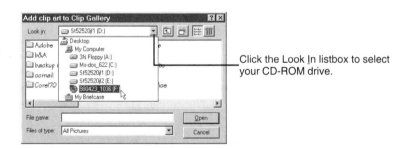

Click the Look In listbox to select your CD-ROM drive.

6. Double-click the file you want to import, or click it once and click the Open button.

7. The Clip Properties dialog box opens, in which you can enter Keywords (to use for searching for appropriate Gallery items later) and choose any Categories in which you want to place the imported file (see Figure 3.6).

8. Click OK to close the Clip Properties dialog box. Your clip art, sound, or video file now appears in the tab, represented by an icon. Figure 3.7 shows a video object added to that tab.

9. Repeat steps 3–8 for any other CD files you want to add to the Clip Gallery.

10. Click Close in the Microsoft Clip Gallery dialog box.

FIG. 3.6
Keywords can be useful later to help you search for files that are appropriate for your documents. This is most useful in PowerPoint, when you're looking for objects to enhance a slideshow.

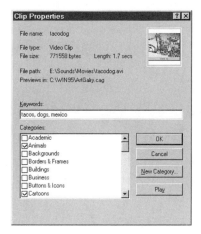

FIG. 3.7
A still from the video serves as an icon to remind you of the content of the video. Double-click the icon to select it for insertion in a document, spread-sheet, or presentation.

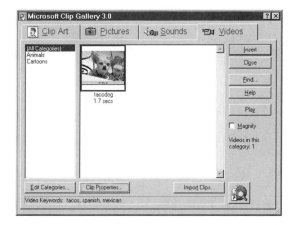

CAUTION

Don't be too quick to copy all the CD's files to your computer. The graphics, sounds, and especially videos will take up a lot of your hard drive space. Using the CD as the storage device adds a few minutes to the process of inserting the files into your Office documents, but you don't compromise valuable space on your PC.

CHAPTER 4

Understanding OLE (Object Linking and Embedding)

Linking and Embedding Within Microsoft Office

One of Windows' most time- and labor-saving devices is the Clipboard, which enables users to take a document (or portion thereof) and use it in another document. The time and margin for error in retyping is eliminated, and consistency is retained. Although the Clipboard is available to and between all Windows applications, you'll find it especially useful within the Microsoft Office suite of programs.

An even more powerful tool is *Object Linking and Embedding (OLE)*. This tool takes the cut/copy and paste relationship between documents and does it one better—the document that provided the Clipboard content (the *source*) remains linked to the document into which the content (object) is pasted (the *target*).

Why establish such a link? It keeps the target updated whenever changes are made to the source. If you use OLE to link a section of an Excel spreadsheet to a report done in Word, when the spreadsheet content changes, the pasted content in Word changes too. You can control when and how these changes take place, however, so you needn't update information unless you want to. Some examples of the uses of OLE within Microsoft Office:

■ Create a chart in Excel and link it to a report in Word or a slide in PowerPoint. If you already have your numeric data in Excel, why not build the chart there, and then use it in the other applications as needed? You can link it to one or many other documents.

■ Use sections of one Word document in other Word documents such as contracts, leases, and other legal documents. When exact wording matters, using the Clipboard is the only way to go. Establishing a link between the original and other documents assures you that even the most minor changes in content are reflected in all documents that use the text.

■ Use an Excel list or Access table to build a table within a Word document. Rather than reenter rows and rows of information in Word, link it from the application where the data was originally entered. Use Word to format and polish the appearance of the text, and know that changes in the data can be updated in the document. This is great for employee lists, phone/extension databases, and price lists that you distribute to customers.

Linking a Source and Target

When linking two documents, one document must be designated the source and the other the target. The source content can appear as part of the target file (inserted at the cursor as though it were a graphic), or as an icon to be clicked when the user is viewing the target file. This option saves space, and allows the user to choose whether he or she wants to see the source content. Another option is to have the source content appear as a floating object, perhaps obscuring existing target file content. This is the least desirable option. To link a document or section of the document to another, follow these steps:

1. Open both your source and target documents.

2. Switch to the source document, and select the section that you want to link to the target.

TIP In Word, Excel, and PowerPoint, you can press Ctrl+A to select the entire document.

3. Choose <u>E</u>dit, <u>C</u>opy from the menu bar, or press Ctrl+C.

 TIP You don't use Cu<u>t</u> when linking, because the source content would be removed from the source document.

4. Switch to the target document. Position your cursor within that document at the point where you want to place the source content.

5. Choose <u>E</u>dit, Paste <u>S</u>pecial from the menu. The Paste Special dialog box opens.

6. Click the Paste <u>L</u>ink option, and select the type of object that youíre linking from the <u>A</u>s box. Figure 4.1 shows an Excel object being selected for placement in a Word document.

FIG. 4.1

Choose Paste Link from the Paste Special dialog box to establish a link between the source document and the target document.

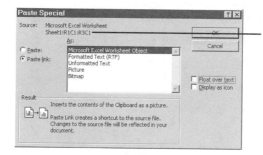

Selected range of cell addresses in Excel document

7. By default, your linked content will be inserted at the cursor in your target document's existing text. In Word, you can choose to have the linked content Float Over <u>T</u>ext or <u>D</u>isplay as an Icon instead. Click the appropriate box next to one or both of these options.

 TIP If you choose the <u>D</u>isplay as Icon option for your linked content, you can click the Change <u>I</u>con button to choose from a palette of icons to represent the content in your target document.

8. Click OK to insert the source content and close the Paste Special dialog box.

NOTE When establishing a link between Excel or Word and PowerPoint, be aware of the slide element that is selected at the time you attempt to create the link. The Clipboard content must be compatible with the selected element—for example, if you're linking text, a text placeholder must be selected. Excel charts or numeric data for a PowerPoint datasheet are typical objects linked to a PowerPoint presentation.

▶ **See** "Copying Excel Data to Create a PowerPoint Chart," **p. 217**

▶ **See** "Pasting an Existing Excel Chart," **p. 218**

Maintaining and Updating Links

After you place linked content in a document, whenever you open the document, you'll be asked if you want to update the link. This question is really asking if you want to update the content to match the source document. If you do, click <u>Y</u>es; if not, click <u>N</u>o. Figure 4.2 shows the Update Links prompt.

Part

I

Ch

4

FIG. 4.2

Links can be updated when you open the target file.

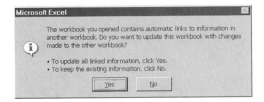

If you choose not to update the link, you can update it the next time you open the file, or at any time that the target file is open by choosing Edit, Links. The Links dialog box gives you the opportunity to update links, open the source document, change the source document, and in Word, break the link between documents. Figure 4.3 shows Word's Links dialog box.

FIG. 4.3

The Links dialog box (generally the same in Word, Excel, and PowerPoint) enables you to control the link between documents and perform updates from the source to the target.

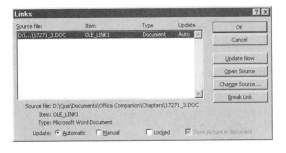

 If you want to temporarily stop all links from being updated, choose Edit, Links, and click the Locked check box. While this box is checked, the Update Now option will be unavailable.

Embedding Applications

Embedding, the third component of OLE, places an entire application in the target document. Instead of pasting a section of an Excel spreadsheet into a Word document, you can embed the Excel application in the Word document, putting all of Excel's tools at your disposal for creating and editing a spreadsheet within the Word window.

But why would you do this? You can have both Word and Excel open at the same time, and you could simply paste or paste link the Excel data into your Word document. Consider these reasons for embedding rather than linking:

  ■ *You don't need both source and target documents.* Your one document becomes both because it actually contains the source application and whatever content you create with it.

  ■ *Some applications require it.* The applets that run within Office—WordArt, MSGraph, and MSOrgchart—are automatically embedded in your document when you add one of their components, such as a logo, a pie chart, or a PowerPoint organization chart. These applications cannot exist on their own.

■ *When sharing a document with another user, he or she needn't have both applications.* If you know someone who only has Word, embed Excel and/or an Excel file in your Word document before you send it to them, and they can view the Excel content within the Word document without having Excel loaded on their PC.

Embedding a New Blank Object

If you only know that you need one application's tools in another application's file but have no specific content to embed, you can embed the object in a blank state. For example, a blank Excel worksheet can be embedded in a Word document (or PowerPoint slide), and its cells can be filled with data at some future time. By embedding the blank worksheet, you place Excel's tools at your fast and easy disposal without having to build the data in Excel beforehand.

Although embedding is a powerful and useful tool, the procedure for performing it is relatively simple. Follow these steps:

1. Open the target document—the document into which you want to embed another application.

2. Position your cursor at the point where you want to place the embedded content.

3. Choose Insert, Object. The Object dialog box opens.

4. To insert an application with no specific content (you'll build that later), click the Create New tab (see Figure 4.4).

FIG. 4.4

Choose which application to embed, and how the embedded object will appear within your target document.

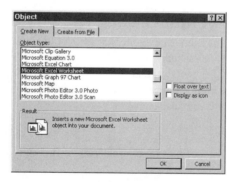

5. Select the application you want to embed from the Object Type box.

6. Choose your display options—Float Over Text, or Display as Icon.

7. Click the OK button. The embedded application opens, and its toolbars and menus take over your target application window.

You can work in the embedded application right away, or click outside of the embedded object box to deactivate the embedded application. The target application's tools reappear. Figure 4.5 shows an embedded Excel object in an Word document.

Part

I

Ch

4

FIG. 4.5

After it's embedded, the source application takes over the target window. Click outside of the embedded object to return to the target application's tools and menus.

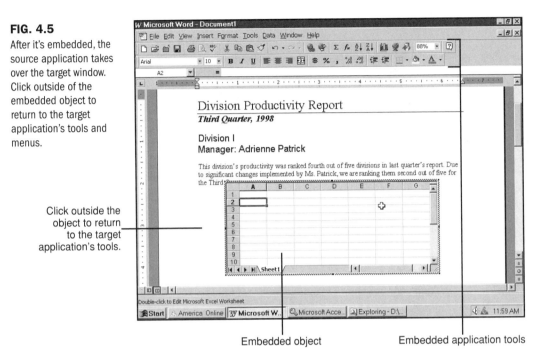

Click outside the object to return to the target application's tools.

Embedded object   Embedded application tools

Embedding an Application with Existing File Content

There will be times that you have an existing file that you want to embed in an application. Perhaps you want your Excel Sales Analysis worksheet to be embedded in your Word Sales Report document so the recipients of the report need only activate the Excel object to make any changes or play with the numbers on their own. The original sales worksheet remains intact, and only the embedded version is changed.

To embed an existing file, follow these steps:

1. In your target document, position your cursor where you want to place the embedded file.

2. Choose Insert, Object. The Object dialog box opens.

3. Click the Create from File tab (see Figure 4.6).

4. Type the path and filename of the file you want to embed, or click the Browse button to find and select it.

5. Choose your display options: Float Over Text or Display as Icon.

6. If you want to create a link between the embedded file and the original file, click Link to File.

FIG. 4.6

Embed an application and an existing file at the same time with the Create from File tab.

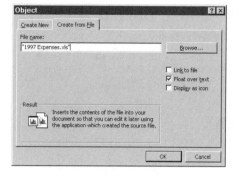

CAUTION

If you choose to Link to File, you cannot play with the embedded content without risk of changing the original file. If you will be distributing the document that contains the embedded file, it's a good idea *not* to invoke the link.

7. Click OK. Your embedded object appears in the target document. Figure 4.7 shows an embedded Excel object in a Word document.

Part
I

Ch
4

FIG. 4.7

Double-click the embedded file to activate the embedded application's tools in the target window.

Object handles show that it is selected, but not active.

Embedded file content

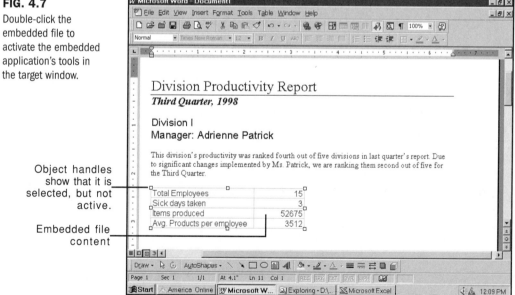

N O T E Choosing to Display as Icon saves space in your target document, especially if there is a lot of content in your embedded object. In addition, other users of the file can choose whether to look at the embedded content, double-clicking the icon if they want to see or use the embedded file and application.

Moving and Deleting Embedded Objects

To move or delete an embedded object, the target application must be active. Click once on the object to select it without activating the embedded application. The object will have handles on all four corners and along its sides (refer to Figure 4.7). You can then perform the following actions:

- To move the object within the currently visible area of the document, point to the edge of the object (not on a handle) and watch for your mouse pointer to turn to a four-headed arrow. Click and drag the object to the desired location.

- If you want to move the object to another page within the document, use the Clipboard to Cut and Paste it to its new location.

- To delete the object, select it (without activating the embedded application), and press the Delete key. ●

Getting Your Word's Worth

Enhancing Document Appearance

In this chapter

Formatting Text with Styles

As the song says, "you gotta have style." Word's Style feature saves time, gives you formatting consistency within and among documents, and simplifies the creation process. The lyrics must be true!

A *Style* is a collection of formats—the font, size, alignment, and other formats—applied to text. Word comes with a series of heading and paragraph text styles, designed to support your creation of standard business documents. You can use them as they are, change them to suit your specific needs, or create styles of your own.

Why use styles? Imagine that you're writing an employee handbook. Throughout the book, you've chosen to use centered Arial 16 point bold text, with a bottom border and 20% shading for all your chapter headings. That's six different character and paragraph formats that you'll have to apply to each of the headings. Yes, you could use the Format Painter to apply the formats you've applied to one heading and apply them to the rest. But that requires a lot of clicking and scrolling around in your document, and the margin for error is great. Creating a style called "Chapter Heading" would be a much faster, more productive way to go. You build the style once, and then apply it throughout the document with a series of quick, simple commands.

Styles are normally part of the template used to create the document. The styles that come with Word are part of the Blank Document template, also known as the Normal template. You can reformat these styles and have the changes apply only to the open document, or make the changes part of the Normal template, making the changed styles available in any new, blank document. The styles you create on your own can also be applied to one document or made part of the Normal template for use in future documents.

Using Heading Styles

Word's Blank Document template contains a series of three Heading styles—Heading 1, Heading 2, and Heading 3 (see Figure 5.1). Each one contains character and paragraph formats that you can instantly apply to selected text. These styles appear in the Style listbox in What You See is What You Get (WYSIWYG) format, so you know what to expect when they're applied to text.

FIG. 5.1

Word's Heading styles enable you to quickly apply several character and paragraph formats with one simple command.

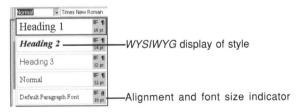

WYSIWYG display of style

Alignment and font size indicator

To apply a Heading style, perform the following steps:

1. Place your cursor in the text in which you want to apply the Heading style.

2. Click the Style drop-down list, and choose the Heading style you want to use. The style is applied to the selected text (see Figure 5.2).

FIG. 5.2
Use Heading styles 1, 2, and 3 hierarchically in your document to indicate levels of importance.

FILM NOIR DETECTIVES ——— Heading 1 used for main title

an essay by Robert Fuller ——— Heading 2 used for subtitle

July 7, 1997 ———

Heading 3 used for least important information in title

"Down these mean street a man must go who is not himself mean, who is neither tarnished or afraid. The detective in this kind of story must be such a man. He is the hero; he is everything. He must be a complete man and a common man, and yet an unusual man. He must be, to use a weathered phrase, a man of honor—by instinct, by inevitability, without thought of it, and certainly without saying it. He must be the best man in his world, and a good enough man in any world."

~ Raymond Chandler

CAUTION

Heading styles are *Paragraph styles*, meaning that they are applied to entire paragraphs, not individual words or phrases within a paragraph. Even if you only select one or two words when you apply the style, the style's formats are apply to all text within the paragraph.

Modifying Styles

If the existing Heading styles don't meet your needs, you can change them—choose a different font, increase or decrease the font size, or change any of the other formats that are included in the style. To change a Heading style, follow these steps:

1. Select the text to which the Heading style is applied.
2. Choose Format, Style to open the Style dialog box (see Figure 5.3).

FIG. 5.3
Use the Format Style dialog box to select the style that you want to modify or delete.

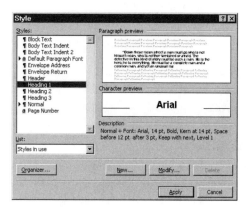

3. Check to make certain the desired Heading style is selected in the Styles box. View the Paragraph and Character Preview boxes.
4. Click the Modify button. The Modify Style dialog box opens (see Figure 5.4).

Part

II

Ch

5

FIG. 5.4

The Modify Style dialog box gives you access to the formatting tools you'll need to change the formatting of the selected style.

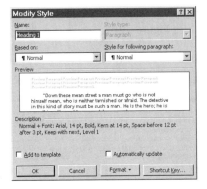

5. Click the F̲ormat button. A list of the areas available for reformatting appears.

6. Select F̲ont or P̲aragraph, depending on the attribute you want to change.

N O T E Your options in the Format list are Font, Paragraph, Tabs, Border, Language, Frame, and Numbering. You can use these options to change anything about the way the style will look and/or function with other text when applied in your document.

7. Make your desired changes in either the Font or Paragraph dialog boxes, and click OK to return to the Modify Style dialog box.

8. If you want to make the changes to the Heading style part of the Normal template (and therefore available on all new, blank documents), click the A̲dd to Template check box.

N O T E You can assign a *shortcut key* to the selected style by clicking the Shortcut K̲ey button in the Modify Style dialog box. Press the keys you want to use as the keyboard command that will apply your style. Click the A̲ssign button, and then click Close. After assigning the shortcut keys, you can use them to quickly apply your style to selected text.

9. If you want to apply the changes to all text in the current document to which this style has already been applied, click the A̲utomatically Update check box.

10. Click OK to return to the Style dialog box. Repeat steps 4–9 for any other styles listed in the Styles box that you want to change.

11. Click A̲pply to return to your document.

Modifying Styles by Example

A faster way of making simple modifications to your styles (both the installed styles and those that you create on your own) is to change the formatting of text to which it's been applied and use the new appearance of your text as an example. Follow these steps to quickly modify any style:

1. Select text in your document, and apply the style of your choice from the Style drop-down list on the Formatting toolbar.

2. With the text still highlighted, reformat it as desired—change the font, make it bigger or smaller, make it bold, or change its color. Apply as many formatting changes as you want.

3. Double-click the style name in the Style box on the toolbar. The name appears highlighted.

T I P If the style name (such as Heading 1) is in two or more parts, you may have to drag through the name instead of double-clicking it.

4. Press Enter. The Modify Style dialog box opens (see Figure 5.5). Do not confuse this dialog box with the one described in the previous procedure.

FIG. 5.5

Changing styles by example is a fast and easy way to reformat a style you'll use often in your current document.

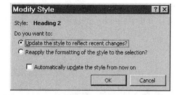

5. Click the Update the Style to Reflect Recent Changes option. This will change the applied style's formats to match the current formatting of the selected text.

6. If you want to have styles automatically update when you reformat text to which styles have been applied, click the check box next to the Automatically Update the Style from Now On Option.

7. Click OK or press Enter to return to your document.

Creating Styles by Example

Just as you can change a style by example, you can format text and use the formatting as an example to build a new style. Follow these steps to build your own new style from formatted text:

1. Select text in your document (it can be any text, although it's best to select text to which you intend to apply the new style).

2. Make certain that Normal is the style appearing in the Style box on the toolbar.

T I P Why start with Normal? So that your new style is based on Normal, the most "vanilla" of styles, and no unexpected or unwanted formats crop up when you use the style later.

3. Format the selected text using any font and/or paragraph formats that you want.

4. Double-click the word Normal in the Style box on the toolbar. The word becomes highlighted.

5. Type a new name for your new style. Although the name can be up to 255 characters long and it can include spaces, keep the name short enough to entirely show in the box, if possible.

6. Press Enter. Your new style is created, and is available in this document to be applied to any text you choose.

NOTE   If you want to make this new style available to all new, blank documents, choose Format, Style, and select your style from the Styles list. Click the Modify button, and choose the Add to Template option. Click OK to return to the Style dialog box. Click OK again to close the box and apply your changes.

CAUTION

Word won't allow you to use the "by example" method to alter the Normal style. You must use the Format, Style procedure to change it, and do so with care—your changes will apply to all regular paragraph text. Do not choose the Add to Template option unless you're absolutely sure the new Normal style will be appropriate for all of your new documents.

Controlling Your Document with the Ruler

Many veteran self-taught Word users neglect one of the most powerful tools in the Word window: the Ruler. The Ruler can be used for virtually anything that applies to how text falls on the page:

- *Tabs.* Set, move, and delete them from the ruler.
- *Indents.* Set and adjust them on the ruler, using the small triangles.
- *Margins.* New margins are just a click and drag away. No need to open the Page Setup dialog box.
- *Bullets and Numbers.* Adjust the distance between the bullet or number and the accompanying text, be it an item in a list or an entire paragraph.

Figure 5.6 shows the ruler and its various tools and features.

 TIP   To make full use of your Ruler, make sure both rulers are showing by choosing View, Page Layout from the menu, or click the Page Layout View button on the View toolbar. A vertical ruler appears on the left side of your screen.

Changing Margins

The most important skill to master in adjusting your margins from the ruler is mouse control. Figure 5.7 shows the top margin in the process of adjustment—the user is dragging the edge of the margin toward the center of the ruler, increasing the margin.

FIG. 5.6

Use the ruler to set tabs, adjust indents and margins, and move text horizontally and vertically on your page.

Tab stop indicator

Top Margin (Bottom Margin guide is out of view)

Left indents (first line and body of paragraph)

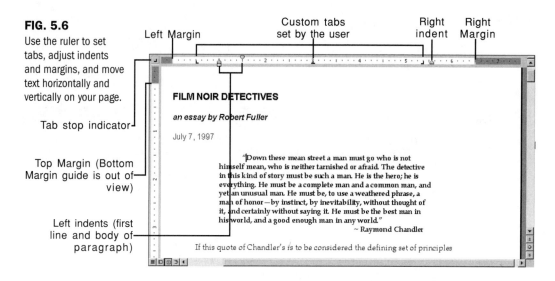

Although changing margins with the ruler is a simple dragging operation, you should keep the following points in mind:

- Use the horizontal ruler to change the left and right margins.
- Use the vertical ruler to change top and bottom margins.
- To increase a margin, drag toward the center of the ruler.
- To decrease a margin, drag away from the center of the ruler.
- Watch the calibrations on the ruler to check the size of the new margin.

FIG. 5.7

Click and drag the margin guides to increase or decrease your margin settings. Exact measurements are difficult to achieve, but the difference between a 1.5 inch and a 1.46 inch margin is rarely significant.

Mouse must be a two-headed arrow to drag the margin guides

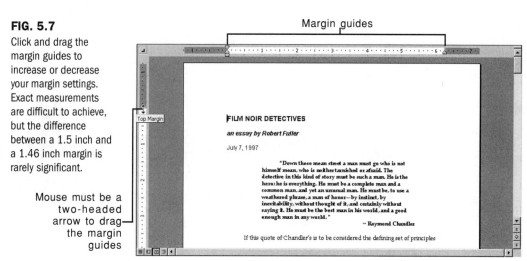

To adjust your margins, follow these simple steps:

1. Point to the spot on the ruler where it turns from white to gray (refer to Figure 5.7). The gray area represents your margin.

2. When your mouse pointer turns to a two-headed arrow, drag the mouse.

> **CAUTION**
>
> Don't decrease any margin beyond .25 inches on the ruler, as this quarter-inch border around the paper cannot be printed on by many laser and inkjet printers.

3. When the desired margin is achieved, release the mouse.

N O T E If, after setting your margins on the ruler, you want to check your new measurements or make sure they've been set to a very specific number, choose File, Page Setup. Click the Margins tab, and view your Left, Right, Top, and Bottom margin measurements. You can adjust them as needed in this dialog box and click OK to apply them to the document.

Setting Indents

Indents are the distance between the margin and your text. The most typically used indent is a first line indent, used at the beginning of a paragraph. Figure 5.8 shows some common indents.

FIG. 5.8

The ruler can be used to set and adjust your left and right indents, adjusting the horizontal position of your text.

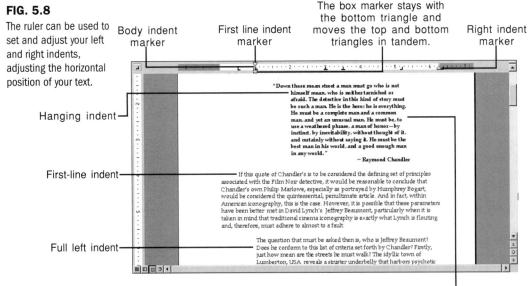

Body indent marker

First line indent marker

The box marker stays with the bottom triangle and moves the top and bottom triangles in tandem.

Right indent marker

Hanging indent

First-line indent

Full left indent

Text indented from left and right

To apply an indent to your text with the ruler's indent markers, click anywhere within the paragraph you want to indent, and drag the triangles to the desired ruler positions. The top and bottom triangles move independently, but the box marker is permanently attached to the bottom triangle. If you drag the box, both triangles come with you, keeping their current relative positions.

 T I P Create a quick first-line indent with the Tab key.

If you want to apply an indent to several contiguous paragraphs, select them all and then move the indent markers as needed.

You can also set indents before you start typing. If you do, the indents you set will apply to all paragraphs typed from that point on, until and unless new indents are set.

N O T E Equally fast, but not as flexible, are the indent keyboard shortcuts: Ctrl+M for a full 1/2-inch indent, Ctrl+T for a hanging indent, and Ctrl+Q to remove all indents and return the text to the margins.

The indent markers can also be used to adjust the space between bullets or numbers and their accompanying text. When bulleted or numbered text is selected, the top triangle on the left represents the bullet or number, and the bottom triangle represents the text. Drag the bottom triangle toward the center of the ruler to increase the distance between the bullet/number and the text.

CAUTION

Be careful when dragging indent markers toward the margin guides. Unexpected and usually unwanted results occur when you drag the indent markers into the margin area.

Part
II

Ch
5

Creating Quick Tabs

Your new, blank documents come with tabs set at every half inch. The text typed beneath these default tabs will be left aligned. For most documents, these tabs are all you need for typing simple multi-column lists and indenting paragraphs. If, however, your tab requirements become more complex, you can set tabs on the ruler by following these steps:

1. Before typing your tabbed text, position the cursor where the text will be started.
2. Click the tab stop indicator (see Figure 5.9), and continue to click it until the alignment you need is displayed. You can cycle through the alignment indicators; they are shown in the following table.

Table 5.1 Tab Stop Alignment Indicators

Tab Alignment Indicator	Alignment
⌊L⌋	Left-aligned tab
⊥	Center-aligned tab
⌐J⌐	Right-aligned tab
⊥	Decimal-aligned tab

3. When the desired alignment indicator is showing, click the ruler at the place where you want to set the tab. A tab symbol (matching the indicator button) appears on the ruler.

4. Continue choosing tab indicators and placing tabs on the ruler until all your desired tabs are set.

5. Type your text, remembering to press the Tab key before each word or phrase that should appear under one of your set tabs. Figure 5.9 shows a column list typed under a series of custom tabs.

N O T E So what's a Decimal tab? Some people use them for numbers, especially currency. They're not really necessary, however, unless your numbers have a varying number of digits to the right of the decimal (as in scientific notation), and you want them lined up vertically under each number's decimal point. For currency, use the Right aligned tab.

FIG. 5.9
Set custom tabs when your tabbing needs are not met by the default left-aligned tabs that are set at every half inch

Tab stop indicator   Tab symbols

Tabbed text

TIP If you require special tabs such as dot leader or bar tabs, you can use the Format, Tabs command and set tabs using the Tabs dialog box.

Moving Tabs on the Ruler

After you've set your tabs, you can move them by simply dragging them on the ruler. Be sure that any tabbed text that was typed using these tabs is selected before you move the tab symbols, or the text will not move with them.

Separate tabs can be set throughout a document. Figure 5.10 shows a page with two different sets of tabs and tabbed text.

FIG. 5.10

Create as many sets of tabs as you need throughout your document.

Previously typed text is aligned under different tabs.

Tab markers for the second set of tabbed lines

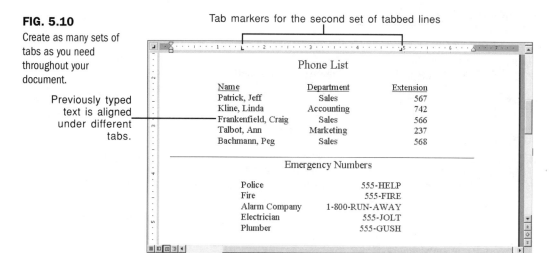

Using the Ruler to Adjust Tab Alignment

After you've set your tabs, you may decide that the text you've typed should be aligned differently. Perhaps you forgot to use a right-aligned tab for a column of tabbed currency amounts, or you want to center a list of dates. To adjust your tabs' alignment on the ruler, follow these steps:

1. Select the tabbed text that was typed under the tabs that you want to change. You have to select full lines of text even if not all of the text on the line will be changed.

2. Click the tab marker that you want to change, and drag it down and off the ruler. The text becomes "scrambled," but don't worry.

3. Click the tab indicator button until the desired alignment is displayed.

4. Click the ruler to place your new tab marker. Your tabbed text falls back into place, realigned to match the alignment of the replaced tab.

Part
II

Ch
5

Removing Tabs from the Ruler

Getting rid of tabs is easy—so easy, in fact, that you must be careful not to do it by mistake when moving tabs! Simply drag the tab marker you want to remove down and off the ruler.

> **CAUTION**
>
> If you don't want your tabbed text to be affected by the tab marker's removal, make certain your cursor is at least one blank line below the tabbed text. If your cursor is on the text that was typed under the removed tab, the text will move when the marker is deleted.

Adding Visual Impact

Word makes it easy to change the appearance of your text and overall document. Between the toolbars, ruler, and user-friendly menus and dialog boxes, changing fonts, aligning text, changing line spacing, and an incredible variety of formatting changes are easy to apply.

However, one of the most powerful visual changes you can make—in terms of its impact on a document's appearance and effectiveness—is the use of colors for text and shading, and the addition of borders to paragraphs and pages.

As more and more documents are never printed—they're viewed on the Web, attached to email and viewed onscreen—color becomes something that anyone can use, not just those of us with color printers! Color helps draw attention to important text, and shading lines or paragraphs of text not only draws the reader's eye, but it also gives the entire document a graphical, polished look. The use of borders is as essential to the effectiveness of some documents as putting a picture in a frame. Figure 5.11 shows a document with colored and shaded text, and a border under an important heading.

FIG. 5.11
Although not visually dynamic in this black-and-white image, the use of color and borders makes onscreen viewing of a document more interesting for the reader.

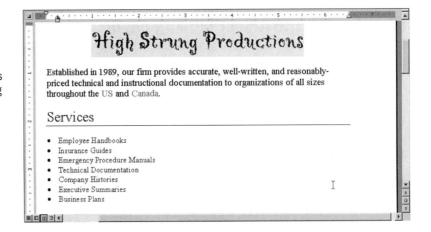

Applying Borders and Shading

Users of Office 97 and Office 95 will find that there are differences between the toolbar methods of applying borders and shading in these two versions of Office. To eliminate confusion, we'll cover the menu command method, which is more consistent between versions.

Borders can be applied to paragraphs or to the entire page of a document. Shading is also applicable to individual words, lines of text, or whole paragraphs. You could apply shading to an entire page, but it isn't advisable—you'll waste printer's toner or ink, and if you make photocopies of the page or attempt to fax the document, the results will be undesirable.

N O T E If you'd prefer to apply borders and shading by using the toolbar:

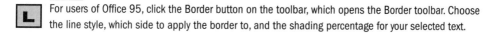

For users of Office 95, click the Border button on the toolbar, which opens the Border toolbar. Choose the line style, which side to apply the border to, and the shading percentage for your selected text.

For users of Office 97, click the Borders and Tables button, opening the Tables and Borders toolbar. Apply a line style, color, and shading color for your selected text.

To apply a border to paragraph text, follow these steps:

1. Place your cursor in the paragraph around which you want to place a border. You do not need to select the paragraph.
2. Choose F*o*rmat, *B*orders and Shading.
3. In the Borders and Shading dialog box, click the Borders tab (see Figure 5.12).

FIG. 5.12

Use the Borders and Shading dialog box to set and customize borders for your paragraph text.

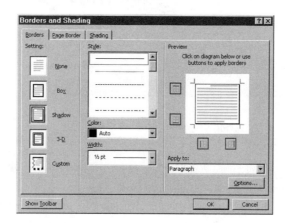

4. Choose the Setting for your border—*N*one, Bo*x*, Sh*a*dow, 3-*D*, or C*u*stom.
5. Choose a St*y*le (solid, dashed, dotted, or multiple lines).
6. Select a *C*olor.
7. Set the *W*idth of your line. This setting refers to the weight or thickness of your line, not its horizontal width as the name implies.

8. In the Preview area, click the sides of the box (top, bottom, left, and/or right) on which you want borders placed.

9. Click the Options button if you want to adjust the distance between the border(s) and the text. After making any changes, click OK to return to the Borders and Shading dialog box.

10. Click OK to apply the borders to your text.

Page borders on a single-page document are easy to apply—you need only place your cursor on the page and perform the steps that follow this paragraph. If, however, you're placing borders on pages in a multi-page document, you must either place them on all pages or add section breaks to your document to control the pages on which borders are applied.

1. Place your cursor on the page (or within the section) around which you want to place a border.

2. Choose Format, Borders and Shading.

3. In the Borders and Shading dialog box, click the Page Border tab (see Figure 5.13).

FIG. 5.13
Page borders apply to all the pages in your document unless you've inserted section breaks. You can apply borders to specific sections, and omit them on the first page of the section.

An Art border selected

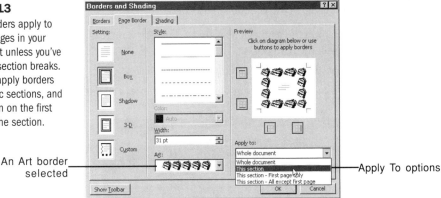

Apply To options

4. Choose a Setting for your page border.

5. Select a line Style.

6. Choose a Color for your border.

7. Select a line Width (weight or thickness).

8. Choose from the Art drop-down list to form a border of small repeated pictures.

9. In the Preview section, click the edges of the display to choose where the border is to be applied.

10. Click the Apply To drop-down list and choose to apply the borders to the Whole Document or to a specific section.

N O T E Click the Options button in the Borders and Shading dialog box to make changes to the placement of the borders. By default, the borders will be placed .24 inches from the edge of the paper. You can choose to measure from the edge of the paper or from the text. Click OK to return to the Borders and Shading dialog box.

11. Click OK to apply your borders as specified.

You can edit your applied borders at any time. Place your cursor within the text that is bordered (or on a page that has a border on it) and choose F<u>o</u>rmat, <u>B</u>orders and Shading. Change the style of your lines, add/or delete sides of the border, or remove the border altogether by choosing <u>N</u>one.

 N O T E Office 97 has a powerful Tables and Borders toolbar which opens when you click the Tables and Borders button on the Standard toolbar. Apply borders, shading, and create tables from this floating toolbar.

Shading can be applied from the Borders and Shading dialog box—click the Shading tab and choose a Fill color and Pattern (see Figure 5.14).

FIG. 5.14
Shading places a colored and/or patterned fill on your page behind text or on blank lines. You can also apply shading to cells within tables.

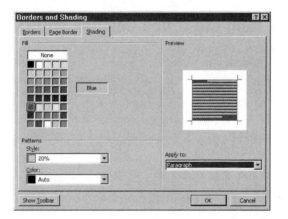

The St<u>y</u>le options allow you to pick a percentage of shading to apply. When applying shading behind text, use a light percentage (20% or less) so the shading doesn't visually compete with the text. You can also choose from several simple geometric patterns by scrolling to the bottom of the St<u>y</u>le list. Of course, you donít want to use patterns behind text unless you want to render the text illegible!

 Shading is an excellent tool for improving the appearance of tables, and for preventing accidental usage of reserved cells in a fill-in form.

Working with Colored Text

Shading and borders can be applied in color, as discussed in the previous section, but color can also be applied to text. Using colored text has obvious uses—change the color of an important paragraph so no one forgets to read it or make your headings a bright color to draw attention to major topics in your document. Of course color can be used for purely aesthetic reasons—to add visual interest or create a festive or exciting feeling. You can apply color in a variety of ways:

- Text color can be applied to selected text by using the Format, Font command to open the Font dialog box. Click the Color drop-down list, and choose a color from the palette.

- Use the Font color button on the Word 97 Formatting toolbar.

- Apply a color to one selection of text, and then turn on the Format Painter to apply it to other text in the document. You'll want to double-click the Format Painter if you want to copy the color to more than one selection.

- Make color part of a style, and then apply the style as needed.

N O T E Word 97 offers another color-oriented format for text—animation! Choose Format, Font, and click the Animation tab. Choose from several animation effects, viewing samples in the Preview box. Click OK to apply your chosen animation to the selected text.

Inserting Graphics from the Office Companion CD

The CD that accompanies this book contains many graphic files—clip art images, photographs, and animated .gifs. These files were included in the CD to enhance the available options for making your documents look more technically polished and visually interesting.

Use the clip art and photographs as backgrounds to add all-over color to documents, whether they're destined to be Web pages or simply documents that will be viewed onscreen. You can print files with backgrounds, but depending on the background colors and color of your text, the output may not be desirable.

To use a background from the CD, follow these steps:

1. With your document open, choose Format, Background. A palette appears.
2. Click Fill Effects.
3. In the Fill Effects dialog box, click the Picture tab.
4. Click the Select Picture button.
5. In the resulting dialog box, navigate to your CD-ROM drive and open the folder that contains the file you want to use. You'll find clip art in the \clipart folder and photographs in the \photos folder.
6. Click the Preview button in the Select Picture dialog box, so you can view each of the backgrounds before selecting one.
7. Double-click the one you want to apply, or click it once and click the OK button. The dialog box closes, and the selected background fills your page, behind your text.

N O T E   You'll notice that as soon as you apply a background, your view changes to Online Layout. This is because the background feature was designed for Web page design. It can be used for documents not destined for the Web, however, so feel free to switch to any of the other views for any text editing or formatting you need to do. Your background will only be visible in Online Layout view, although it remains in effect even when you can't see it.

Clip art and/or animated .gif files are included in the CD to give you a more interesting array of images to add to your documents. As the saying goes, a picture's worth a thousand words—your readers will sit up and take notice when they receive a document that includes graphics, and they'll remember the document after reading it!

To insert any of the clip art or animated .gifs from the CD, follow these steps:

1. Position your cursor at the place where you want to add the graphic file.
2. Choose Insert, Picture, From File. The Insert Picture dialog box opens.
3. Navigate to your CD-ROM drive, and open the folder entitled \clipart for clip art images, or \animgifs for animated .gif files.
4. Click the Preview button in the Select Picture dialog box so that you can see each of the files as you click them.
5. When you've found the image you want to use, double-click it or click it once and click OK.

After inserting the graphic, it appears in your document with handles on its corners and sides. Use these handles to resize the graphic by dragging them away from the center to increase the image size, or toward the center of the image to make it smaller. While resizing, your mouse pointer will appear as a two-headed arrow.

To move the graphic, point to its border (visible only when the graphic is selected) and watch for your mouse pointer to turn to a four-headed arrow. When it does, click and drag to position the graphic in a new location. If you want to move it beyond the visible area of your document, use the Clipboard to Cut and Paste it to a new spot.

T I P   In Word 97, you can open and use the Picture toolbar to format your graphic. To open the toolbar, right-click any toolbar and choose Picture from the pop-up menu.

Part

II

Ch

5

Structuring Documents with Tables

Creating Complex Document Formats with Tables

This may sound like a strong statement, but tables may be the most powerful, useful, and effective tool in the entire Word application. Tables can be used to create column lists (for which you would otherwise have to set custom tabs), intricate documents such as resumes and contracts (eliminating your need to set up complex indents and paragraph formats), and fill-in forms for surveys, questionnaires, and other information-gathering documents. Figure 6.1 shows a document that contains a fill-in form and a set of parallel paragraphs, formatted by their placement in a table.

FIG. 6.1

Instead of setting tabs or custom indents for lists, forms, or paragraphs, use tables to control the placement of text.

Employee Evaluation Form

Name _____
Department _____
Supervisor Name
Date of Last Review ▓▓▓▓▓▓▓▓▓▓▓▓▓▓▓▓▓▓

Position	Description
Administrative Assistant	Responsible for all written, faxed, and emailed information coming out of the Accounting department. Must keep all files up-to-date, and maintain a database of customers and their current and overdue balances. Phone skills, computer literacy and bookkeeping experience are required for any applicants for this position. Experience in the Insurance industry is a plus.

Tables are simple to set up, fill in, and format for aesthetic and functional appeal. Using the Clipboard, Word tables can be easily translated into Excel worksheets, and Excel worksheets can be easily converted into Word tables. Word tables are also useful in PowerPoint presentations, and can serve as databases for form letters.

You can format your cell contents just as you would paragraph text—use your font, size, alignment, and style tools as usual. You can apply any paragraph formats to your cell content, as well as bullets and numbers, color, shading, and borders.

Building and Formatting Tables

Tables can be inserted from the toolbar or menu by following these simple steps:

1. To create a table from the Standard toolbar, place your cursor in your document at the point where you want to insert the table. Click the Insert Table button.

2. A grid appears. Drag your mouse through the grid, starting with the block in the upper-left corner. Drag across to select the number of columns, and drag down to select the number of rows (see Figure 6.2).

T I P Although the Insert Table grid appears showing only 20 blocks (for a 5×4 table), as you drag your mouse, the grid expands, enabling you to create a table with dimensions as large as 18 rows by 12 columns.

FIG. 6.2

Drag through the Insert Table tool's grid to determine the dimensions of your new table.

CAUTION

To avoid having to adjust column widths and potentially reformat your entire table later, try to have an accurate count of the columns you'll need for your table before you create it. Although columns can be added later, adding them can create problems for your table's layout.

3. Release the mouse to insert the table.

CAUTION

Be careful when creating new tables in a document that already contains a table—if you're too close to the existing table (one blank line above or below it), the new table will be added to the existing table as additional rows and columns. To make sure your new table is separate from the existing table, put two or more blank lines between them.

To insert a table from the menu, follow these steps:

1. Position your cursor where you want the new table inserted.
2. Choose Table, Insert Table from the menu bar. The Insert Table dialog box opens (see Figure 6.3).

FIG. 6.3

A more methodical method of creating a table is to use the Insert Table dialog box.

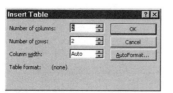

3. Enter the number of columns and rows you need, and click OK.

Your new table is inserted, and you can begin entering text into the cells, or formatting the columns and rows.

Navigating a Table

Your table is automatically sized (in terms of column width) to fit the width of your document. To move through the table, press the Tab key. This will move you left to right, one cell at a time. When you reach the last cell in a row, the Tab key will move you to the first cell in the next row down. If you want to move backward, use the Shift+Tab key combination.

Part

II

Ch

6

To move quickly from the first cell in a row to the last, press Alt+End. To move from the last cell to the first cell in a row, press Alt+Home.

 T I P It's tempting to use the arrow keys to move through your table's cells. This works fine until you have text in the cells—then the arrow keys move among the text, not from cell to cell.

Selecting Cells, Columns, and Rows

Before you apply formatting to cells in your table, you must select the cells that you want to set up. Selecting cells within your table is simple, and you can do it in any of the following ways:

- To select a column, point to the top border of the column and watch for your mouse pointer to turn to a black, down-pointing arrow (see Figure 6.4). When it does, click once. The entire column is selected. Drag through adjoining columns to select more than one.

FIG. 6.4

Watch for the appropriate mouse pointer, and then drag through your columns to select them.

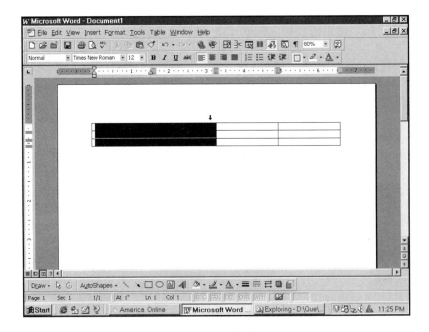

- To select a row, point to the left margin outside the table, next to the row you want to select. When your mouse pointer points to the right, click (see Figure 6.5). The row is selected. Drag up or down to select adjoining rows.
- Click and drag through rows, columns, or blocks of cells. You can select one or more cells this way.

N O T E Text entry in a table is the same as typing normal paragraph text, except for the fact that the Tab key takes you to the next cell instead of indenting your cursor. If you need to insert tabs within a cell, press Ctrl+Tab.

FIG. 6.5
Use the left margin to select one or more rows.

Adjusting Column Width and Row Height

The key to making a table do what you want it to do is to adjust the width of your columns and the height of your rows. Column width can be adjusted in any of the following ways:

■ Position your mouse on the right side border of the column. When the mouse pointer turns to a horizontal two-headed arrow (see Figure 6.6), drag to the right to widen the column, drag to the left to make it narrower.

FIG. 6.6
Drag your column borders to increase or decrease column width.

A dashed vertical guide appears as you drag the mouse to adjust column width.

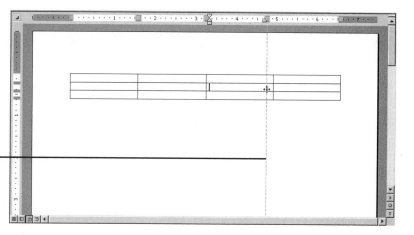

■ Select a column or columns and choose Table, Cell Height and Width. In the resulting dialog box, click the Column tab and enter a width for your column(s) (see Figure 6.7).

FIG. 6.7
Use the Cell Height and Width dialog box to make precise adjustments to your column width.

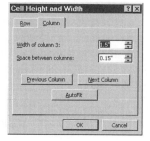

Part
II

Ch
6

 T I P Click the AutoFit button in the Column tab to automatically adjust the width of your selected columns to fit the widest entry.

■ Drag the table column markers on the ruler. When your mouse pointer turns to a white two-headed arrow, point to the small boxes on the ruler (above the column borders) and drag them right to widen the column, left to narrow it (see Figure 6.8).

FIG. 6.8

Your ruler's column markers can be used to adjust column width.

Drag the column marker.

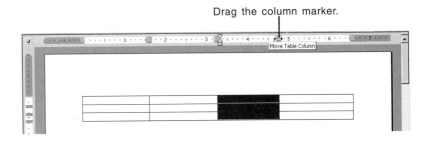

Row height is adjusted automatically when you enlarge text in a cell or when you add blank lines with the Enter key or type continuous wrapped paragraphs within a cell. You can also manually adjust row height using the following methods. Try doing it both ways—you'll find that one may be preferable to the other, depending on your comfort level with the mouse or fondness for the methodical procedures found in menu commands.:

■ Row heights can be adjusted by dragging the bottom border of a row. When you point to this border, the mouse turns to a vertical two-headed arrow (see Figure 6.9). Drag down to make the row taller, drag up to make it shorter.

FIG. 6.9

Drag your row borders to adjust row height manually.

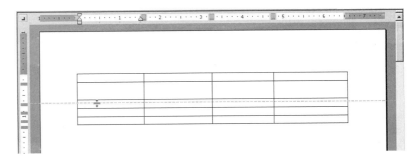

■ Adjust your row heights by selecting a row or rows and choosing Table, Cell Height and Width. Click the Row tab and enter a measurement for the row(s) (see Figure 6.10). You can enter inches (type the inch marks ["] after the number) or points, typing a number only. Don't type "points" or "pts"—Word assumes the points measuring system when numbers are typed with no inch marks after them.

■ There are table markers on the vertical ruler just as there are on the horizontal ruler. If you're in Page Layout view, click and drag the row markers on the vertical ruler to adjust row height.

FIG. 6.10

Enter your row height measurements in inches or points by using the Cell Height and Width dialog box.

N O T E You can center your entire table horizontally, relative to the page, by placing your cursor in the table and choosing Table, Cell Height and Width. In the Row tab, click the Center option in the Alignment section. Click OK to close the dialog box and apply the alignment setting.

Using Tables Instead of Indents and Tabs

Tables are an excellent tool for controlling the placement of parallel paragraphs—columns of words or phrases accompanied by paragraph text, such as you find in resumes, leases and contracts, or other complex reports. Figure 6.11 shows a resume that was constructed with a table.

FIG. 6.11

Use a table to control the placement of text in two or more columns.

Width of column controls wrap of paragraph text, as though an indent were set

Bullets used within a cell

Alignment of text within the table's column mimics tabbed text

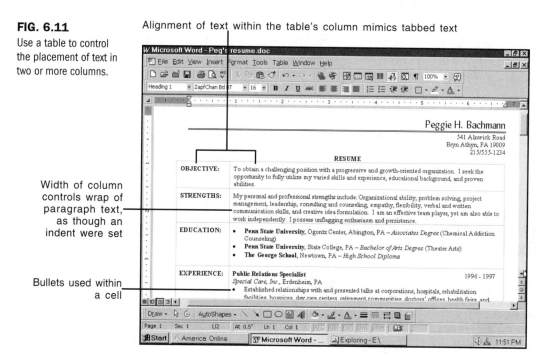

Generally, documents containing parallel paragraphs have two columns and as many rows as there are items, such as topics or headings in a report or resume. By adjusting the width of these columns, you can create the appearance of indents and tabs.

Part
II

Ch
6

Column lists, such as a list of people and their phone numbers can have any number of columns, and as many rows as there are people to be listed. When created with a table, this list will look like it was created with tabs, but the columns (and the alignment applied to individual columns) eliminates the need to set tabs, and is much easier to accomplish and control. Figure 6.12 shows a list of employees and their departments and phone numbers. The visible gridlines will not print, creating the look of a tabbed list.

FIG. 6.12

Turn off your borders so only you know that a table was used to create the look of tabs or indents.

Headings formatted to stand out

Company Phone List

NAME		DEPARTMENT	EXTENSION NUMBER
Joan	Mattaliano	Accounting	546
Ken	Cook	Marketing	468
Miriam	Elmaleh	Sales	359
Dave	Mermelstein	Sales	362
Ken	Hoelzle	Accounting	558
Greg	Such	Janitorial	221
Carol	Barbieri	Marketing	472

Alignment applied within columns

Cells split to create two columns under one single cell.

Inserting Columns and Rows

Even the most well thought-out, carefully planned table is bound to require more columns than you expected; and if you forget to include any of the items you want in a table (which nearly always happens), you'll have to go back and add additional rows. Luckily, there are simple ways to add them, even after you've added text to the existing columns and rows:

- To insert a column, select the column to the right of where you want the new one to be, and choose Table, Insert Columns.
- To add several columns at once, select one column and choose Table, Split Cells. Enter the number of columns you need to add, and click OK (see Figure 6.13). The selected column is divided into several columns (the number of columns you specified). You can widen these columns as necessary (use the techniques we covered in the earlier section, "Adjusting Column Width and Row Height").

TIP Turn off the Merge Cells Before Split option if your cells already contain text. This will save you having to move or retype the content in the cells that were split.

FIG. 6.13

Split existing columns and rows into two or more new columns and rows, increasing the dimensions of your table, but not the space it takes up on the page. Adjust column widths as needed afterward.

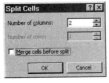

- To add a row or rows, select the row below where you want the new rows to be added, and choose T<u>a</u>ble, <u>I</u>nsert Rows.

- To add several rows, select one row (below where you want the new rows to be added), and choose T<u>a</u>ble, S<u>p</u>lit Cells (refer to Figure 6.13). Enter the number of columns you already have (so it doesn't split your columns) and enter the number of rows you want to add. Click OK.

CAUTION

Rarely will the addition of rows and columns not result in some unwanted width or placement results. Be prepared to Undo your action and try again, or spend some time adjusting your column widths.

Applying Borders and Shading

Borders and shading make your table look more polished and professional, but they also serve functional purposes. In the case of fill-in forms, the use of shading (with solid colors or pattern fills) can help users steer clear of cells that they shouldn't use. Borders can become signature lines on a form, or dividers in a multi-part document. Figure 6.14 shows a document with a variety of table shading and border formatting applied.

FIG. 6.14
Borders and shading can be applied for aesthetic and/or functional purposes.

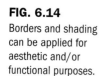
Shaded column highlights important information

Shaded row breaks column headings from remainder of table

Shaded blocks indicate item not selected

Part
II

Ch
6

CAUTION

When you insert a table, it has visible and printable borders around each cell. You can leave them as they are, or delete them in the whole table or on a cell-by-cell basis to achieve your desired visual effect. Once you've deleted them, be sure your T<u>a</u>ble, <u>G</u>ridlines command is set ON (a check mark next to it), or you won't be able to tell which cell you're in as you move through the table.

T I P

In Word 97, the T<u>a</u>ble, <u>G</u>ridlines command actually appears as Hide <u>G</u>ridlines when gridlines are showing, and Show <u>G</u>ridlines when they've been turned off.

To apply borders to your table cells, follow these steps:

1. Select the cell or cells around which you want to add or delete a border.

2. Choose Format, Borders and Shading. The Borders and Shading dialog box opens (see Figure 6.15).

FIG. 6.15

The Borders and Shading dialog box gives you options for the appearance and placement of your table's borders.

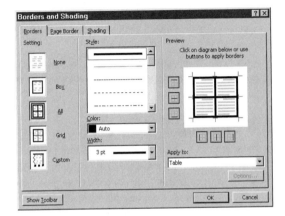

3. Click the Borders tab.

4. Choose the type of borders you want for the selected cells from the Settings options.

T I P For detailed information on each of the Settings options, click the What's This? Help (?) button in the upper-right corner of the dialog box, and then click the Settings option for which you need details.

5. Choose a Style, Color, and Width for your borders.

6. Use the border buttons in the Preview section to determine which borders you want to add or delete. You can apply top, bottom, inside horizontal, left, and right borders.

7. Click the Apply To drop-down list, and choose Cell to apply the borders to only the selected cell(s). Choose Table to apply them to the entire table, regardless of which cells are selected.

8. Click OK to apply your border changes and close the dialog box.

To apply shading to your cells, follow these steps:

1. Select the cells you want to fill with color or pattern, and choose Format, Borders and Shading.

2. Click the Shading tab (see Figure 6.16).

FIG. 6.16

Add a solid color or patterned fill to cells to protect cells from use in fill-in forms, or to create a graphical block in any table-based document.

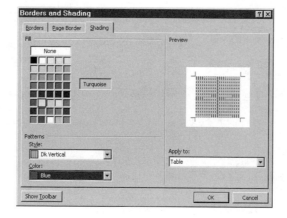

3. In the Fill section, choose a color. This color will serve as a solid color if you choose a percentage shading effect, or as the background color if you select a patterned fill.

4. In the Patterns section, click the Style drop-down list and select a percentage shading for your color. You can also scroll down in the list to choose from a variety of simple patterns.

5. Choose a Color for your pattern (this box only becomes available if a pattern is selected).

6. Click the Apply To drop-down list and choose Cell to apply the fill to the selected cells or Table to apply it to the entire table.

7. Click OK to apply your shading or pattern and close the dialog box.

N O T E A fast and easy (yet not terribly flexible) method of applying both borders and shading to a table is to use the Table, Table AutoFormat command. This feature provides a list of predesigned table formats that you can select and preview, as well as options for which parts of the formats to apply. When you find one that meets your needs, click OK.

▶ **See** "Applying Borders and Shading," **p. 57**

Sorting Table Data

Tables that store lists of information—rows of names and addresses, for example—can be sorted like a true database. You can sort your table by one or more *fields*, which are the categories found in each column of your table.

Figure 6.17 shows a table that contains a list of people and the events they're sponsoring for a fund-raising campaign. This list can be sorted by name, event, or funds raised. It can also be sorted by two or more of those fields at the same time, resulting in a list sorted by names, and for each name, the events that person is responsible for in order by how much money was raised. Figure 6.18 shows the table after this sort has been performed.

FIG. 6.17

A table that contains a list can be sorted so the records appear in a relevant order.

Name	Event	Funds Raised
Ulrich, Karl	Herbal Healing Day	$7,620.00
Frankenfield, Craig	Golf Workshop – Beginners	$32,460.00
Kline, John	Real Estate Seminar	$2,590.50
Frankenfield, Craig	Golf Workshop -- Advanced	$35,585.50
Kline, John	Money Management Class	$12,350.00
Ulrich, Karl	Reflexology Class	$5,270.00
Kline, John	Financial Planning Seminar	$15,640.00

Items in the list are in the order in which they were entered.

FIG. 6.18

After sorting by person, then by funds raised, the table's records are in a useful order.

Name	Event	Funds Raised
Frankenfield, Craig	Golf Workshop – Beginners	$32,460.00
Frankenfield, Craig	Golf Workshop -- Advanced	$35,585.50
Kline, John	Real Estate Seminar	$2,590.50
Kline, John	Money Management Class	$12,350.00
Kline, John	Financial Planning Seminar	$15,640.00
Ulrich, Karl	Reflexology Class	$5,270.00
Ulrich, Karl	Herbal Healing Day	$7,620.00

To sort a table, first determine whether your table has a *header row*. This is the top row of the table, and the cells contain the category or field names for the information stored in the table. For example, in a name and address list, the header row would contain First Name in the first cell, Last Name in the next, Address in the third cell, and so forth. If your table has a header row, Word will probably detect it automatically when you invoke the Sort command—if it doesn't you can tell it that you have a header row, and that row will be left at the top of the table and not sorted in with the other rows.

If your table cannot have a header row (normally for aesthetic reasons), it will not affect your sorting capability.

To sort your list table, follow these steps:

1. Click in any cell in your table. Don't select any cells, or Word will think you only want to sort those particular cells and not the whole table.

2. Choose Table, Sort.

3. The Sort dialog box opens (see Figure 6.19).

4. Choose the first field by which to sort.

FIG. 6.19

Sort by one, two, or three fields in your table. To sort on more than one field, there must be duplicate data in one or more fields.

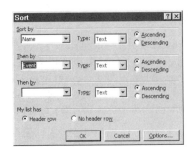

Your category names should appear in the Sort By listbox—if they don't, click Header Row in the My List Has section.

5. If you want to perform a second-level sort, click the Then By listbox, and choose the next field by which to sort.

6. Set a third level (Then By) sort if needed, and click OK.

 Make sure each of your sort levels is set to the right order—Ascending or Descending. This applies to alphabetical or numeric data.

Your table is sorted, and can be resorted as necessary by repeating the previous steps.

▶ **See** "Sorting Lists," **p. 186**

Performing Calculations in Tables

Tables that are used to store numeric data—the total billed in an invoice, for example—don't require you to do math externally and then type your calculation results into the cells manually. Word's Table menu contains a Formula command that enables you to use Excel-like formula construction techniques for summing, counting, or averaging numbers in columns and rows.

To perform a calculation in a table, follow these steps:

1. Click in the cell that should contain the result of the formula.

2. Choose Table, Formula. The Formula dialog box opens (see Figure 6.20).

FIG. 6.20

Use the Table, Formula command to perform simple calculations in your Word table.

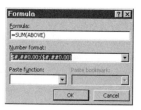

3. If your cell is at the foot of a column or in the last cell of a row, Word assumes you want to SUM the column or row. This formula will appear in the Formula box. You can edit this box as desired.

4. If the assumed function and cell selection (=SUM(ABOVE) or =SUM(LEFT)) is correct, click OK and your total appears in the selected cell.

5. If you need to change to another function, click the Paste Function listbox and choose from one of 18 different functions.

6. Click the Number Format listbox and choose a format for your formula's result.

7. Click OK to perform the calculation and insert the result in the selected cell (see Figure 6.21).

Part
II

Ch
6

FIG. 6.21

The result of the sum of the cells in the column appears in the selected cell, in currency format.

Name	Event	Funds Raised
Frankenfield, Craig	Golf Workshop – Beginners	$32,460.00
Frankenfield, Craig	Golf Workshop -- Advanced	$35,585.50
Kline, John	Real Estate Seminar	$2,590.50
Kline, John	Money Management Class	$12,350.00
Kline, John	Financial Planning Seminar	$15,640.00
Ulrich, Karl	Reflexology Class	$5,270.00
Ulrich, Karl	Herbal Healing Day	$7,620.00
	TOTAL FUNDS RAISED:	$111,516.00

CAUTION

Word's use of mathematical functions is not as helpful as the Function Wizard in Excel—there will be no help for you in constructing the formulas if you must supply cell addresses or external numbers to complete the formula. Stick to simple sums, counts, and averages for Word table calculations. If a more complex function is required, perform it in Excel, and paste the cells into your Word document.

If you change the contents of any cells that contributed to your formula, you can update the result of the formula by selecting the cell that contains the formula result and pressing the F9 key. This can also be used if you add rows or columns within the range of cells being summed, counted, or averaged and want their amounts to be included in the result. ●

Working with Long Documents

Understanding Sections

Rarely seen or needed in single-page documents, *sections* are divisions within a long document that break the entire document into separate parts. The points at which these sections are divided are called *section breaks*. Some section breaks occur naturally, through the addition of certain elements to your document:

■ *New margins for a single page or portion of the document.* Unless you choose the Whole Document option when changing margins or reset your margins from the rulers (which changes them for the whole document), you will add a section break for the portion of the document with the new margins. If the portion of your document that has new margins is preceded by and followed by pages with no changes to the original margins, you will end up with three sections.

■ *New orientation.* If you switch to Landscape (from Portrait), or to Portrait (from Landscape) for a single page within your document, a section break will be added at the beginning of the page and at the end of the page, creating a total of three sections.

■ *Page numbers with no number on the first page.* By separating the first page and specifying that it have no page number, a section break is added after the first page, dividing your document into two sections—the first page, and then everything after it.

If a section break can be added unintentionally, how do you know you've added one? Check your status bar. Figure 7.1 shows a Print Preview of a naturally occurring section break in a five-page document.

FIG. 7.1
Section breaks are added by Word when you change the rules for a portion of the document.

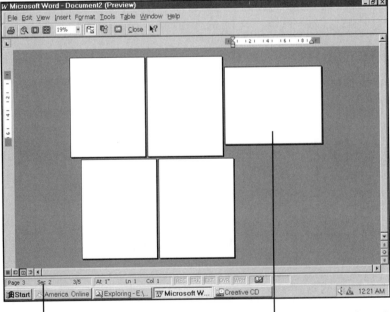

Section indicator on the status bar

A single page changed to Landscape orientation

Inserting Section Breaks

Some section breaks are purposely added by the user so that separate parts of a single document can be treated differently. Imagine an employee handbook with a cover page, a table of contents, the main handbook pages, and an index. Following the index is a Notes page for the employee to fill with handwritten notes about any procedural updates. As each of these five conceptual sections will require special handling—no page numbers or headers/footers on the cover page, for example—each conceptual section will have to be separated from the rest of the sections with a section break.

Section breaks enable you to apply page numbering or headers and footers to certain sections and not to others. You can have section breaks between chapters, and number each chapter differently. You can suppress your header and footer on the cover page by placing a section break at the end of that page. For any document that you don't want formatted the same way throughout, section breaks are essential, giving you the ability to create a complex document with visually distinct sections.

To insert a section break, follow these steps:

1. Turn on Word's Show/Hide view by clicking the Show/Hide button on the Standard toolbar, or by choosing View, Show All from the menu bar.

NOTE   Always turn Show/Hide on when adding section breaks to make sure they've been placed where you intended. When you're ready to return to typing or editing your document, you can turn off your Show/Hide feature if you find that the codes clutter your screen. To turn off Show/Hide, click the Show/Hide button again, or choose View, Show All.

2. With your hard returns, spaces, tabs, and other non-printing codes now visible, place your cursor at the point where you want to place the page break.

3. Choose Insert, Break. The Break dialog box opens (see Figure 7.2).

FIG. 7.2

Inserting your own section breaks gives you control of your document's conceptual divisions.

4. Click Continuous or Next Page in the Section Breaks portion of the dialog box.

5. Click OK to close the dialog box and insert your section break.

NOTE   Continuous section breaks are added at the cursor and do not interrupt the flow of text before and after their position in the document. Next Page section breaks insert not only a section break but a page break as well, following the section break. This type of section break is useful when building a document from a series of blank pages, before any text has been typed.

Part
II
Ch
7

Working with Page Numbers

Any document in excess of a single page should probably contain page numbers, if only to help a reader who has dropped the printed document and wants to put the pages back in order! Business letters should be numbered starting with page two, even if page two is the last page.

Page numbers can be applied to individual sections of your document, all pages but the first, or to all your pages without any deviation.

To insert page numbers on all pages of your document, follow these steps:

1. Place your cursor at the top of the document by pressing Ctrl+Home.
2. Choose Insert, Page Numbers. The Page Numbers dialog box opens (see Figure 7.3).

FIG. 7.3

Place your page numbers at the top or bottom of the page, on the left, right, or centered horizontally.

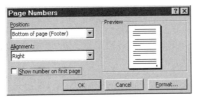

3. By default, page numbers are placed at the bottom of the page (in the footer), on the right side of the page. Change these settings as desired.
4. For most business documents, there should be no page number on the first page. Turn the Show Number on First Page option off.
5. Click OK to insert your page numbers and close the dialog box.

 If you can't see your page numbers onscreen, switch to Page Layout view by choosing View, Page Layout from the menu bar, or by clicking the Page Layout View button on the View toolbar. Your page numbers will appear dimmed at either the top or bottom of your pages. They are also visible in Print Preview.

Defining Page Number Formats

By default, your page numbers appear in Arabic numerals (1,2,3), accompanied by no other text or symbols. You can change them to upper- or lowercase Roman numerals or letters of the alphabet. These formats can be applied to all your page numbers, or to numbers within certain sections of your document.

To change your existing page number formats or to insert page numbers and simultaneously apply special formatting to the page numbers in your entire document, follow these steps:

1. With your cursor on a numbered page, choose Insert, Page Numbers. The Page Numbers dialog box appears.
2. Choose or change the position of your page numbers on the page, if necessary.
3. Click the Format button.

4. In the Page Number Format dialog box, choose a Number Format for your page numbers. Figure 7.4 shows the list of number formats displayed.

FIG. 7.4

Your page numbers can appear as Arabic or Roman numerals, or as letters of the alphabet. Normally, a table of contents is numbered with lowercase Roman numerals.

5. Click OK to close the dialog box and apply your page number formats.

N O T E   By default, your page numbers will be in the font and size of the rest of the text in your document. You can change the character formats of your page numbers by double-clicking a page number on any page. This opens the header or footer area of the document. Click the page number—handles will appear around it—and choose the desired font and size from the Formatting toolbar. Double-click back in the main portion of the document page to exit the header/footer.

The desire to remove page numbers usually arises when you've applied page numbers to an entire document and then want to break the document into sections, some of which you want to number differently or not number at all. To remove page numbers from your entire document, follow these steps:

1. Double-click a page number on any page in your document. Your document's text dims, and a dashed box appears around the top or bottom of your page.

2. Click once on the page number. A slashed border with small black graphic *handles* appears around the number (see Figure 7.5).

    If the slashed border appears without handles, click the slashed border. Eight handles will appear on the border.

FIG. 7.5

Your page number is inserted as an object, a movable, resizable box that contains the number. Click once to select it for moving, resizing, or deletion.

Page number object handles

3. Press the Delete key. The number disappears.

4. To return to your main document, double-click anywhere on the page outside of the dashed box.

 Surprisingly, this is the only way to remove page numbers. There is no Remove button or function within the Insert Page Numbers dialog box. If, however, your addition of page numbers was your last action, you can use Edit, Undo or press Ctrl+Z.

Varying Page Numbers Between Sections

Many times, the primary motivation for inserting section breaks is to enable you to either omit page numbers in one or more sections, or to have the format of the numbers themselves vary between sections. By default, page numbers span section breaks without altering their appearance within the sections. Even if the section breaks were added by Word due to formatting changes applied to selected portions of the document, your page numbers will continue, unchanged, across landscape pages or pages with different margins.

If you want to change the format of page numbers in a particular section or sections of your document, you must turn off the connection between sections, and then deal with the page numbering in each section.

If you want to remove the page numbers, the method you'll use depends on the method you used to insert them. If you inserted them through the Header and Footer toolbar (discussed later in this chapter), you must remove them through the use of that toolbar. If you inserted them by using the Insert, Page Numbers command, use the following steps to remove them and then reapply numbers to the active section:

1. Double-click the page number on any page in the section you want to change.
2. Click once on the page number. Handles appear around the number, showing that it is selected.
3. Press the Delete key. The number disappears. All your page numbers throughout the entire document have also disappeared.
4. Move to the adjoining section that you want to have numbered.
5. Choose Insert, Page Numbers. In the Page Numbers dialog box, click the Format button.
6. In the Page Numbering section of the Page Number Format dialog box, click the Start At option, and enter the page number you want to use for the first page of the current section. This turns off the Continue from Previous Section option.
7. Choose a Number Format, if necessary.
8. Click OK to close the dialog box and insert your numbers in the current section.

To change the format of page numbers in a section of your document, follow these steps:

1. Turn on your nonprinting codes so that you can see your section breaks, by choosing View, Show All.

2. Position your cursor in the section that should have different page numbers than the previous section.

TIP When altering existing section page numbers, work from the end of your document—the commands for breaking the connection between sections' page numbering pertain to the previous section.

3. Choose Insert, Page Numbers.
4. In the Page Numbers dialog box, click the Format button.
5. In the Page Numbering section of the Page Number Format dialog box, click the Start At option and enter the starting number for the first page of the current section.
6. Choose an alternative Number Format.
7. Click OK. The page numbers in the current section change according to your latest settings.
8. Repeat steps 2–7 for all sections that should be different from their previous sections.

N O T E When setting up different page numbering styles for different sections of your document, it's best to plan ahead. Going back and changing things after all your sections have been numbered results in too much repetitive work and unwanted results. Create your section breaks before you apply any page numbering, and then apply page numbers to each section individually, using the Start At option in the Format Page Numbers dialog box to assure that each section's page numbers are set up as you need them.

Using Headers and Footers

If you've added page numbers to your document, you've already used the header or footer portion of your document. Each document consists of two layers—the text layer, where you type your main document content, and the header/footer layer, where page numbers and other content to be repeated on every page are typed.

Although page numbers are the most common header/footer content, you can also place copyright information, chapter titles, dates, times, or author names in this area. Graphics, such as company logos, are also placed in the header or footer area to give each page and/or section of a document a polished, desktop-published look.

TIP Placing a border below your header text and above your footer text helps visually separate the header/footer content from the rest of your document text.

Part
II

Ch
7

Inserting Header and Footer Content

To add header and/or footer content, you must activate that portion of the document. This can be done in one of two ways:

- Choose <u>V</u>iew, <u>H</u>eader and Footer.
- Double-click any existing header or footer content, such as a page number. If there is no such content, double-click the very top or bottom of the page while in Page Layout view.

Either technique will result in the opening of the Header and Footer floating toolbar, as shown in Figure 7.6.

FIG. 7.6

Headers and footers are repeated on every page in your entire document or within sections you specify. They can vary between sections as desired.

Your document's main text (if any) becomes dimmed when the Header and Footer toolbar appears. The Header or Footer portion of the document is activated, and has a dashed border around it. Figure 7.7 shows a document header with a centered page number.

FIG. 7.7

Add the word Page before existing page numbers in your header or footer.

To create Header or Footer content, type in the dash-bordered box. You'll notice that preset tabs appear on the ruler, giving you left-, center-, and right-aligned tabs, distributed evenly over the header or footer box.

 When you've finished entering header content, click the Switch Between Header and Footer button to view the footer box. To return to the text layer, click the <u>C</u>lose button on the Header and Footer toolbar, or double-click the page outside of the dashed header or footer box.

Varying Headers and Footers Between Sections

 One of the most important buttons on the Header and Footer toolbar is the Same as Previous button. This button, turned on by default, can be used to break the link between sections when you want the header and footer content to vary between sections.

To change headers and/or footers in a section of your document, follow these steps:

1. Move to the section of your document that you want to change, and click to place your cursor in it.
2. Choose <u>V</u>iew, <u>H</u>eader and Footer.

3. On the Header and Footer toolbar, click the Same as Previous button to turn this feature off. This breaks the link between your current section and the one before it.

4. Delete or change the content of your header, as desired.

5. If necessary, switch to the footer by clicking the Switch Between Header and Footer button.

6. Click the Same as Previous button to break the link between the footer of the current section and that of the previous section.

7. Delete or change your footer content as desired, and click Close.

CAUTION

Never make changes to one section's header or footer content before you've turned off the Same As Previous button—if you make changes before doing so, your changes will apply to the previous section as well.

Creating a Table of Contents

Imagine opening a reference book, even a short one, and not finding a table of contents. How would you find the topic you're looking for without leafing through the whole book? Just as a book needs a table of contents, so do many of your longer documents. Any document that people will use in parts—looking up one topic or another for reference—should have an accurate table of contents to use in finding topics and page numbers.

Luckily, these very useful items are easy to create, provided you perform some simple supporting tasks during the creation of your document, or just before generating the table of contents.

Word builds a table of contents for you, based on the heading styles (or other styles you select) that are used within your document. For example, if you have used Heading 1, Heading 2, and Heading 3 styles throughout your document for main-, sub-, and low-level headings, the text that is formatted in these styles will become entries in your table of contents, along with the page number on which the text is found.

Be sure not to format the words **Table of Contents** at the top of that page with the Heading 1, 2, or 3 style, or the table of contents will end up listed inside itself.

To build a table of contents for a document containing appropriately applied heading styles, follow these steps:

1. Position your cursor at the point in your document where you would like to place your table of contents.

2. Choose Insert, Index and Tables. The Index and Tables dialog box opens.

3. Click the Table of Contents tab (see Figure 7.8).

Part

II

Ch

7

FIG. 7.8

A table of contents is built by Word searching your documents for your use of the Heading 1, 2, and 3 styles in your document.

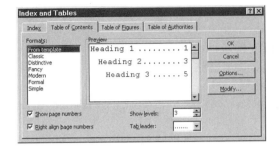

4. From the Formats list, choose from a series of predesigned table of contents layouts. As you click the formats, see a Preview on the right.

5. If you want to adjust the number of levels in your table of contents (how much detail it will contain), click the Show Levels spin box, and enter the number you need.

6. Click OK to generate the table and close the dialog box.

N O T E When choosing the number of levels to show in your table of contents, consider how illustrative your main topic headings are. If they're not terribly revealing, you will want to use two or three heading levels, so your low-level headings (which are hopefully more revealing of the content they precede) will make the table of contents more useful.

What if you add or delete content after generating the table and your text is no longer on the pages that are listed? Select the table of contents (double-click anywhere in the listings) and press the F9 key to update the table with your current page numbers.

If you want to use styles other than the default Heading 1, 2, and 3 styles, follow these steps:

1. With your cursor at the point where you want to place your table of contents, choose Insert, Index and Tables.

2. Click the Table of Contents tab.

3. Click the Options button.

4. In the Table of Contents Options dialog box (see Figure 7.9), choose from the Available Styles those styles that you want to use for your Table of Contents entries by typing the level (1, 2, or 3) in the TOC Level box next to the desired style.

FIG. 7.9

You can use any style from the active document's template to build your table of contents entries.

User-created style to be TOC level 1

Headings 2 and 3 will still be used.

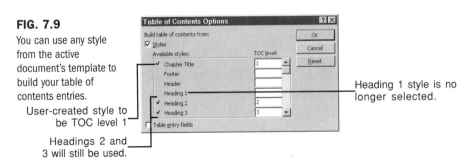

Heading 1 style is no longer selected.

5. To deselect the heading styles you don't want to use, delete the TOC level number next to the unwanted styles.

6. Click OK to return to the Index and Tables dialog box.

7. Click OK to create your table of contents using the specified styles.

> **CAUTION**
>
> Although you can change the styles that Word will look for in building your table of contents, make sure these styles have been consistently applied to your heading text, and that they are not in use on any text that you don't want in the table of contents.

▶ **See** "Using Heading Styles," **p. 46**

Building an Index

An index is an incredibly useful tool in a book, manual, or any very long document. You know your document needs an index if there are important topics covered within it that you know your readers will want to find but aren't listed in or easily found using the table of contents. An index can also indicate related topics (see also) or topics within a topic, also known as subentries.

Like a table of contents, an index requires some preparatory work on your part. Unlike a table of contents, Word will not simply look for text in a certain style and make entries for it. You must mark your index entries and make careful choices for their use and appearance in the index.

Marking index entries requires going through your document and selecting words and phrases that you think people will want to look up in your document. While highlighted, these selections will be marked as index entries, and later, when you choose to generate the index, these entries will be listed, along with their page numbers.

You can start at the beginning, end, or anywhere in your document and continue to build entries throughout the document. To mark your index entries, follow these steps:

1. Select to highlight your first intended index entry.

2. Press Alt+Shift+X. This marks the entry and opens the Mark Index Entry dialog box (see Figure 7.10).

3. Your selected text appears in the Main Entry text box. You can edit this as necessary.

4. Type any Subentry text, such as *Accumulated*, under a main entry of *Vacation Days*.

5. In most cases, the default Current Page option is the simplest choice, so leave this selected.

Part

II

Ch

7

TIP
If you choose to create a Cross-reference, you must enter the text to which the current entry should also refer. Make sure you also separately mark the cross-referenced text so that it also appears as an entry in the index.

FIG. 7.10

Highlight text that you think will help your readers find information quickly by using your index. Press Alt+Shift+X to mark the selected text as an index entry.

6. Apply Bold and/or Italic formatting to your page numbers.

7. Click the Mark button to mark this one occurrence of the text, or click Mark All if you want every occurrence of the selected text to be marked and thus have an entry in the index.

8. The dialog box remains onscreen, awaiting your continued selections and markings for the rest of your document's index entries. You must repress Alt+Shift+X for each entry you select.

9. When you finish selecting and marking entries, close the dialog box by clicking the Close (x) button.

After you've marked all your entries, you can generate the index by following these steps:

1. Position your cursor where you want to place your index in the document.

2. Choose Insert, Index and Tables. The Index and Tables dialog box opens.

3. Click the Index tab (see Figure 7.11).

FIG. 7.11

After you've marked your index entries, choose the visual layout for your index, and generate it through the Index and Tables dialog box.

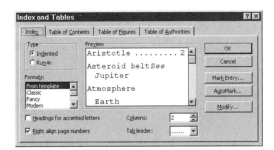

4. Choose from the list of Formats to determine the appearance of your index.

5. Specify the number of Columns for your index.

6. Click OK to generate the index and close the dialog box. Figure 7.12 shows a small index generated in an employee manual.

If your document changes and your existing index entries have become invalid due to additions, deletions, or rearranged text, select the entire index and press the F9 key. Your index is automatically updated in place, and the updated entries appear for your marked text.

FIG. 7.12
Index entries can be marked once or you can choose to mark all occurrences of a given word or phrase. It's best to mark only those that will be of real use to the reader.

Index title created by user

Subentry text

Cross reference

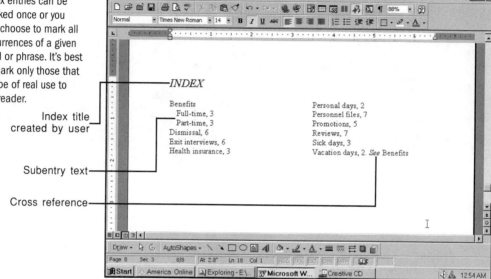

Harnessing the Power of Templates

Using Installed Templates

Before we discuss the templates that Word has already installed for you, let's start by clarifying what a template is. A template is essentially a cookie cutter for documents. Just like a cookie cutter is used to create many identically-shaped cookies, a template is used to create many uniform documents. You can apply icing, sprinkles, or even add things like nuts and raisins into the cookie dough, but the overall shape is the same, thanks to the cookie cutter. Documents created with templates can have lots of extra things added to them to make them more informative or interesting, but their overall appearance is dictated by the template on which they are based.

Word's installed templates can be used for building several types of documents, including letters, memos, resumes, and newsletters. To see the complete group of available templates, choose File, New from the menu, and click the various tabs in the New dialog box (see Figure 8.1). These tabs house Word templates by category.

TIP The New button on Word's Standard toolbar does not open the New dialog box. Instead, it gives you a blank document based on the Normal template, no questions asked.

FIG. 8.1
Word gives you a variety of templates for the most commonly-created business and personal documents.

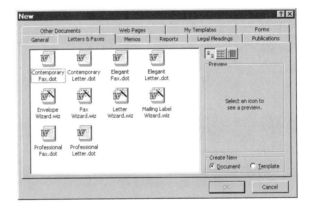

When you start a new document with a template, you're not actually opening the template—you're using the template as a foundation for the document. You'll notice that your new document's name on the title bar (until you save it) is Document1 (or another number if you've opened other new documents in your current Word session). The template itself is not open, and therefore is not going to be altered in any way by the content you add or formatting you apply to your new document. The template remains intact for the next time you need it.

To start a Word document with a template, follow these steps:

1. Choose File, New. The New dialog box opens (as shown previously in Figure 8.1).
2. Click the tab that contains the template you want to use.
3. Double-click the template icon, or click it once and click OK.

Your new document opens, containing any text and formatting that was built-in to the template. Many of Word's templates contain instructive text, as shown in Figure 8.2. You replace this text with your own content.

FIG. 8.2
Highlight the instructive text in your template-based document and replace it with your own content, such as names and fax/phone numbers for a fax cover sheet.

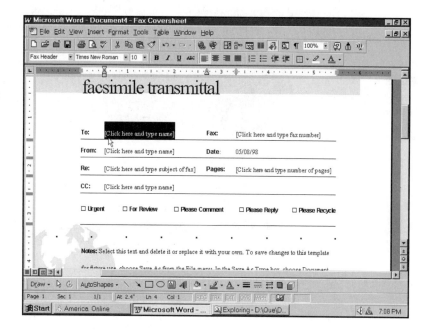

📄 **N O T E**   You'll notice an icon called Blank Document in the General tab of the New dialog box. This template isn't really blank, although it contains no text or graphics. It contains all the formatting—margins, tabs, default fonts, and line spacing that you rely on for new, blank documents. This is the template that is invoked when you click the New button on the Standard toolbar.

▶ **See** "Quick Starts with a Presentation Design," **p. 204**

Working with Wizards

Wizards are a variation of the template. Instead of simply opening a partially built or instructional document for you to use in building your own document, a wizard asks you a series of questions about your new document, and based on your answers, builds a document that is virtually complete.

Some wizards are more trouble than they're worth—dealing with the steps and dialog boxes that take you through the process of building your document can take longer than building it from scratch.

To use a wizard to build a document, follow these steps:

1. Choose File, New.

2. Click the tab that contains the wizard of your choice. Wizard icons contain the image of a magic wand.

3. Double-click the Wizard icon, or click the icon once and then click OK.

4. The wizard begins, showing a series of steps on the left side of its first dialog box (see Figure 8.3). These are the steps you'll have to go through to complete the wizard process. Click Next.

FIG. 8.3

The first step asks for the name of the document(s) you want to send, and assumes you want a cover sheet.

Click any step to go directly to it.

View the steps that the wizard will require for completion.

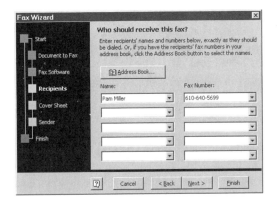

5. Answer questions in each successive dialog box, clicking Next to move on to the next step, or Back as needed to go backward to a previous step. Figure 8.4 shows Step 3 of the Fax Wizard.

FIG. 8.4

Each step in the wizard process is important, although you can skip any that pertain to information you don't know at the time or don't intend to use on the fax cover sheet.

6. On the last step, you can click Finish to tell the wizard that you have completed the steps you want to perform, and are ready to have your document created for you.

In the case of the Fax Wizard, the only typing you'll have to do after completing the wizard process involves any comments you have about the document that accompanies the fax cover. Figure 8.5 shows a completed fax cover sheet, ready to be faxed to the recipient.

FIG. 8.5
You can choose your fax modem by choosing File, Print, or by invoking a preferred faxing software program to send your cover sheet and any other documents.

If you have fax software, you may see this floating toolbar.

Using the Templates from the Companion CD

The CD that accompanies this book contains several templates designed to enhance your use of Word by increasing the variety of templates available to you for business and personal use. You can copy the ones you want to use from the CD to your hard drive by following these steps:

1. Insert the CD into your CD-ROM drive.

2. Using Windows Explorer or My Computer, open the CD-ROM drive and view its contents.

3. Open the Templates folder.

4. You can select a single template by clicking it once, or hold down the Ctrl key as you click additional templates. When you've selected all the template files you want, release the Ctrl key.

5. With one or several template files selected, choose Edit, Copy from the menu bar, or press Ctrl+C.

6. Open the Templates folder in your MSOffice (or Microsoft Office) folder. The path on your local drive will probably be: C:\program files\msoffice\templates\.

7. With that folder open, choose Edit, Paste from the menu bar, or press Ctrl+V.

You can also copy and paste files by right-clicking the source files (files to be copied) and choosing Copy from the pop-up menu. Right-click the target folder (destination), and choose Paste from that pop-up menu.

> **CAUTION**
>
> It is absolutely essential that you copy these templates to the Templates folder in your Microsoft Office folder. If you copy them to any other folder, they won't be available through the File, New command.

Creating Your Own Templates

It's hard to imagine, but even after installing the templates that come with the companion CD, you may find that the available templates don't meet your needs. If this occurs, you can easily make templates of your own, complete with formatting, any uniform content, instructive text, and even a bit of automation to speed their use.

Your templates can be created from scratch, by formatting a blank document, or by typing any content that would be seen in every use of the template. You can also create a template from an existing document, if that document's content would be appropriate in every use of the template.

To create your own basic template, follow these steps:

1. Create a new, blank document or open an existing document that you want to use as the basis of your template.
2. If using an existing document, go through it and remove any content that you don't want to appear in all future uses of the document as a template.
3. If using a new, blank document, type any content that you want to have on each new document based on the template, such as the words To:, From:, Subject:, and Date: on a memo template.
4. Apply any formatting, such as new margins, tabs, line spacing, fonts, and style changes.
5. Choose File, Save As.
6. Click the Save as Type drop-down list, and select Document Template (*.dot).
7. Word automatically places you in the Templates folder, displaying subfolders that correspond to the tabs of the New dialog box (see Figure 8.6).
8. You can either save your new template to the main Templates folder, or double-click one of the subfolders to choose a tab for your template icon to appear on in the New dialog box.
9. Give your template a name. Do not type the file extension; Word inserts the .dot for you.
10. Click Save.
11. Close your open template file by choosing File, Close or by pressing Ctrl+F4.

To use your new template, choose File, New, and find it in the tab that corresponds with the folder into which you saved it. If you saved it to the main Templates folder, it will be on the General tab.

FIG. 8.6
The subfolders of the Templates folder correspond to the tabs in the New dialog box.

User-created folders

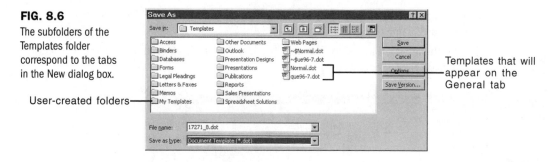

Templates that will appear on the General tab

Automating Templates

The process of automating a template can take two forms:

- *Create a macro to invoke the template.* Any template, be it one of the installed Word templates, a template from the companion CD, or one that you've created yourself, can be made easier to use by creating a macro that performs the steps involved in using the template to start a new document. The macro can then be assigned to the toolbar or a keyboard shortcut, further simplifying the template's use.

- *Add automated features to the template itself, such as fill-in forms with check boxes and drop-down lists.* Especially useful in time sheets, surveys, and questionnaire forms, these dialog box features can be added to any document to make filling in a form easier.

Creating a Template Macro

Using a macro to invoke a template saves you the time involved in opening the New dialog box, finding, and selecting the template. To assign a template to a keyboard shortcut or toolbar button, follow these steps:

1. With any document open, choose Tools, Macro, Record New Macro. The Record New Macro dialog box opens (see Figure 8.7).

2. Type a name for your macro to replace the numbered name that appears by default. Your macro name can be up to 255 characters long, but don't use any spaces.

FIG. 8.7
Give your macro a name (no spaces) and tell Word how you want to invoke it—from the toolbar or keyboard.

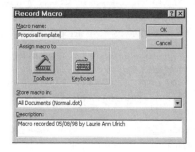

3. To assign the macro to the keyboard, click the <u>K</u>eyboard button. The Customize Keyboard dialog box opens (see Figure 8.8).

4. Type the intended keyboard shortcut (such as Alt+Q for a Questionnaire template) into the Press <u>N</u>ew Shortcut Key text box.

FIG. 8.8

Choose a shortcut key combination that includes a letter of the alphabet or a number between 0 and 9 that you'll find easy to remember.

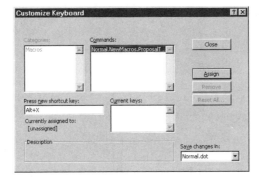

CAUTION

If your keyboard shortcut is already assigned to another macro or command, the existing command will appear below the Press <u>N</u>ew Shortcut Key text box. Make sure the keys you press are designated [unassigned]. The Alt+(letter or number) combinations are usually your best bet.

5. Click <u>A</u>ssign, and then click <u>C</u>lose.

6. Your macro is now recording, indicated by the appearance of the floating Stop and Pause buttons in the Macro toolbar (see Figure 8.9).

7. Go about the process of creating a new document based on your template—choose <u>F</u>ile, <u>N</u>ew, and go to the tab that contains your template icon.

8. Double-click the icon, opening a new document.

9. Click the Stop button to stop recording. Your macro is complete.

Keyboard shortcuts can be hard to remember, and if other people will be using your computer and/or your templates, you'll want to make it easy for them to use your macro. A toolbar macro is your best bet if failing memory or another user's ease are priorities.

To assign your macro to a toolbar, follow these steps:

1. With any document open, choose <u>T</u>ools, <u>M</u>acro, <u>R</u>ecord New Macro.

2. In the Record Macro dialog box type your <u>M</u>acro Name, and click the <u>T</u>oolbars button.

N O T E   Your Record Macro dialog box has a <u>D</u>escription text box into which you can type a short or long paragraph description of your macro. The description can include the macro's purpose, the date, your name—whatever will help distinguish it from similar macros.

Part

II

Ch

8

FIG. 8.9
Click the Pause button
if you need to take a
brief break in recording.
Stop closes the macro
program with your last
action.

Stop button

Mouse pointer
indicates that the
macro is recording

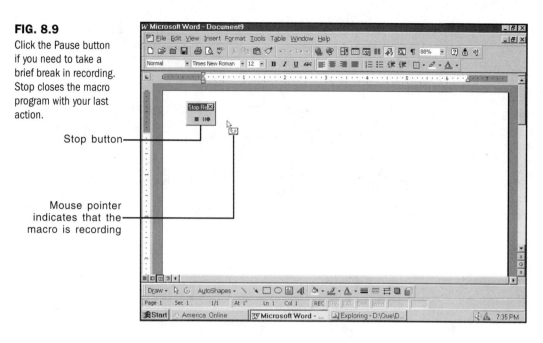

3. The Customize dialog box opens (see Figure 8.10), displaying a list of Categories and a list of Commands. Your macro may be the only one in the list. Drag the command for your macro up to the toolbar.

FIG. 8.10
Drag the macro
command name from
the Commands list up
to the spot on your
toolbar where you'd like
the button to appear.

Macro command
added to toolbar

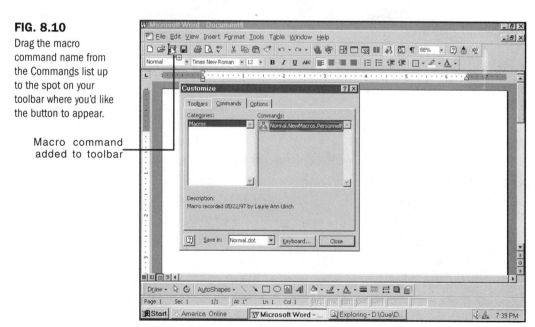

4. You can place the command anywhere on the toolbar—between existing buttons, or at the end or beginning of either your Standard or Formatting toolbar. When you're pointing to the desired location, release the mouse. Figure 8.11 shows the macro moved into position on the toolbar.

FIG. 8.11

If your toolbar moves when you place the long text button on it, don't worry. As soon as you replace the button's text face with a picture, the toolbar returns to normal.

New button with command text

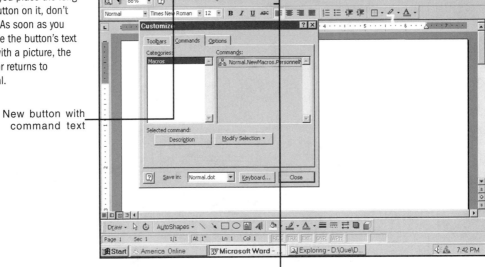

Existing toolbar buttons moved aside and down

5. The text of your macro name appears on the button face. To change to a picture button, click the Modify Selection button, and choose Text Only (in Menus) from the menu.

6. To replace the command symbol now appearing on your new button, click the Modify Selection button again, and choose Change Button Image. A palette of button images appears (see Figure 8.12).

7. Click one of the images in the palette. That face will appear on your macro button.

8. Click the Close button to begin recording your macro.

9. Choose File, New to open the New dialog box.

10. Click the tab that contains the template you want to use for your new document.

11. Double-click the template icon, or click it once and click the OK button.

12. As soon as your new document is open onscreen, click the Stop button on the Macro toolbar (see Figure 8.13).

To start a new document with your new macro, you can now invoke it from the toolbar button or keyboard shortcut you assigned. The macro only opens the document—it goes no further than that, assuming you followed the previous instructions.

FIG. 8.12

It's not always possible to choose a picture that's relevant to the macro that it represents. Just pick one you like!

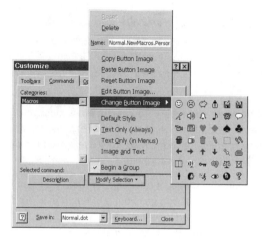

FIG. 8.13

When your new document is open, click the Stop button so that your macro's last command is the selection of the desired template.

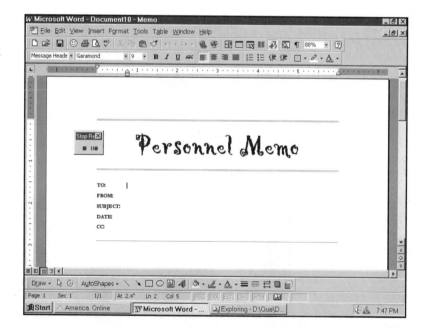

CAUTION

You don't want to create a macro to start a wizard—the Wizard dialog box being onscreen prohibits your ability to click the Macro toolbar Stop button, so you'll end up recording the entire wizard process. Because that process varies each time you use the wizard, it's not something that you'd want to automate with a macro.

Adding Check Boxes and Drop-Down Lists to a Template

Documents that serve as fill-in forms are some of the most effective and useful documents you can create in Word. Saving a form as a template makes a form even more useful, because each time it's filled out, the user can save it as their own, leaving the original (blank) form intact for the next user.

To make a form, you normally use tables. Tables can be used for questionnaire, survey, and similar forms that require a combination of typed text responses and check boxes. Word also gives you drop-down lists, enabling you to offer your users a list of possible responses. This increases the accuracy and clarity of your forms.

To build a form, it's a good idea to map it out on paper first. After you know what questions and options you'll want on the form, you can go about building it in a Word document. Assuming you've read Chapter 6, "Structuring Documents with Tables," you can begin the following procedure with your table and question text inserted as shown in Figure 8.14.

FIG. 8.14

A well-structured form should start with a table. You'll use the cells to house your automated fields.

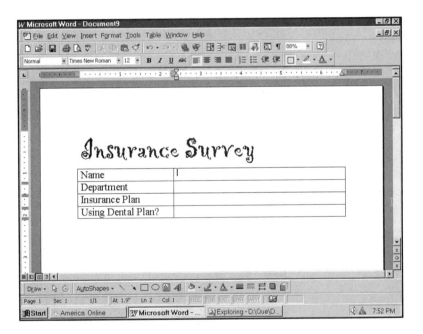

To add check boxes and drop-down lists to your form template, follow these steps:

1. Click in the table cell to which you want to add a check box or drop-down list.

2. Choose View, Toolbars, Forms. This opens the Forms toolbar, as shown in Figure 8.15.

3. Click the Text Form Field, Check Box Form Field, or Drop-Down Form Field button. A gray shaded box appears in the cell.

4. Click the Form Field Options button to customize the automated field you've just created. Figure 8.16 shows the Drop-Down Form Field Options dialog box.

FIG. 8.15
Use the Forms toolbar
to add text boxes,
check boxes, and drop-
down lists to your table
form.

Text added by the user

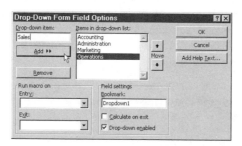

Check boxes   Drop-down list fields

FIG. 8.16
Type the list of words or
phrases from which the
user will choose when
using this drop-down
list. Click Add after
each one.

5. After entering the text or drop-down list options (you don't need to set any options for standard check boxes), click OK in the Drop-Down Form Field Options dialog box.

6. Continue to move to the other cells in your form table that require automated fields, adding them as described in steps 3–6.

7. Click the Protect Form button to make your fields useable when the template is used to create a new form.

 TIP If you don't want your field to appear shaded on the form, make sure it is selected, and click the Form Field Shading button. On by default, clicking it now will turn it off.

8. If your form hasn't been saved as a template previously, choose <u>F</u>ile, Save <u>A</u>s.

9. In the Save as <u>T</u>ype drop-down list, choose Document Template (*.dot). The Templates folder automatically appears in the Save <u>I</u>n box.

10. Name your template, leaving off the extension (.dot)—Word adds it for you.

11. Save your file to the Templates folder or one of its subfolders.

12. Click <u>S</u>ave.

Your form is now available for use by you or any other users with access to your computer. If Microsoft Office is running on a network, your Templates folder may be on a network drive, in which case your template will be available to other users on your network.

ON THE WEB

http://pobox.upenn.edu/~tech/ulcs/concept.html If your computer is infected with the Word Concept virus, use SCANPROT, available from this University of Pennsylvania site, to cure the virus. The Word Concept virus, although not destructive, does cause all saved documents to be saved as templates, whether you want them to be or not.

Modifying Templates

Many templates contain names, prices, product numbers, phone numbers, and so forth—information which tends to change over time. Using the insurance questionnaire used in the previous section as an example, if the company decided to offer other types of insurance, the drop-down list options would have to be changed for the automated fields so the new offerings would be represented on the form.

Although it's a good idea to build as little time-sensitive information as you can into a template, it can't be totally avoided. To open and change your template's content or formatting, follow these steps:

1. Choose <u>F</u>ile, <u>O</u>pen. The Open dialog box appears (see Figure 8.17).

FIG. 8.17
By default, the Open dialog box looks for .doc documents. Choose Document Templates (*.dot) from the list of file types.

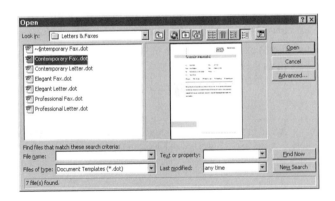

2. Under Files of Type, choose Document Templates (*.dot) from the drop-down list.

3. Using the Look In box, navigate to the Templates folder in your MSOffice (or Microsoft Office) folder.

4. When your Templates folder is displayed, double-click the icon for your template (if it was saved to the Templates folder directly). If you saved it to one of the Templates subfolders, double-click the subfolder that corresponds with the tab in which you normally find the template icon. Double-click the icon for the template you want to open.

5. With your template displayed onscreen, make whatever changes are required—edit the text, reformat your character or paragraph settings, or change your page setup.

 N O T E If the changes pertain to an automated field on a form template, you must turn off the form protection before you can make any changes to your field options. Open the Forms toolbar, and select your entire form. Click the Protect Form button to turn off the protection. You can now make changes to your fields, including changing types, adding drop-down list selections, or changing your shading settings. Remember to reprotect your form before saving the template!

 6. When you've finished making your changes, click the Save button on the toolbar, or press Ctrl+S. Your template ID saved, still in the .dot format.

Organizing Templates

Throughout the step-by-step procedures in this chapter, saving templates to a very select group of folders has been described. All templates must be saved to the Templates folder (a subfolder of your Microsoft Office folder), or to one of the Templates folder's subfolders. If your templates are not in one of these folders, they won't be available when you choose File, New.

If, however, you have saved a template to one of the Templates subfolders and decide you want to save it to a different one, or if you want to create a new subfolder (and thus a new tab in the New dialog box), you can do so through the Windows Explorer or My Computer programs. Both of these programs make it easy to copy or move files, and to create new folders. If you'd prefer to perform these tasks from within Word, use the following procedures.

To move a template from one Templates subfolder to another, follow these steps:

1. Choose File, New.

2. In the New dialog box, click the tab that currently contains the template icon you want to move.

3. Right-click the icon, and choose Cut from the shortcut menu.

4. Click the tab to which you want to move the icon.

5. Right-click an empty space in the box that displays the current icons on that tab.

6. Choose Paste from the shortcut menu. Your icon appears in that tab.

7. Click Cancel to close the New dialog box.

CAUTION

Be sure to close any open documents that are based on the template that you want to move (Cut) to a new location. While these documents are open, the template cannot be moved or deleted.

If you want to add a new tab, and thus a new template category, follow these steps:

1. Choose File, Save As.

2. Navigate to the Templates folder, under MSOffice (or Microsoft Office).

3. Click the Create New Folder button.

4. The New Folder dialog box opens (see Figure 8.18). Type the name of the new folder. Remember that this name will appear on the tab in the New dialog box, so choose something short and relevant.

FIG. 8.18

Give your new folder a short and relevant name that you'll want to see on one of the New dialog box tabs.

5. Click OK.

6. In the Save As dialog box, your new folder appears among the existing Templates subfolders.

7. Click the Cancel button. This cancels the Save As process, but not the creation of your new folder.

After creating a new folder, you can use it as a place to save new templates, or following the steps found earlier in this section, you can move existing template files from one Templates subfolder to another. ●

CHAPTER 9

Using Word's Powerful Automatic Features

In this chapter

Working with Find and Replace

Webster's Dictionary defines automatic as "Operating or able to operate with little or no external control." Word has several such features, the Find and Replace commands being just two of them. To be a real power user of Word (or Excel or PowerPoint, both of which offer the same tools), it is important to understand these features.

Find and Replace can be used in several ways:

■ *To look for a specific combination of letters (a portion of a word), a word, or a short phrase.* This use of the Find command merely locates the text. What you do with the found content is then a separate function.

■ *To make global changes to a document, finding every use of a word or phrase and changing it to something else.* For example, if you're updating last year's catalog, using Replace to change all uses of the number 1997 to 1998 would help to turn it into this year's catalog.

■ *To replace special characters.* You can look for tabs and replace them with hard returns, or look for two spaces after a period and replace them with one space.

■ *To replace formatted text.* Look for all text that is bold, 14 points, and italic, and change it to bold, 16 points, and italic. If you've used a style throughout your document, you can replace it with another one.

As you can see in these examples, Find can work alone, but Replace requires Find. For this reason, you'll see that the Find and Replace dialog box is one entity—a multi-tabbed dialog box that enables you to perform both a Find and a Replace in one place. This is rather convenient, as many times a process that began as a simple Find turns into a Replace.

In Office 97, the Find and Replace dialog box also contains the Go To tab. This tab enables you to look for and go to specific items within a document, such as a page, section, or bookmark.

To find text, follow these steps:

1. In the document containing the content you want to find, press Ctrl+Home to go to the top of the document.

Although Find and Replace can be started at any point in the document and set up to search backward, forward, or in only a selected portion of your document, it's easier to start at the beginning of a document and search forward.

2. Choose Edit, Find. The Find and Replace dialog box opens (see Figure 9.1).

FIG. 9.1

The Find command can help you search through a long document for text that you might miss if you were proofreading manually.

3. The Fi**n**d tab is in front. Type the text you want to find in the Fi**n**d What text box.

4. Click the **F**ind Next button, and the first occurrence of the text you're seeking will be highlighted.

5. If you think there may be more occurrences of the text, continue to click the **F**ind Next button until you are prompted that no more occurrences of your text can be found. Click OK to close the prompt.

6. Click Cancel in the Find and Replace dialog box to close it and return to your document.

If the text you're looking for appears in several locations, you can stop at any one of them and perform any editing or formatting you choose. The Find and Replace dialog box remains onscreen, and you can restart the search by clicking the **F**ind Next button again.

> **CAUTION**
>
> The only editing that cannot be performed while the Find and Replace dialog box is onscreen is drag and drop. You can use the Clipboard by issuing Cu**t**, **C**opy, or **P**aste commands, but you cannot move or copy text with the mouse while this (or any) dialog box is open onscreen.

Changing Content with Replace

Replace is by nature a more powerful tool than Find, because it actually performs a task for you—it doesn't just look for the year 1997 in last year's catalog, it can be set to change that number to 1998 without any further direction from you.

To replace text in your document, follow these steps:

1. In the document in which you want to replace text, press Ctrl+Home to position your cursor at the top of the document.

2. Choose **E**dit, **R**eplace. The Find and Replace dialog box opens, with the Re**p**lace tab in front (see Figure 9.2).

FIG. 9.2

When finding and replacing text, if plural forms of the word are found, they are replaced with plural forms of the replacement text, even if both your Fi**n**d What and Replace W**i**th text is in the singular form.

3. Enter the text you want to find in the Fi**n**d What text box. Press Tab.

4. Enter the text with which you want to replace the found text in the Replace W**i**th box.

5. To replace all occurrences of the found text with your replacement text, click the Replace All button. To find each occurrence one at a time and replace only some of them, click Find Next to go to the first occurrence of the text. Figure 9.3 shows the word employee found, and about to be replaced by the word associate.

FIG. 9.3

Word tenses, plural forms of the word, and uses of the word as part of another word are all situations where you'll be glad you didn't use Replace All.

The word employee will be changed to associate.

The word employees has been skipped by the user.

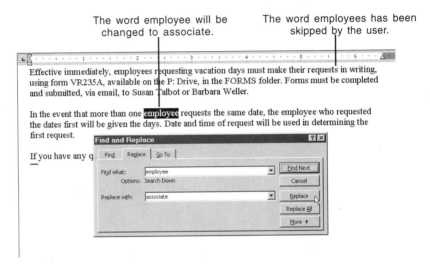

CAUTION

Replace All is a drastic move. Use it only when you're absolutely sure that every occurrence of your found text should be replaced. Even though moving through your document with the Find Next and Replace buttons takes longer, you're less likely to regret a replacement.

6. As you find each occurrence, choose to skip it (click Find Next again to move on) or Replace and then Find Next to change and then continue to the next occurrence.

7. Continue skipping and replacing occurrences of your text until Word prompts you that no more occurrences are found (see Figure 9.4). Click OK to close the prompt.

FIG. 9.4

Word tells you when you've come to the end of the document and no more occurrences of your text can be found.

8. Click the Cancel button in the Find and Replace dialog box.

  If you performed a Replace All and realize quickly that it was a mistake, use Undo (Ctrl+Z).

▶ **See** "Using Find and Replace to Make Global Changes," **p. 150**

Using Replace to Reformat Your Document

If you've used a particular style or applied certain formats throughout your document, you can use Find and Replace to change them to another style or to apply different formats. You can also change the flow of your text throughout a document by replacing special characters such as tabs, hard returns (paragraph marks), spaces, and page breaks with other special characters.

To Find and Replace special characters, character formats, paragraph formats, or styles in your document, follow these steps:

1. In the document that contains the content you want to change, press Ctrl+Home to position your cursor at the top of the document.

2. Choose Edit, Replace. The Find and Replace dialog box opens, with the Replace tab in front.

3. Click the More button to expand the dialog box (see Figure 9.5).

FIG. 9.5

Click the More button to expand the Find and Replace dialog box. Note that the More button changes to the Less button after you've clicked it.

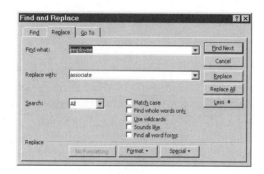

4. With your cursor in the Find What box, click either the Format button (to find character or paragraph formats, styles, or tabs) or the Special button to select special characters such as spaces, hard returns, page breaks, or section breaks. Figure 9.6 shows the list of Format button options.

FIG. 9.6

Choose the format you'd like to search for, and an appropriate formatting dialog box opens. Make your choices in that box, and then click OK to return to the Find and Replace dialog box.

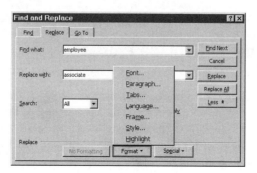

5. Click in the Replace With box, and select either the Format button or the Special button to enter the replacement content. Figure 9.7 shows the list of Special characters.

FIG. 9.7
Special characters are both printing (en and em dashes) and non-printing (hard returns and tabs).

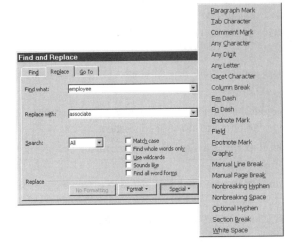

TIP   Although text, format, and special character replacements are normally done separately, you can search for text that is formatted in a certain way and followed by a certain special character and replace it with another text/format/special character combination as needed.

6. Click the Replace All button to make a global change without any further interaction required from you. You can also replace the occurrences of the formats/special characters one at a time by using the Find Next and Replace buttons.

7. When you are prompted that there are no more occurrences of the content, click OK to close the prompt, and then Cancel to close the Find and Replace dialog box.

TIP   You needn't see any Find and Replace session through to the end—you can stop at any time by clicking the Cancel button.

▶ **See** "Formatting Text with Styles," **p. 46**

Fine-Tuning the Find and Replace Process

When you issue the Find or Replace commands, some default actions are set to take place:

■ *The entire document is searched, starting wherever the cursor is when the command is issued.* At the end of the document, the program goes back to the beginning and works forward again, until it meets the point where the search started.

■ *The case of text is ignored.* If you search for the word employee, Employee and EMPLOYEE are considered matches.

■ *All word forms are considered matches.* If you search for the word employee, employee and employees both meet the search criteria.

After clicking the More button in the Find and Replace dialog box, options for changing these default actions are offered. Click the check boxes next to the options you want to use, and adjust your search direction by clicking the Search drop-down list.

After adjusting your settings, you can proceed with your Find or Replace procedure as described previously in this section.

N O T E If you're not sure how one of the options will affect your search, get more information about the option by clicking the What's This? (?) help button in the upper-right corner of the Find and Replace dialog box. Then, with a question mark appended to your mouse pointer, click the option about which you need more detail. A pop-up description of that feature will be displayed.

Using AutoCorrect

When Office 95 was released, everyone was excited about the fact that Word could underline your spelling errors as you type, and the excitement was understandable. For those of us who occasionally forget to run spell check before printing and distributing documents, it's been a real lifesaver—the red underlines serve as a reminder that there are errors to be corrected.

AutoCorrect takes that level of automation up a notch by fixing your spelling mistakes as you type. As if that weren't enough, AutoCorrect can also convert punctuation to symbols (:-) becomes a smiley face), initials to names or phrases (AMT becomes Ann Miller Talbot), and spelling errors to correctly spelled words (teh becomes the). The list of corrections that AutoCorrect makes as installed is impressive. The fact that you can add as many entries of your own as you need makes it a tool you can't live without!

AutoCorrect works without your doing anything—as soon as you type a combination of characters that it finds in its list, the corresponding correction is made. No commands need to be issued or options turned on. To view the current list of AutoCorrect entries, choose Tools, AutoCorrect. The AutoCorrect dialog box opens (see Figure 9.8).

FIG. 9.8

AutoCorrect can fix your accidental use of the CapsLock key and make sure you don't forget to type the days of the week in title case.

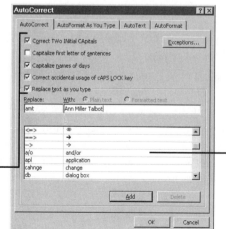

Default AutoCorrect settings for punctuation and capitalization

List of symbols, abbreviations, and commonly misspelled words and their replacements/ corrections

Scroll through the list of AutoCorrect entries to see if any of your favorites are there. The list starts with symbol replacements and then moves into an alphabetical list of misspellings and abbreviations.

Building AutoCorrect Entries

To add a word you always misspell or an abbreviation or acronym that you normally type in full text, follow these steps:

1. In any document, choose Tools, AutoCorrect.
2. In the Replace text box, type the misspelling or abbreviation.

 TIP If the misspelling or abbreviation is already typed in your current document, highlight it with your mouse prior to opening the AutoCorrect dialog box. When you open the dialog box, the selected text appears in the Replace text box.

3. Press Tab or click in the With text box.

CAUTION

Be careful when building AutoCorrect entries that your Replace text isn't a real word or an abbreviation that you don't want to type in full text. For example, if your name is Bill Edmonds, using "be" as the Replace text results in your name replacing the word "be" in any sentence.

4. Type the correct spelling or full text of the abbreviation.
5. Click the Add button.

NOTE Another way to build an AutoCorrect entry is to use a misspelled word that is currently underlined in red, Word's way of telling you that the word is spelled incorrectly. Right-click the word, and choose AutoCorrect from the shortcut menu. A submenu appears, offering alternative spellings for your word. Choose one. The AutoCorrect entry is made, with your misspelling and its corresponding correction, all without opening the AutoCorrect dialog box.

6. If you want to add another entry, double-click your last misspelling or abbreviation in the Replace box and type the new entry.
7. Press Tab to select the With box contents, and type the correction/full text replacement for the new entry.
8. Click Add. You can continue this cycle for all the entries you want to add at this time.
9. Click the OK button when you are ready to close the AutoCorrect dialog box.

NOTE You can create AutoCorrect entries for symbols as well as text. Choose Insert, Symbol, and select the symbol you want to use. Click the AutoCorrect button, and then proceed to store the entry as usual.

The first thing most people want to do is test their new entry. To make sure you entered it correctly, type the misspelling or abbreviation, and then press either the Spacebar or the Enter key, both of which indicate that the word is complete. Watch for the replacement that is inserted by AutoCorrect.

Changing and Deleting AutoCorrect Entries

What if you made an error in setting up an AutoCorrect entry? Imagine you were trying to build an entry for a coworker's name and you misspelled it. Now when you type LK, instead of getting Linda Kline, you get Linda Klone. It's easy to fix your entry so the right correction is made in the future:

Part

II

Ch

9

1. In your open document, choose Tools, AutoCorrect.
2. In the Replace box, type the misspelling or abbreviation you need to fix, or scroll through the list of entries and select the entry.
3. Tab to the With box and type the correctly spelled word or name.
4. Click the Replace button. Your entry is fixed.
5. Click OK to close the AutoCorrect dialog box.

Deleting an AutoCorrect entry is just as simple. Open the AutoCorrect dialog box and select the entry you want to delete. Click the Delete button. Your entry is removed from the list.

Setting Up AutoCorrect Exceptions

As the saying goes, "There's an exception to every rule." AutoCorrect is an example of that! If need be, you can set up exceptions that cover you for situations in which the current AutoCorrect settings and entries will do more harm than good.

If, for example, you want AutoCorrect to fix it when you type two initial capitals (THank You), but you don't want it to fix it when you type PRnumber, you can build that particular word into AutoCorrect's list of Exceptions.

To create exceptions to AutoCorrect's entries and settings, follow these steps:

1. Choose Tools, AutoCorrect.
2. Click the Exceptions button.
3. In the AutoCorrect Exceptions dialog box, click either the First Letter or INitial CAps tab (see Figure 9.9).
4. Type your exception text in the Don't Capitalize After box (for First Letter exceptions) or Don't Correct box (for INitial CAps exceptions).
5. Click the Add button.
6. Click OK to exit the AutoCorrect Exceptions dialog box.
7. Click OK in the AutoCorrect dialog box to close the dialog box and return to your document.

FIG. 9.9

Instead of turning off an AutoCorrect setting or deleting an entry, build an exception to the rule.

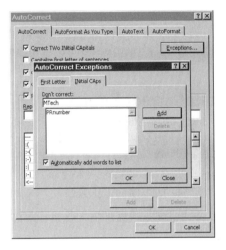

ON THE WEB

http://www6.zdnet.com/cgi-bin/texis/swlib/hotfiles/search.html   This page contains many shareware programs for Microsoft Word, past and current versions.

Building a Document with AutoText

Many of the documents we create contain sections that are the same as those that we've typed in previous documents—the disclaimer about prices being subject to change without notice that you type at the end of a proposal, the clause in a lease about not allowing pets that you use repeatedly. Any time you type something into a document and know you could use it again in a future document, you'll save yourself a lot of work if you turn that text into an AutoText entry.

Any text can become AutoText. AutoText entries can be as short and simple as a letter closing (from the Very truly yours to the typist's initials) or as long and complex as a contract. To turn existing text into an AutoText entry, follow these steps:

1. Select the text that you want to reuse as AutoText.

T I P   If you're selecting a paragraph or group of paragraphs as your AutoText and you want there to be blank lines before and/or after it when it is inserted in the future, select any paragraph marks that precede and follow the text.

2. Choose Insert, AutoText, New. The Create AutoText dialog box opens (see Figure 9.10).

3. Type a name for the AutoText entry, a brief word, phrase, or abbreviation that represents the entry.

4. Click OK. Your AutoText entry is stored, and can be used at any time, in any document.

To insert AutoText, type the entry name that you assigned to the AutoText when you created the entry. After typing it, press the F3 key. The full AutoText entry replaces the entry's name.

FIG. 9.10

The shorter your AutoText abbreviation, the more typing it will save you in the future.

Selected text that will become AutoText

A list of installed generic AutoText entries is available by choosing Insert, AutoText. The AutoText submenu offers a wide variety of salutations and letter closings, as well as any AutoText entries that you've created (see Figure 9.11). If you forget your entry names, look for them in this submenu.

FIG. 9.11

Check the AutoText submenu for a list of installed AutoText as well as the AutoText entries that you've created.

Point to the AutoText entries and categories in the submenu to see samples of the AutoText they represent.

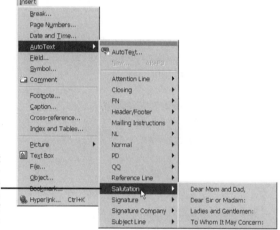

Understanding Your AutoFormat Options

Just as AutoCorrect improves the accuracy of your document by fixing your spelling errors or replacing abbreviations with full text, AutoFormat works to make your documents more consistent and more polished. AutoFormat works by interpreting your content and changing it to more appropriate formats, such as changing $1/2$ to ? symbol. AutoFormat can be applied as you work, or all at once to an existing document.

To view the automatic settings that are applied while you work in Word, choose Tools, AutoCorrect, and click the AutoFormat As You Type tab (see Figure 9.12).

To change your AutoFormat settings, remove the check mark next to the option you want to turn off, or click the check box to turn on an item that is currently not in use. The AutoFormat settings are designed to make replacements that meet the needs of most users—if your special needs are at odds with these automatic formats, be sure to turn them off in both the AutoFormat As You Type and the AutoFormat tabs.

FIG. 9.12

You can turn your AutoFormat settings off as needed, but most of them are labor-saving features that save time and improve the appearance of your documents.

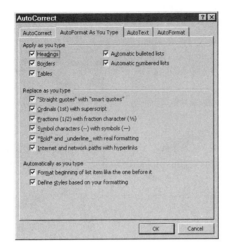

The AutoFormat tab contains settings that can be applied to an existing document by choosing Format, AutoFormat. Choose Tools, AutoCorrect and click the AutoFormat tab to view and change these settings as needed (see Figure 9.13).

FIG. 9.13

Your AutoFormat settings move your text and apply styles to it.

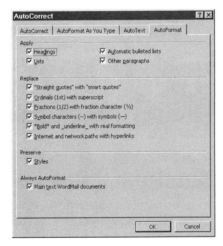

To control the way AutoFormat manipulates your existing document, follow these steps:

1. In the document you want to AutoFormat, press Ctrl+Home to move to the top of the document.

2. Choose Format, AutoFormat. The AutoFormat dialog box opens (see Figure 9.14).

3. Choose to apply the AutoFormats all at once with no interaction from you (AutoFormat Now) or to see each potential change and decide on each one individually (AutoFormat and Review Each Change).

FIG. 9.14

Although accepting all AutoFormat changes is faster, you may find it safer to review each change one at a time.

4. Indicate the type of document you're working on so AutoFormat applies the most appropriate formats. Click the Please Select a Document Type... drop-down list and select General, Letter, or Email.

5. To check your AutoFormat settings before applying them, click the Options button—the AutoCorrect dialog box opens, displaying the AutoFormat tab. Make any desired changes and click OK to return to the AutoFormat dialog box.

6. Click OK to begin the AutoFormat process and close the dialog box.

If you elect to review all the AutoFormats (see Figure 9.15), you can scroll through the document to see the proposed changes. After viewing the changes, you can click the Accept All or Reject All buttons.

FIG. 9.15

The proposed AutoFormat changes appear in color, and any deletions in strikethrough style.

If some of the changes are appropriate and some are not, click the Review Changes button rather than making an overall acceptance or rejection. The Review AutoFormat Changes dialog box opens (see Figure 9.16).

FIG. 9.16

Use the Find buttons to move forward and backward in your document, change by change.

As you move through the document (by clicking the Find buttons), you'll see a description of each intended change in the dialog box, and you can also see the change within the context of your document. This will assist you in deciding to perform the change and move on by clicking the Find buttons or Reject the change.

T I P Don't use the Hide Marks button, because this removes the strikethrough and color effects of the AutoFormat changes, and you won't be able to see your original content versus the proposed changes.

When all AutoFormat changes have been reviewed, Word prompts you, asking if you want to start again at the beginning, and continues to tell you that each time it has cycled through all the changes. To end the process normally (without having to click Cancel), you must resolve all the changes by either accepting or rejecting them. ●

CHAPTER 10

Customizing Word Options

In this chapter

Customizing Word's Toolbars

Your toolbars give you the quickest access to the most powerful commands that Word has to offer. Word's designers chose the commands and features that people need and use most often, and assigned them to the Standard and Formatting toolbars, but you needn't be restricted by this limited offering.

Word offers a list of 11 additional toolbars, accessible from the View, Toolbars command or by right-clicking any displayed toolbar, as shown in Figure 10.1.

FIG. 10.1
Select the toolbar that offers commands that match your task, such as Drawing or Forms.

For most documents, the Standard and Formatting toolbars offer the tools you need. There will be times, however, when you need a more focused set of tools—perhaps to work with graphics (the Picture toolbar) or to create a fill-in form (the Forms toolbar). Adding these task-specific toolbars to your screen, however, takes up a lot of space. If you open four or five toolbars at the same time, you can reduce the visible space for your document by almost three inches!

What if you could pick the one or two most important buttons from each of the other toolbars and add them to your two basic toolbars? You'd have the functions you need, but you wouldn't have to take up so much space on your screen.

 T I P   In addition to the other toolbars' buttons, you can add buttons to your main toolbars that represent menu commands and macros that are not currently shown on any toolbars.

Adding Toolbar Buttons

Adding toolbar buttons is easy—deciding which buttons you need is the hard part! The list of existing buttons and buttons that you can create for every conceivable menu command is so long, you may be tempted to add too many new buttons to your toolbars. Remember, the idea is to select the tools that you'll use often, or that are cumbersome to get to using the menus.

> **N O T E**   If you share your computer with others, consider creating your own custom toolbar to accommodate your toolbar customization needs rather than making potentially confusing additions and changes to the existing toolbars. Techniques for creating your own toolbar are discussed later in this chapter.

To add a button to your Standard or Formatting toolbar, follow these steps:

1. Choose Tools, Customize.

2. Click the Commands tab to see a list of all the available menus and toolbars (see Figure 10.2).

FIG. 10.2

When choosing commands to add to your toolbars, select only those commands that you use most often.

3. Click one of the Categories to see a list of the commands found in that category.

4. Scroll through the Commands; when you find the one you want to assign as a button on the toolbar, drag it up to the toolbar with your mouse.

 The All Commands category contains a list of every menu command, all in one list.

5. When you release the mouse, the button (with its assigned button face) appears on the toolbar.

6. Continue to select categories and drag commands up to your toolbars until you've added all the buttons you need.

7. Click OK.

CAUTION

Try not to place your new buttons haphazardly—you want to group your buttons (and the functions they represent) in logical clusters. Keep file-related functions (like Close, or Close All) at the left end of the Standard toolbar with the existing Open and Save commands. Add your new formatting tools (Outline, Strikethrough) next to the existing Bold, Italic, and Underline buttons. This will help you continue to benefit from the original designers' placement of the basic tools.

If the command you chose doesn't have an assigned button face (graphic image on the button), you can choose one of your own:

1. Choose Tools, Customize.

2. On the toolbar, click once on the button for which you need a graphic button face.

Part
II

Ch
10

3. In the Customize dialog box, click the Commands button.

4. Click the Modify button, and choose Change Button Image. A palette of button faces is displayed (see Figure 10.3).

FIG. 10.3
Choose a button face that matches your button's function, if possible.

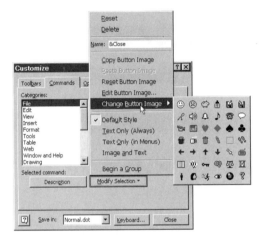

5. Click the button face you want to use. That image appears on your button.

6. If text also appears on the button (a command or macro name, for example), click the Modify button again, and choose Text Only (in Menus). The text will disappear from the button face, leaving only your selected graphic button image.

7. Click OK to close the Customize dialog box.

Moving and Deleting Toolbar Buttons

Your toolbar buttons can be rearranged, and buttons you've added can be removed if you decide you don't need them. To make changes to your toolbars, the toolbars must be displayed, and the Customize dialog box must be open. You open the Customize dialog box by choosing Tools, Customize.

N O T E If anyone other than you uses your computer, it's a good idea not to remove any of the Standard or Formatting toolbars' original buttons—doing so can make it hard for other users to find familiar commands.

While the Customize dialog box is open, the toolbars become changeable—you can drag buttons from one place to another, moving them to the left or right of their current location, or dragging them between displayed toolbars.

If you want to delete a button, merely drag it off the toolbar and release the mouse.

After you've made your changes and deletions, close the Customize dialog box by clicking the OK button.

N O T E You can rearrange and delete your toolbar buttons without opening the Customize dialog box. Press and hold the Alt key, and drag buttons around to rearrange them, or drag them off the toolbars to remove them. Release the Alt key when you've completed your changes.

Creating Custom Toolbars

Although it might seem like Word offers all the toolbars you could ever need, you may decide that rather than (or in addition to) customizing the existing toolbars, you'd like to create a collection of buttons of your own—a group of toolbar buttons to give you access to the functions you perform in your regular activities in Word.

To create your own toolbar, follow these steps:

1. Choose Tools, Customize.
2. Click the Toolbars tab (see Figure 10.4).

FIG. 10.4

Use the Toolbars tab to start the process of creating your own new toolbar.

3. Click the New button. The New Toolbar dialog box opens (see Figure 10.5).

FIG. 10.5

Give your new toolbar a short and relevant name.

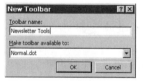

4. Type a Toolbar name and select a template from the Make Toolbar Available To drop-down list.

T I P Choose the default template (Normal.dot) in the Make Toolbar Available To drop-down list. This will make your new toolbar accessible in all documents.

5. Click OK.
6. A floating toolbar appears on your screen, with your new toolbar's name on its title bar (see Figure 10.6).

Part

II

Ch

10

FIG. 10.6

Drag commands to your new toolbar, selecting the ones you'll use most often.

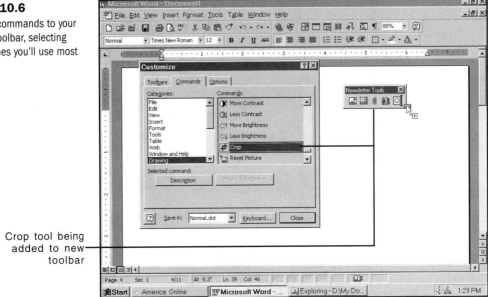

Crop tool being added to new toolbar

7. Using the Commands tab, select menu and toolbar commands and drag them to your new toolbar.

8. While the Customize dialog box is open, your new toolbar's buttons can be rearranged or deleted (if you change your mind about them). Finish making your Commands selections and setting up your toolbar buttons.

9. Click OK to close the Customize dialog box.

Your new toolbar can now be dragged up to the top of the screen to join your Standard and Formatting toolbars. Perhaps your new toolbar can replace one of them.

You can close your toolbar at any time by right-clicking it. Select the toolbar's name, and it disappears from the screen. You can redisplay it by right-clicking any displayed toolbar. Choose your toolbar from the list.

To delete any custom toolbar, choose Tools, Customize and click the Toolbars tab. Select the toolbar and click the Delete button.

CAUTION

You'll notice that Word won't let you delete one of its original 14 toolbars—the Delete button is dimmed unless you select a user-created toolbar from the list. Although Word won't stop you from deleting toolbar buttons on any toolbar, you should restrict toolbar button deletions to the buttons you've added to the installed toolbars and the toolbars you've built on your own.

Working with Word's Defaults

Word's defaults are what make it possible for you to sit down at your computer, start Word, and begin typing immediately on Document1. This blank document contains many defaults that are built into the Normal template—settings for everything from your font size to the type of bullet you get when you apply bullets to your text.

Changing these defaults should always be considered carefully. Never change a default for a unique document or for a situation that you aren't sure will arise in 90 percent or more of your documents. When considering default changes, keep a few things in mind:

- *Will this change work in most, if not all, of my documents?* Making changes that won't benefit nearly all your typical documents will only increase your work and waste time when you have to make formatting changes to work around your new defaults.

- *How many steps does it save me if I make this new setting a default?* Don't make a change to a default setting to save accessing a menu command or using a simple dialog box. The possible ramifications of changing most defaults could create more work and waste more time than you'll save.

- *If others use my computer, will these changes create problems for them?* Don't make changes that won't benefit everyone who uses your computer. If you are working in a shared environment, you shouldn't make changes that help only you.

- *Do the changes apply to templates, macros, or other files that are stored on a network?* Making changes to files that other people access on public network drives can create problems for people who rely on Word's original default settings.

What Word defaults can you safely change? The following list gives you the answers:

- *Your AutoFormat settings.* These are an obvious choice because they are easily reset to the original settings.

- *Your AutoCorrect options for capitalization and punctuation.* These, like AutoFormats, are easy to reset if you don't like your new defaults.

- *The default font and font size for documents based on the Normal.dot template.* Click the <u>D</u>efault button in the Font dialog box to make the selected font formats the default setting for documents based on the Normal template (see Figure 10.7).

> **CAUTION**
>
> If you decide to change your default font (or to choose a new font for one of the Normal template's styles), be aware that other users may not have your new font on their computers. If they don't, Word will substitute another font for yours when your document is opened on the other user's computer. It's a good idea to pick standard fonts that most people have, such as Arial, Courier, or Times New Roman.

- *Styles.* If you choose the <u>A</u>pply to Template option when creating new styles or modifying existing styles, the changes become part of the Normal template.

- *Default tabs stops.* The Normal template has left-aligned tabs at every half-inch. You can change this increment in the dialog box that appears when you choose F<u>o</u>rmat, <u>T</u>abs.

Part
II

Ch
10

FIG. 10.7
Choose a new default font with care! Make sure it doesn't clash with your stationery or fax and make your message illegible.

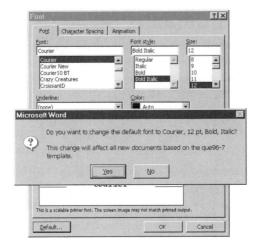

As most of the defaults in the preceding list apply only to the appearance of text, they are safe areas to manipulate in your quest to make Word even more flexible and productive than it already is.

> **CAUTION**
> If you're making a change to any default setting, it's a good idea to jot down what settings were in place before you made changes—that way, if anything unwanted results from your modifications, you know what settings to restore.

▶ **See** "Modifying Styles" **p. 47**
▶ **See** "Using AutoCorrect" **p. 113**
▶ **See** "Understanding AutoFormat Options" **p. 117**

Setting File Locations

Be default, Word saves all normal documents (files with a .doc extension) to the My Documents folder on your local drive. The My Documents folder was created when Windows 95 was installed on your computer, and all Microsoft Office applications default to this folder when a file is saved.

Most users create subfolders within the My Documents folder to categorize their files—subfolders such as "Letters," "Staff Memos," and "Reports" help classify the different documents they create. These categories don't work for all documents, however, so they should not be made the default folder.

If you're using Word in a Windows NT environment, you may find that you're prompted to place your files in a personal folder stored in your user profile.

If, however, you must save to a network drive or if you share your computer with another user, you may want to create a folder for yourself and make that your default folder. The folder can be named after you ("Bob's Files") or your job function ("Sales Documents"). By making this the new default folder for saved files, you can save yourself time navigating to this folder from the My Documents folder each time you save a file for the first time.

N O T E If your computer is on a network, your rights to certain folders are determined by your login, as set up by your system administrator. Windows gives you the ability, if you're on a network, to determine the sharing settings for certain folders. Use My Computer and choose File, Properties. Click the Sharing tab to see and change the current settings for the selected folder.

To choose a new default folder for documents, follow these steps:

1. Choose Tools, Options.
2. Click the File Locations tab (see Figure 10.8).

Part

II

Ch

10

FIG. 10.8

The File Locations tab lists the various types of files you can create in Word and enables you to change their default storage locations.

3. In the File Types list, click Documents.
4. Click the Modify button.
5. In the Modify Location dialog box, navigate to the folder that you want to make the default. Figure 10.9 shows the user selecting a folder called Robert's Files.
6. Double-click the folder, and click OK.
7. Click OK to close the Options dialog box.

CAUTION

Do not change the default location for templates in Word or any other Office application. To do so can result in not being able to access them when creating new documents.

FIG. 10.9
If you share your
computer with another
user, create and select a
default documents
folder with your name
on it.

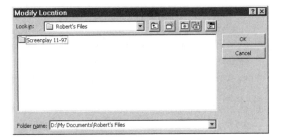

Configuring Word's Proofing Tools

Word processors that can check your spelling—and more recently, check your grammar—are probably the most productivity-enhancing tools to be added to anyone's software arsenal. For most people, Word's spelling and grammar-checking tools are configured "just right," and with the exception of adding words to the user's custom dictionary, there is no need to change the way these tools work.

Some users, however, have special needs that require some fine-tuning of Word's Spelling and Grammar feature. Word gives you the ability to completely customize the way both spelling and grammar are used to proof your documents.

> **CAUTION**
> The decision to tweak Word's spelling and grammar tools should not be made lightly—as in resetting defaults, making changes to how Word proofs your document's content should be made with the needs of your most common documents in mind.

Customizing Spell Check with an Exclusions List

One way to make Word's spelling feature work the way you do is to add a list of words that the Spelling and Grammar program should stop on when doing a spell check, even if they're spelled correctly. For example, imagine you prefer the more formal spelling of "catalogue" to the more colloquial "catalog". By adding `catalog` to the exclusion list, you can force Word to question you each time you type `catalog`, giving you the change to replace it with the preferred spelling.

This feature can be especially useful if you find yourself typing the wrong word spelled correctly, such as "form" instead of "from", or "lust" instead of "list". Add `form` and `lust` to the exclusions list, and Word will stop to ask you about these words whenever you use them.

To build an exclusions list, follow these steps:

1. Choose File, New and select the Blank document template, or click the New button on the toolbar.

2. Type your list of words, pressing Enter after each one. Figure 10.10 shows a list of exclusions.

FIG. 10.10

If you prefer "grey" to "gray" or "colour" to "color," build the versions you don't like into your exclusions list.

Insert all forms of any word that you tend to use incorrectly.

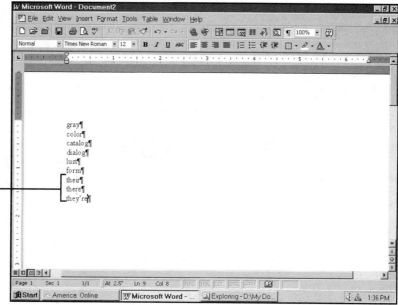

3. When your list is complete, choose File, Save As.

4. Navigate to the folder where your main dictionary is stored. This is either in C:\Program Files\Common Files\Microsoft Shared\Proof or C:\Windows\MSApps\Proof.

5. Name your exclusion list with the same filename as your main dictionary, but give it an .exc extension (rather than the .lex extension you'll find on the main dictionary file). The main dictionary file is named Mssp2_en.lex.

6. In the Save File as Type list, choose the Text Only (.txt) format.

7. Click Save.

8. Close the Mssp2_en.exc file so it can be used when you run your next spell check.

You can easily add words to this exclusions list at any time by opening the document and inserting words. Resave the file, making sure to retain the Text Only format and to keep the filename and location intact.

ON THE WEB

http://www.spellex.com/   If you work in the pharmaceutical, medical, dental, legal, or other industry that has its own jargon, check this site for tools that will enable you to spell-check your esoteric terminology.

Adjusting Grammar Settings

Some people are conversational chameleons—they speak in a formal way when conversing with their boss or anyone in authority, and speak much more informally when conversing with friends or people they don't feel the need to impress.

Word's grammar checking tools enable you to customize the grammatical standards that are applied to your documents just like you might customize your speech patterns for different groups of people.

To choose which grammatical rules will be applied to your documents, follow these steps:

1. Choose Tools, Options.
2. Click the Spelling & Grammar tab (see Figure 10.11).

FIG. 10.11

You can thoroughly customize your spelling and grammar settings to fit any type of document and any type of reader.

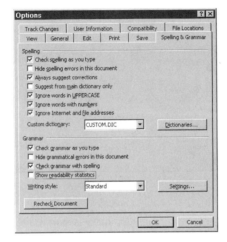

3. In the Grammar section of the dialog box, click the Writing Style drop-down list and choose the style that matches the audience of your current document.
4. Click the Settings button. This opens the Grammar Settings dialog box (see Figure 10.12).

FIG. 10.12

Choose which standards are important to you for the selected writing style.

5. For your selected writing style, choose the Grammar and Style Options that you want used (make sure they're checked) and ignored (remove the check mark).

6. Set your standards for Commas Before Last List Item, Punctuation with Quotes, and Spaces Between Sentences.

7. Click OK to put your new grammatical standards into effect and return to the Options dialog box.

8. Click OK in the Options dialog box.

Your goal in setting your grammar options is to pick the settings that will work for most of your documents. You can, of course, reset them for every document if the nature of your documents and the audience for them change frequently. ●

Part

II

Ch

10

Picking Up the Pace with Excel

Building an Efficient Spreadsheet

In this chapter

Entering Content More Efficiently

The key to effective and productive use of Excel doesn't lie entirely in your math or accounting skills. It doesn't have anything to do with knowing the latest tax codes or what the prime rate is. The people who get the most from Excel are those who can move around in a workbook quickly and enter their spreadsheet content with confidence.

N O T E   If you're not using it already, get comfortable with the numeric keypad on your keyboard. Use it for entering all numbers, mathematical operators (/,*,+,-), and decimal points. The Enter key works like an equal sign! Before using it, make sure your NumLock is on (look for a light over the keypad). Turning on the NumLock feature turns this cluster of keys from a navigational keypad to a numeric keypad.

Keyboard Navigation

The shortest distance between two points is a straight line, and certainly a workbook—being made up of nice, straight columns and rows—should lend itself to getting from place to place quickly. Whether you're entering data or finding a specific cell in your worksheet, you'll find the keyboard shortcuts in Table 11.1 helpful.

Table 11.1   Keyboard Shortcuts Navigating Excel

To Do This	Press These Shortcut Keys
Move one cell to the left, right, up, or down	Arrow keys
To move from left to right, one cell at a time, while entering content	Tab
To move to the cell directly below the active cell	Enter
To move from right to left, one cell at a time, while entering content	Shift+Tab
Move to the beginning of the row you are in	Home
Move to cell A1, from anywhere in the worksheet	Ctrl+Home
Move down one screen	Page Down
Move up one screen	Page Up
Move to the right, one full screen	Alt+Page Down
Move to the left, one full screen	Alt+Page Up
Move to the next sheet in the workbook	Ctrl+Page Down
Move to the previous worksheet	Ctrl+Page Up
Move to the last cell in the current row	Ctrl+right arrow
Move to the last cell in the current column	Ctrl+down arrow

To Do This	Press These Shortcut Keys
Move to the last cell that contains data	Ctrl+End

 T I P When entering rows of data, you'll find that due to its location on the keyboard, using the Tab key to move from left to right is faster than using the arrow keys. When you're ready for the next row/record, press Home, and then press the down arrow or Enter key once; you're at the beginning of the next row!

To move to a particular cell address, press Ctrl+G or the F5 key. Either method opens the Go To dialog box (see Figure 11.1). Enter the cell address to which you want to go, and press Enter or click OK.

FIG. 11.1
Go to a specific cell that's out of your current view by pressing Ctrl+G and entering the cell address.

Selecting Cell Ranges

Just as highlighting text in Word indicates which text you're about to edit, format, or delete, you must select cells in Excel before you edit, format, or delete their contents. You'll also need to select cells before using the Clipboard (to cut, copy, or paste cells), and when choosing a range of cells to sum or average.

You can select a single cell by clicking in it with your mouse or using the arrow keys to move to the desired cell. Table 11.1 earlier in this chapter defines all the methods of moving to a particular cell. The cell on your worksheet with the thick outline is the selected cell (see Figure 11.2).

You can also select a block (range) of cells by clicking and dragging through them. The first cell in the range (where you clicked before dragging) remains white, and the rest of the selected range turns black. Figure 11.3 shows a selected range of cells.

T I P To select the entire worksheet, press Ctrl+A.

Selected cells need not be contiguous. You can use your Ctrl key to gather single cells or ranges of cells, selecting them all over the active worksheet. Figure 11.4 shows a series of selected ranges. The first cell in the last range you select remains white. All the other selected cells turn black.

FIG. 11.2
Click once in any cell to select it.

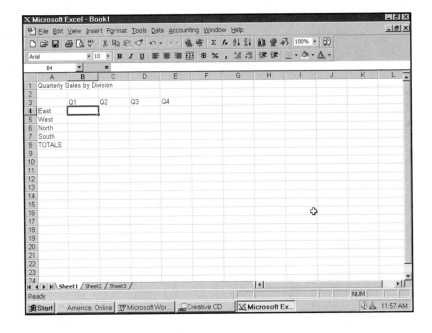

FIG. 11.3
A block of selected cells can be as small as two cells or as large as the entire worksheet.

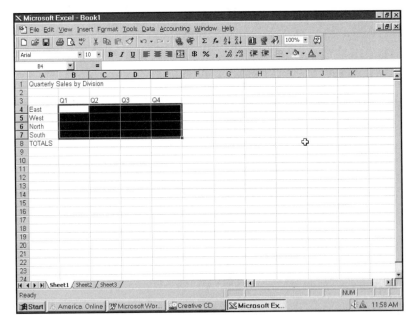

N O T E Users who either can't or don't like to use the mouse can select cells by using the arrow keys in conjunction with the Shift key. Hold the Shift key down as you click the up, down, left, and right arrow keys, selecting the desired range of cells. When the selection is complete, release the Shift key.

FIG. 11.4

To apply formats or delete the content in several areas at once, select multiple ranges with the Ctrl key.

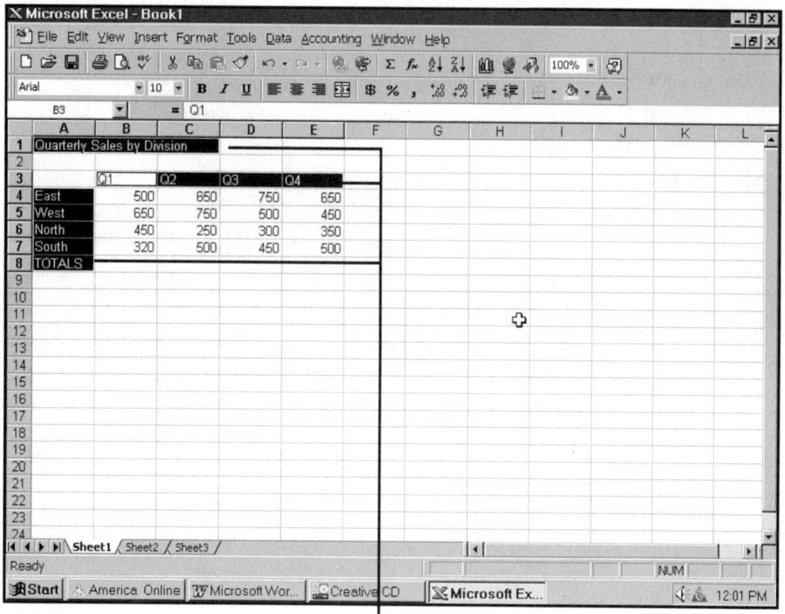

Multiple ranges selected for text formatting

Naming Ranges for Fast Access

Unless your worksheet's content is housed within one screen's worth of cells, you can't simply click a particular cell when you want to—you have to look up and down, left and right, with your keyboard or mouse until you spot the cell you're looking for, right? Wrong. If you name the important or often-accessed cells in your worksheet, you can go to these cells (or ranges of cells) quickly and easily.

First, you must name the cell or range of cells. Typically, the name is a short description of what's in the cell(s), such as First Quarter Projections or Northwest Division Expense Total. After you've named your worksheet's key areas, you can dispense with trying to remember cell addresses.

To name a range (which can be one cell or a contiguous range of cells), follow these steps:

1. Select the cell or range of cells that you want to name.

2. Choose Insert, Name, Define.

3. In the Define Name dialog box (see Figure 11.5), type the name of the range in the Names in Workbook text box.

4. Click Add.

5. You can keep the dialog box open and move throughout your workbook, naming ranges. Click the Shrink button at the end of the Refers To text box to shrink the dialog box.

Part III

Ch 11

FIG. 11.5
Naming a range makes it easy to find it without having to remember the cell addresses.

Previously named ranges

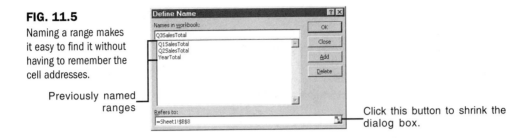

Click this button to shrink the dialog box.

N O T E In lieu of physically selecting your other ranges, you can type their cell address/range address in the Refers To box. =Sheet1!$C$8:$D$9 would select a range of four cells on Sheet1. The dollar signs indicate that this named range will stay in these cells, even if the content is moved. If you want the named range to move if the cell contents are moved, don't type the dollar signs.

6. Scroll or move to the next desired range, and select it.

7. Click the Expand button to expand the Define Name dialog box, and enter a name for the current cell/range.

8. Click Add.

9. Continue repeating steps 5–8 until all your cells/ranges are named. Click Close when you are ready to exit the Define Name dialog box.

To access the list of named ranges in your worksheet, click the Name listbox, and select your named range from the list. Figure 11.6 shows the Name list and a range selected.

FIG. 11.6
Pick your named ranges from this handy listbox to move quickly to the cell or range you need.

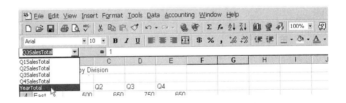

Creating Column and Row Labels with a Series

An Excel series is a list of words or numbers that are intuitively created by Excel when just the first one or two items in the list are provided. These Custom List series are usually used to create a set of column or row labels, as shown in Figure 11.7.

Excel contains the following Custom Lists, which you can use to build a series in a column, row, or block of cells:

■ *The days of the month.* You can fill them in as abbreviations (Jan, Feb, Mar, and so on) or in full text (January, February, March, and so on). You can start with any month and create a series as long as you want. When the series reaches December, it will begin again in the next cell with January.

FIG. 11.7

Excel's Custom List feature enables you to set up headings that contain the months of the year in one simple step.

■ *Days of the week.* You can choose from abbreviated days (Mon, Tues, Wed) or full text (Monday, Tuesday, Wednesday). You can start the series on any day of the week—when it reaches Sun (or Sunday), it will start again with Monday in the next cell.

 Don't type a period at the end of the abbreviated days of the week or months of the year. Excel doesn't recognize them.

To fill a series, follow these steps:

1. Click in the cell that will be the first cell in the series.
2. Type the first entry—a day of the week or a month of the year.
3. Point to the fill handle, the black box in the lower-right corner of the cell (see Figure 11.8). Your mouse turns into a black cross.

FIG. 11.8

Drag the fill handle to complete your series of days or months.

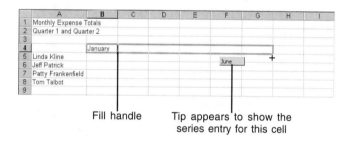

Fill handle   Tip appears to show the series entry for this cell

4. Click and drag the black cross through the cells into which you want to fill the series.
5. When the series is complete, release the mouse.

If you want to create a numeric pattern, such as 1, 2, 3, or 50, 100, 150, you must establish a pattern first and then use the cells containing the pattern as an example. Excel "learns" from these cells and completes the pattern in the cells you indicate. Figure 11.9 shows a numeric pattern established and then completed across a row.

 Even though it isn't listed in the installed Custom Lists box, Excel recognizes a series of fiscal quarters—type Q1, Qtr 1, or Quarter 1, and drag to fill in the series.

You can also create your own Custom Lists for text or numeric patterns. Imagine that your company has 10 divisions, and you're always typing their names across the top row of your spreadsheet. Instead of typing them each time (or copying the row from an existing worksheet), create a Custom List. From then on, you'll need to type only the first division name in a cell and then drag through the remaining nine cells to complete the series.

FIG. 11.9

Create a pattern in two or three cells, and then use them to show Excel how to complete your numeric series.

A pattern established in these cells enables the user to create a series of numbers, each increasing by 10.

To create your own Custom List, follow these steps:

1. Choose Tools, Options.

2. Click the Custom Lists tab (see Figure 11.10).

FIG. 11.10

View the existing Custom Lists and build some of your own to speed the entry of your column and row labels.

Lists created by user

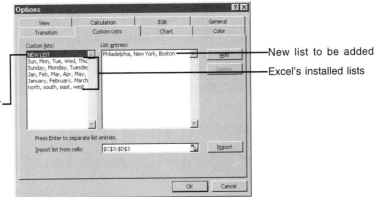

New list to be added

Excel's installed lists

3. Click the NEW LIST item in the Custom Lists box. Your cursor appears in the List Entries box on the right.

4. Type your Custom List, separating each item in the list with a comma. Figure 11.11 shows a list of compass points being added.

5. When your list is complete, click Add.

6. You can add as many Custom Lists as you need, repeating steps 3–5 for each one.

7. When you've added all your Custom Lists, click OK to close the Options dialog box.

Test your new series by typing any word or number from the series and dragging through adjacent cells. The cells are filled with the next item in the list, and begin again with the first item in the list as soon as the last item is used. Figure 11.12 shows the compass points list in use.

FIG. 11.11

Proofread the items in your list before clicking OK.

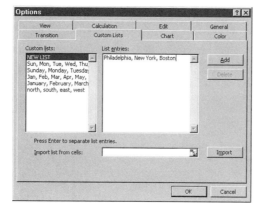

FIG. 11.12

If your company's activities are divided geographically, create a Custom List of global areas.

N O T E If you've already typed a series of column or row labels and you want to use them to create a Custom List, select the cells containing the series and choose Tools, Options. Click the Custom Lists tab, and click the Import button. Your list automatically appears in the List Entries box. Note that you can use this method only with text, not numbers. Numerical custom lists can be created using the Options dialog box, as described in the previous procedure.

ON THE WEB

http://www.decisionanalyst.com/s/   This shareware site contains downloadable programs that enable you to create random numbered lists. A variety of other statistical add-ins are available from this site as well.

Using AutoFill to Enter Data

Excel wants to make your life easy. Every time you type text in a cell, Excel looks at your previous text entries in that column and looks for a match. As soon as Excel sees a match in your previous entries, it inserts that match in the cell into which you're typing. If Excel's guess as to your intended content is correct, press Enter to accept it. This saves you from typing the remainder of the entry. If you want to type something different, just keep typing—you'll insert your content over Excel's assumed content.

This feature is especially useful when entering lists of data that contain a lot of repeated content. Figure 11.13 shows a worksheet in progress and Excel's AutoFill offering suggested content.

FIG. 11.13

To make the most of AutoFill, be careful to spell and/or abbreviate your entries the same way each time when entering repeated data.

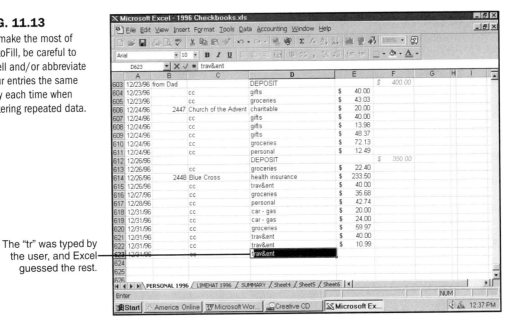

The "tr" was typed by the user, and Excel guessed the rest.

Copying and Moving Cell Content

Your mouse can be a significant ally in the war against wasted effort. If one cell in your worksheet contains data that you want to use or reuse elsewhere but that you don't want to type again, you may not want to bother using Edit, Cut or Edit, Copy to take the data to a new cell or cells.

To use your mouse to move or copy cell content, point to the edge of the cell or range of cells you want to use/reuse. When your mouse pointer turns to a white, left-pointing arrow, drag the cells to a new location (see Figure 11.14). If you want to duplicate them in a new location, press and hold the Ctrl key as you drag the cell(s). When you use the Ctrl key to copy cell content, you'll notice a small plus sign appended to your mouse pointer.

N O T E If you already have some content on the Clipboard that you don't want to lose, dragging the cell content to a new spot is the only way to protect the Clipboard content from replacement.

If you prefer the more methodical method of using the Clipboard to move or copy cell content, try these faster methods:

- Use your right mouse button to open a shortcut menu (see Figure 11.15). The menu offers the Clipboard Cut, Copy, and Paste commands.
- Use the keyboard—Ctrl+X to Cut, Ctrl+C to Copy, and Ctrl+V to Paste.

FIG. 11.14
Save typing and ensure consistency by dragging existing cells to a new location.

Original cell location

Target location

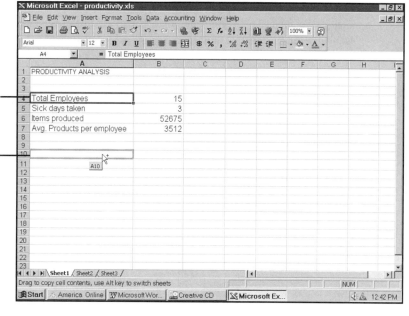

FIG. 11.15
Right-click your source cells and choose Cut or Copy. Then right-click your target cells and choose Paste.

Creating Quick Formulas

Quick Formulas in Excel almost seems redundant—the most powerful aspect of an electronic spreadsheet is the capability to perform calculations quickly and accurately. Some users, however, don't take full advantage of productivity-enhancing techniques for building and using spreadsheet formulas.

Working with Relative Addressing

Relative addressing is the use of cell addresses in formulas rather than real numbers. If your spreadsheet contains sales totals for a series of divisions of your company, the formula that totals all the divisions is going to contain cell addresses, not the actual sales totals for each division. This enables you to change one division's sales, and have their total and the grand company-wide total change simultaneously. The grand total changes *relative* to what is in the cells included in the formula. Figure 11.16 shows a sales report total built with cell addresses.

FIG. 11.16

Click in the cells as you build your formula. Type an operator between them, and press Enter at the end.

Cell address—

Operator—

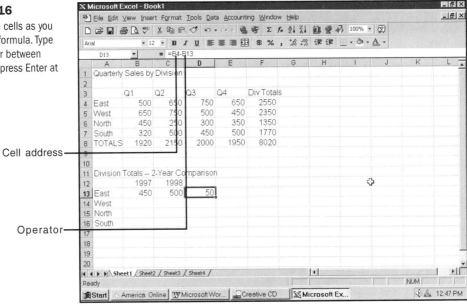

 TIP When building your formulas with cell addresses, it's faster and easier to click in the cells you want to include in your formula than to type them. It also eliminates typos!

Pasting a Formula

When you have more than one column or row to sum, average, or on which you want to perform any calculation, perform that calculation only once, in the first row or column. Then point to the fill handle (see Figure 11.17), and drag the cell that contains the total across the remaining columns or down the remaining rows.

By using the fill handle to paste your formula into other cells, you're reusing the formula—but because relative addressing is also at work here, the results of the calculations are correct for their new location. The formula that summed column B now correctly sums columns C, D, and E, and the formula reflects the proper cell addresses.

Using Absolute References

Absolute is a strong word. It normally indicates a lack of flexibility when someone says he is "absolutely sure." In Excel formulas, use of an absolute reference indicates that one or more of the cell addresses in the formula cannot be changed, and will not be changed, even if the formula is pasted to other cells.

FIG. 11.17
Relative addressing makes it possible to paste a formula from one cell to another and have the formula update itself for its new location.

Formula for column B

The same formula was pasted to these cells to sum these columns.

The fill handle

Quarterly Sales by Division

	Q1	Q2	Q3	Q4	Div Totals
East	500	650	750	650	2550
West	650	750	500	450	2350
North	450	250	300	350	1350
South	320	500	450	500	1770
TOTALS	1920	2150	2000	1950	8020

Division Totals -- 2-Year Comparison

	1997	1998	
East	450	500	50
West			
North			
South			

=SUM(B4:B7)

If Excel's strength lies in its flexibility, why take away from that by building an inflexible formula? Imagine a series of products, accompanied by their current prices. In your spreadsheet, you want to project price increases for all of your products. You're toying with a 15% or 20% increase, and you want to see how the difference in price will affect your other sales numbers. You could create a formula such as =C3*1.20 to show the current price (in cell C3) increased by 20%. But you'd have to repeat it for all your prices. Even if you paste it down the column to update all your prices by 20%, you'll have to redo the formula and re-paste it to see the prices at 15%.

Absolute references avoid all that extra effort when you're playing "what if" games with numbers. To create an absolute reference in your formula, follow these steps:

1. Place your absolute reference number in a stray cell, somewhere off to the side of your main spreadsheet content.
2. Go to the cell that will contain your formula, and begin building the calculation.
3. When you reach the point where you'd type the absolute reference number that you're using in the formula, type or click in the cell address that contains the number.
4. Press the F4 key. You'll see dollar signs appear in front of the column letter and row number in the cell address.
5. Finish your formula as needed, and press Enter.
6. Paste your formula to the remaining cells in the row or column.

When you click in each of the cells that contain your pasted formula, you'll see that while all the other cell addresses updated appropriately for their new location, the stray cell address did not. Now you can experiment with a new number (such as the multiplier 1.15 in our previous example), and see all the numbers change to reflect the contents of the absolute reference cell. No retyping, no re-pasting is required! Figure 11.18 shows a price list with absolute reference.

FIG. 11.18

Play "what if" games with your numbers by putting your variable number in a cell and making that cell an absolute reference in your formula.

An absolute reference as it appears in a formula

The absolute reference cell

 TIP If changes in the layout of your spreadsheet content require you to move the absolute reference cell, use the drag-and-drop method to move it—the formulas that refer to it are updated automatically.

Using Find and Replace to Make Global Changes

The way you deal with numbers isn't likely to change from year to year—your budget will probably contain the same categories; your investments might change, but your calculations for determining their value probably won't. Excel's Find and Replace commands enable you to take advantage of this consistency and search for the things that will change and insert alternative content.

Using Find and Replace can turn last year's sales report into this year's by replacing the name of a sales rep that's no longer on staff, or by changing the quota percentage from last year's 25% increase to this year's optimistic 30%. Using the Replace command to do this eliminates missing one or two occurrences of the content you're looking for, and makes your replacements consistent.

To find and replace worksheet content, follow these steps:

1. Press Ctrl+Home to move to cell A1 in the worksheet you want to search.

 TIP If you want to search only a specific area of your worksheet, select that range of cells before invoking the Find or Replace commands.

2. Choose Edit, Replace. In the Replace dialog box (see Figure 11.19), enter the content for which you're searching in the Find What box.

FIG. 11.19

Use Find and Replace to search for numbers or text in your spreadsheet and delete or change them as needed. Don't rely on a manual search!

3. Press Tab to move to the Replace With box, and type the replacement content.

N O T E The options for where to Search (By Rows or By Columns) and to Match Case or Find Entire Cells Only make it easier to control the outcome of your Find and/or Replace session by fine-tuning the search.

4. Click Find Next to go to the first occurrence of the content.

 If you'd prefer to delete one of the occurrences when you find it, click in the cell (the Find or Replace dialog box stays onscreen) and press Delete. Click back inside the Find or Replace dialog box to reactivate it, and click Find Next to continue the Find/Replace process.

5. Click Replace to change it or Find Next to skip it and move to the next occurrence.

6. If you want to replace every occurrence of the found content with the replacement text and not be prompted for each one, click Replace All.

CAUTION

Be very careful when using Replace All. If, for example, you're replacing 1997 with 1998 to update your titles throughout a spreadsheet, make sure that none of your data includes the number 1997 (for example, $1,997,540.00). To avoid this situation, choose the Find Entire Cells Only option.

▶ **See** "Working with Find and Replace" **p. 108**

Building a Workbook with Grouped Sheets

Every Excel workbook opens with three blank sheets. You can add sheets as needed (Insert, Worksheet), adding up to 255 total sheets in any workbook. Many users, however, never go past Sheet1 in a workbook, finding all the room they need in the 16,777,216 cells (65,536 rows×256 columns). If you do need to use two or more sheets, you can build them independently, or if their content is similar, you can group them and build their common content simultaneously.

 You can rearrange your sheets (by dragging their tabs) and rename them (by double-clicking their tabs and typing a name).

N O T E Excel for Office 95 offers 16 new sheets with every workbook—and because most users don't use them all, Office 97 reduced the default number to three.

To group and build two or more worksheets at the same time, follow these steps:

1. Click the first tab in the intended group. The tab turns white, and that sheet is on top.

2. Press and hold the Ctrl key.

3. Click the other tabs that you want to group. Because you're holding down the Ctrl key as you do so, they all remain selected, although the sheet for the first tab you clicked remains on top. Figure 11.20 shows three grouped sheets.

FIG. 11.20

Achieve consistency by building two or more worksheets simultaneously.

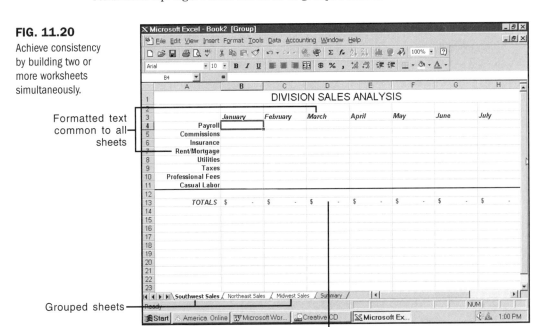

Formatted text common to all sheets

Grouped sheets

Formulas built before any numbers entered

 T I P If you want to quickly select a contiguous series of sheets, use the Shift key. Click the first sheet in the series, and then click the last. The first, last, and all sheets between them are selected.

4. While your sheets are grouped, enter and format all the content that you want on all the grouped sheets. Include formulas and titles, but don't enter any content that is meant for only one of the sheets.

N O T E Sales reports for divisions of your company, product reports (one product or product line per sheet), and budgets (one per sheet) are good candidates for grouped sheets. Just don't type any of the unique content (division or product names, department-specific budget items) until you've ungrouped your sheets.

5. When all your common content is completed, click one of the sheets that was not in your group. This breaks the link that ties the grouped sheets together.

 TIP If you have all your sheets grouped, right-click any one of the sheet tabs and select Ungroup Sheets from the shortcut menu.

6. Go to each of the now ungrouped sheets, and enter the unique content for each sheet.

If you realize you missed some content or formatting that should have been done while the sheets were grouped, you can always go back and regroup them. Make your entries or complete your common formats, and then ungroup the sheets again. ●

Part

III

Ch

11

Formatting Worksheet Appearance

Applying Number Formats

Numbers are your primary worksheet content, whether they represent dollars, units, dates, or serial numbers. How they look can make a big difference in how they are perceived by the people reading and using your worksheets. If your sales worksheet doesn't make it clear, your readers may confuse the 50,000 in sales as the number of items sold rather than dollar volume. Using a dollar sign in front of the number would clear up any confusion.

Excel gives you two methods for formatting your numbers—the Formatting toolbar and the Format Cells dialog box. Excel's designers have placed the most often-used number formatting tools on the toolbar (see Figure 12.1) and have given you the Format Cells dialog box as an alternative for applying other formats and fine-tuning the way all formats are applied.

FIG. 12.1

Click the dollar or percent signs on the Formatting toolbar to apply these number formats to your selected cell(s).

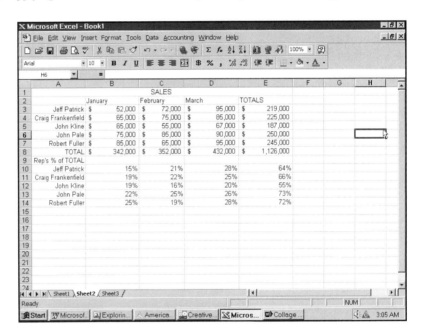

To apply number formats by using the Formatting toolbar, follow these steps:

1. Select the cell or cells to be formatted.

2. Click the Currency Style, Percentage Style, or Comma Style button on the toolbar.

> **TIP** By default, Currency Style adds commas to any numbers in excess of 999.99. If you don't want dollar signs but do want commas, use the Comma Style button instead.

3. If necessary, adjust the number of decimal places showing in the cell by clicking the Increase Decimal or Decrease Decimal buttons.

After converting numbers to currency or adding commas, you may find that your numbers turn to pound signs—don't panic! This happens so you'll know that your column isn't wide enough for the numbers with all the extra formatting. See "Changing Column Width" later in this chapter for more information.

If you want a little more control over just how your currency, percentage, and other numeric formats are applied, follow these steps:

1. Select the cell or cells that you want to format.

N O T E   Rather than dragging through a long row or column to select only the cells that contain (or will contain) numbers, select the entire row or column and then apply your Currency or Percentage Style formats.

2. Choose Format, Cells. The Format Cells dialog box opens (see Figure 12.2).

FIG. 12.2

Choose from several number formats and customize the manner in which they're applied.

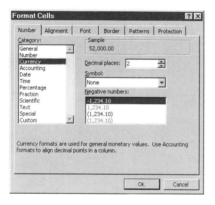

3. Click the Number tab.
4. Choose a number format from the Category list. Depending on the category you select, the remaining area of the dialog box varies.
5. Make your selections, using drop-down lists that enable you to control the number of Decimal Places or how Negative Numbers will appear. View your selection in the Sample box.

T I P   Within the dialog box, a sentence or two appears for each Category, suggesting when and how to use that particular formatting.

6. When the Sample appears as you want your real content to look, click OK to apply your formats.

After you've applied formatting from the toolbar or dialog box, you must use the dialog box to change or remove the formats.

Formatting Text and Titles

Text is generally intended to inform the reader and/or identify the numbers in your worksheet. Some of this text can benefit from a small degree of formatting—the amount of formatting you apply depends on the nature of your data, and in which format your users will be seeing the worksheet. If your worksheet will be viewed onscreen, feel free to use some color. If your worksheet will be printed, the use of color should be limited to what your printer can handle—for example, very light colors (yellow, pink) should be avoided if you can print only in black and white. Figure 12.3 shows a worksheet formatted in color (but shown in black and white). The color choices (medium shades) look good onscreen but also work well when printed on a black and white printer.

FIG. 12.3
By choosing medium to dark colors for your worksheet content, you can create a color scheme that looks good onscreen and when printed in black and white.

Fonts enlarged and bold applied

Colored titles and total numbers

CAUTION

Numbers can be formatted just like text. When changing the font or color of numeric content, make sure your font, size, and color choices don't make it hard to read the numbers.

 TIP When using color, be conservative. You want your visual formatting to enhance your worksheet's content, not distract the reader from it!

The nature of your worksheet's content should also give you some clues as to how colorful it can be. A worksheet on the savings your firm will realize if it downsizes the staff shouldn't have a bright and festive appearance. Conversely, if you're attempting to generate enthusiasm for a new sales incentive program, the worksheet that shows how much a sales rep can earn by exceeding quotas should be visually bright and exciting.

For most worksheets, the amount of visual formatting you apply—font changes, colors, borders, shading, and so forth—should be limited to what's necessary for indicating the important numbers on the worksheet, and making it pleasant and easy to read. Excel gives you toolbar buttons to access the most commonly used formats and dialog boxes for fine-tuning the way your worksheet content looks.

To change the fonts, alignment, and color of your worksheet content, follow these steps:

1. Select the cell or cells that you want to format.
2. Choose Format, Cells. The Format Cells dialog box opens.
3. Click the Font tab (see Figure 12.4).

FIG. 12.4
Your font choices can set the tone for your worksheet—choose simple, clear fonts for the most professional, legible effect.

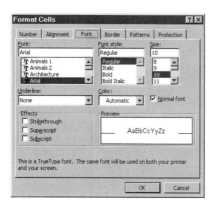

4. Change the Font, Font Style, Size, Underline, and Color attributes of the selected text. Check the Preview box to make sure you like the formats you've selected.
5. Click the Alignment tab, shown in Figure 12.5.

FIG. 12.5
Although you should normally accept Excel's default alignment, Centering headings and titles can be visually effective.

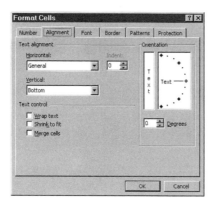

Part
III

Ch
12

TIP A General setting for the Horizontal alignment means that Excel will choose the alignment depending on the nature of the content—left alignment for text, right alignment for numbers.

6. Make your selections to adjust the Horizontal and Vertical alignment.

7. Adjust your content's Orientation by clicking along the clock-like half circle, or by entering a number of Degrees to rotate the content in its cell(s).

TIP Rotating headings by 45 degrees creates flag-like labels above your columns or beside your rows.

8. Make any needed selections in the Text Control section.

9. Click the Border tab (see Figure 12.6). Choose the sides of your cell or cells that you want bordered, and choose the line Style and Color for your border.

FIG. 12.6

Apply a border around your grand total to draw the reader's eye to the "bottom line."

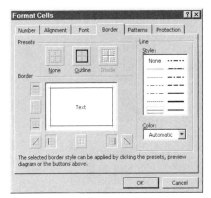

10. Click the Patterns tab (see Figure 12.7). Apply a fill Color to the cell(s), or choose a Pattern. If using a pattern, select a foreground and background color.

TIP Apply fill colors or patterns to empty cells, rows, and columns. Use them for purely cosmetic reasons or to steer a user away from typing in the cells.

11. After you've selected formatting in these four areas, click the OK button to apply them to your cells and close the dialog box. Figure 12.8 shows a spreadsheet with font, color, and alignment formatting applied.

Toolbar Access

Your Formatting toolbar contains buttons for changing the way your content looks. You can use the Font `Arial`, Font Size `10`, or Font Color `A` buttons, and apply styles such as Bold `B`, Italic `I`, and Underline `U`. You can also apply Borders to cells (to emphasize their content over and above the effect of your gridlines), and add color or patterns behind cell content by using a Fill Color.

FIG. 12.7
If you apply a dark fill color to your cell, choose a light color for your font so it can be read against the background.

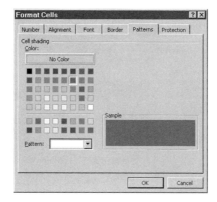

FIG. 12.8
If your column headings are long, choose the Wrap Text option on the Alignment tab or choose to rotate your text by adjusting its orientation.

Title merged and centered

Column headings with a 45 degree rotation

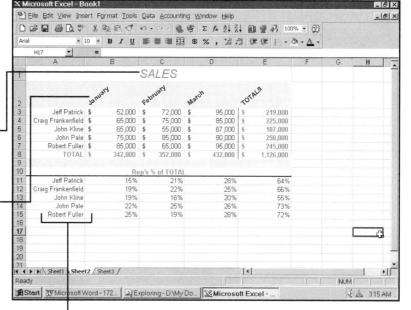

Right-aligned text

 In addition to toolbar buttons that change the color, size, and style of your text, you can also adjust your content's alignment. Excel makes some assumptions about alignment, based on the type of content you enter into a cell—numbers are automatically right-aligned, text is automatically left-aligned. The most common alignment choice is Center, and this alignment is primarily applied to column and row labels, and worksheet titles.

Figure 12.9 shows a worksheet with centered column headings and a title that has been centered across columns using the Merge and Center button.

Part
III

Ch
12

FIG. 12.9
Align your text for clarity and to draw attention to your column headings and worksheet title.

Product Pricing					
Product Number		Current Price			New Price
BT824	$	525.65	$		604.50
JH876	$	458.50	$		527.28
HS247	$	750.25	$		862.79
KJ179	$	650.50	$		748.08
KC297	$	255.00	$		293.25
Average Prices	$	527.98	$		607.18

 N O T E Use Merge and Center to create one long cell across the columns in your worksheet. Select the cell that contains your title (normally in cell A1), and drag across the other cells in that row, above your columns. Click the Merge and Center button.

Keyboard Shortcuts

For users who don't like to use the mouse or who are so focused on data entry that they don't want to take their flying fingers off the keys, the use of keyboard shortcuts can be helpful in the quick formatting of worksheet content. Table 12.1 lists some helpful keyboard shortcuts.

Table 12.1   Keyboard Shortcuts for Visual Formatting

Press These Keys	To Get This Effect
Ctrl+B	Bold
Ctrl+I	Italic
Ctrl+U	Underline
Ctrl+1	Open the Format Cells dialog box
Ctrl+L	Left-align cell content
Ctrl+E	Center cell content
Ctrl+R	Right-align cell content

Although not typically used in a spreadsheet, clip art can be added for visual impact or to make a point for an informal audience.

▶ **See** "Inserting Graphics from the companion CD" **p. 60**

Using the Format Painter

The Format Painter is a tool that enables you to take formatting you've applied in one area of your worksheet and copy it to another area. Using the Format Painter saves time and gives you a consistent look throughout your worksheet.

To use the Format Painter, follow these steps:

1. Select the cell or cells that are formatted as you want to format another area of the worksheet.

2. If you intend to apply these formats to only one other area, click the Format Painter button once. If you need to apply the formats to several areas, double-click the Format Painter button. In either case, a paintbrush appears with your mouse pointer (see Figure 12.10).

FIG. 12.10

The Format Painter copies formatting from one set of cells to any other cells in your worksheet.

Original cells from which the formatting is copied

Target cells to be formatted

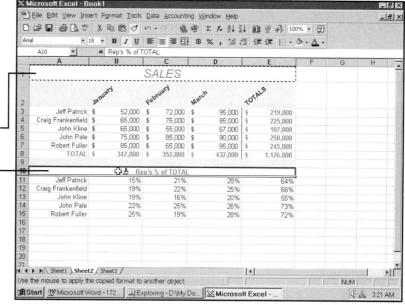

CAUTION

Take the time to remember what formats you applied to the original cells. It's easy to forget, for example, that you decreased your decimal places or chose red for negative numbers. Make sure all the formats you're copying with the Format Painter are appropriate for the target cells.

---

3. Move to and select the cells that you want formatted to match your original selected cells. Any Number, Font, Border, Pattern, and Alignment formats you applied to the original cells will be applied to these new cells.

TIP If you clicked the Format Painter only once to turn it on, it will turn off automatically after one use.

4. If you double-clicked the Format Painter, continue copying the formats to other cells as needed, and then click once on the Format Painter to turn it off.

If you regret your application of the Format Painter, use <u>E</u>dit, <u>U</u>ndo or click the Undo button to reverse your action.

Changing Column Width

The width of your columns can control the legibility of your worksheet, how much content will fit on one printed page, and how loose or tight your entire worksheet looks. Cramped columns that are just wide enough for your text or numbers are hard to read, but spreading things out too much can result in columns that stray onto an unwanted second page. Tweaking column width is one of the easiest ways to improve the overall appearance of your work.

To change the width of a single column, follow these steps:

1. Click the column heading at the top of the column you want to widen or narrow.

TIP   Although not required for adjusting single columns and rows, selecting the column or row by clicking its heading makes it easier for you to focus on one particular component in a visually complex window.

2. Point to the seam between the selected column heading and the column to its right. Your mouse pointer turns into a horizontal two-headed arrow, as shown in Figure 12.11.

FIG. 12.11

Adjusting column width manually is fast and easy, although not precise.

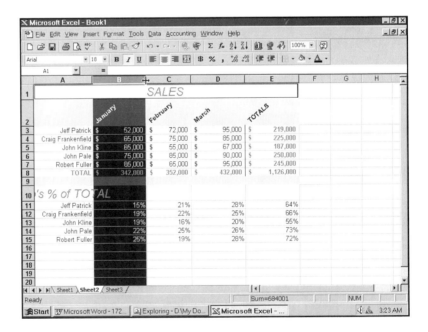

3. Drag to the right to increase column width, or drag to the left to make the column narrower.

> **TIP** Double-click the seam between your selected column and the column on its right to AutoFit your selected column. The column width changes to fit the widest entry in the column.

When your worksheet contains several columns of data that are all approximately the same width, you may want your columns to also be the same width. This uniformity gives your worksheet an organized, structured look and shows you paid attention to details and consistency.

To adjust the width of several columns at the same time, follow these steps:

1. Click the column heading of the first row in your series of columns, and drag through the remaining desired column headings.
2. Point to any interior seam between two of the column headings. Your mouse turns into a horizontal two-headed arrow.
3. Drag the mouse to the right to widen all the selected columns, and drag to the left to narrow them.

Whatever change in width you make by dragging this one seam affects all the columns, leaving them all the same width.

> **TIP** Although it may not make all your selected columns the same width, you can apply AutoFit to your selected columns by double-clicking any interior column heading seam. Each of the selected columns will widen or narrow to fit its own widest entry.

If you prefer a more methodical method that also provides for absolute precision in setting the width of one or more columns, you'll want to use the Column Width dialog box.

Follow these steps to enter an exact measurement for your column width:

1. Select the column or columns for which you want to set a new width.
2. Choose Format, Column, Width. The Column Width dialog box opens (see Figure 12.12).
3. Enter the number of characters wide your column(s) should be.
4. Click OK to apply the new width and close the dialog box.

> **TIP** You can also issue the AutoFit command from the menu. Select your columns and choose Format, Column, AutoFit.

Adjusting Row Height

Row height adjusts automatically—when you increase your font size, the cells get taller to accommodate the text. You can adjust them manually or by using the menu if a specific height is required. Figure 12.13 shows a row made taller by the increase in font size in one of the cells in the row.

Part
III

Ch
12

FIG. 12.12
Although standard column width is 8.43 characters wide, this is rarely wide enough for currency-formatted text.

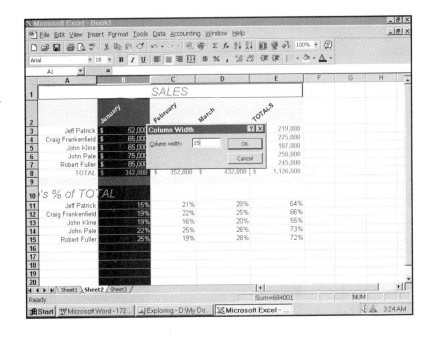

FIG. 12.13
Row height, as with fonts, is measured in points. By increasing font size, your row heights increase automatically.

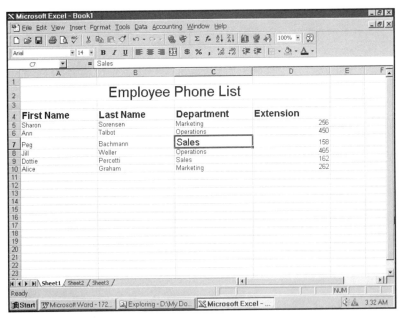

Many users add height to rows even if the text isn't any bigger than the default 10 point font—the taller cells make the worksheet appear roomier, increasing legibility within the cells.

As with column width, row height can be adjusted by dragging the row heading seams or by entering an exact height measurement. Your choice of method should be determined by your needs—if you must have rows that are exactly 16 points high, you'll want to use the menu. If you just want to make the row taller (or shorter, perhaps), you can use the row headings to make a manual adjustment.

To adjust row height manually, follow these steps:

1. Click the row heading for a single row, or drag through several row headings to select a series of rows.

2. Point to an internal seam within the group or the seam on the bottom side of the individual selected row (see Figure 12.14).

 TIP Although not required for adjusting single columns and rows, selecting the column or row by clicking its heading makes it easier for you to focus on one particular component in a visually complex window.

FIG. 12.14
Before adjusting your row height, look for a vertical two-headed arrow on your row heading seam.

Row 9 is directly adjusted, but 7 and 8 will be made taller as well.

Row adjusted automatically through font-size increase

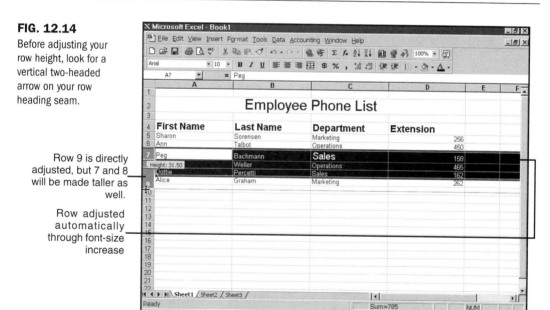

3. Drag down to make your row(s) taller; drag up to make your row(s) shorter.

CAUTION
After you've adjusted a row's height, it will no longer respond to font-size changes by automatically adjusting itself. If you've adjusted a row and then find it too short or tall for your text, use Format, Row, AutoFit with that row selected.

Part
III

Ch
12

If you must set a specific height (measured in points) for your row, follow these steps to use the Row Height dialog box:

1. Select the row or rows that you want to adjust.

2. Choose Format, Row, Height. The Row Height dialog box opens (see Figure 12.15).

FIG. 12.15

Enter a precise point measurement to adjust the height of your selected row(s).

3. Enter a number of points for your row height. It should exceed the point size of your largest font used in the selected row(s) by at least a point.

4. Click OK to apply the new height and close the dialog box.

N O T E The standard row height of 12.5 points is based on the needs of rows containing the default 10 point text. Use this equation (row height = text point size+15%) to determine the proper row height for your text. To avoid having to do this math entirely, let your changes in font size dictate your row heights, and don't tinker with them yourself unless it's absolutely necessary.

CHAPTER 13

Using the Chart Wizard

In this chapter

Creating a Quick Chart

The saying "a picture is worth a thousand words" is especially true when it comes to numerical data. Presenting rows and columns of words and numbers can be both confusing and boring to people who read your spreadsheets. Converting this data to a chart simplifies the information by turning it into a graphical representation of the data. A chart makes it easy for the reader to see, for example, that one division's sales are higher than another's, or that expenses have decreased steadily over the last three years. Figure 13.1 shows a spreadsheet and its accompanying chart. To interpret the spreadsheet, the reader must look at all the numbers and draw his or her own conclusions. The overall meaning of the numbers is immediately clear when viewing the chart.

N O T E   When data in a worksheet is turned into a chart, any changes made to the data will be reflected in the chart. If you want to establish a chart that will remain unchanged, regardless of updates made to the source data, copy the source data to another sheet and then create the chart from that copy of the data. Updates can then be made to the original data (and not the copied version), leaving the chart intact.

FIG. 13.1

See the "big picture" for your data by converting it to a chart.

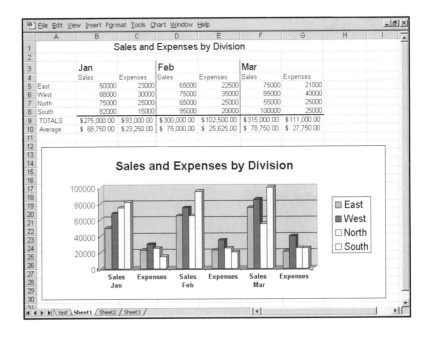

Excel gives you a simple, yet powerful tool for creating and formatting charts. The Chart Wizard takes you step-by-step through the process of building and customizing a chart—from choosing the data that will be charted to applying titles to the chart and its axes. Figure 13.2 shows a chart and its major elements as created by the Chart Wizard.

FIG. 13.2

It's a good idea to recognize the parts of a basic chart before you create one of your own.

Gridlines help the viewer follow a data point from the right side of the chart back to the Value axis on the left.

A data point is the plotted contents of one of the cells in the chart's supporting data. Groups of data points comprise a data series.

The Value axis, also known as the Y axis, shows the range of values represented by the numeric data. This axis normally starts at the bottom with zero, and shows a calibrated range leading to the highest number in the chart data.

Chart and axis titles can contain extra information to help the viewer interpret the chart.

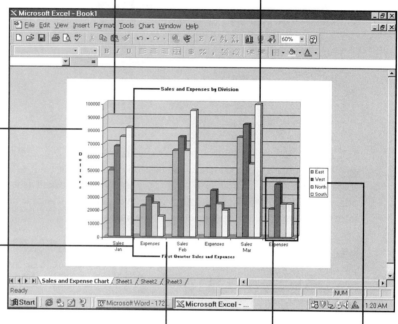

The Category axis, also known as the X axis, shows how the data series are broken down in the chart—by months, or divisions for example.

A data series is any group of related data points, such as years for one division or divisions in a single year.

The legend is used to help the viewer associate the colored lines, bars, and slices with particular data series/categories.

Part III Ch 13

 The Chart Wizard is invoked by clicking the Chart Wizard button on the toolbar or by choosing Insert, Chart from the menu bar.

TIP Although choosing a range of cells to include in the chart is not the first step in the Chart Wizard, it's a good idea to have selected the cells in your chart before invoking the wizard.

Choosing a Chart Type

As soon as the Chart Wizard is invoked, it wants to know what type of chart you want to create. Figure 13.3 shows Step 1 of 4.

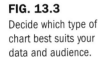

FIG. 13.3

Decide which type of chart best suits your data and audience.

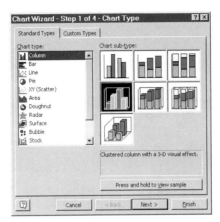

This first dialog box is divided into two main areas—Chart Type and Chart Sub-type. Choose a type on the left, and then choose a sub-type on the right. For each sub-type, a description appears below the Chart Sub-type box. If you want to see your data as it will appear in a particular sub-type, click the Press and Hold to View Sample button. The Chart Sub-type box temporarily shows you your data in the selected sub-type format.

N O T E   The second tab in the Step 1 of 4 dialog box offers a group of custom chart types. Each selected type is displayed on the right side of the dialog box. These custom types are more visually complex than those offered in the Standard Types tab.

When choosing a type and sub-type, keep the following things in mind:

- *How much data will be charted?* If you want to show more than one data series, you can't use a pie chart. Also, combination charts and charts that stack colors can become too confusing if several data series will be presented.
- *How will the chart be viewed?* If this chart will also be viewed in a PowerPoint slide (after pasting it from Excel into PowerPoint), keep it simple. If the chart will be viewed onscreen or paper by one person at a time, you can choose a more elaborate or complex chart type.

After selecting a Chart Type and Chart Sub-type, click the Next button to proceed to Step 2 of 4—Chart Source Data.

Selecting the Correct Data Range

Step 2 of 4 asks you to select or confirm a range of cells to be charted. If you selected your range before invoking the wizard, that range appears in the dialog box (see Figure 13.4).

If you have not yet selected your range, you can do so by typing the range into the dialog box or moving the box out of the way to drag through the cells you want to include in your chart. Figure 13.5 shows a range of cells selected.

FIG. 13.4

Confirm your previously selected range or enter a range of cells to include in your chart.

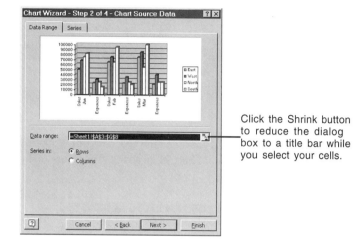

Click the Shrink button to reduce the dialog box to a title bar while you select your cells.

Category axis labels

FIG. 13.5

Remember to include only the columns and rows that you want to see plotted on your chart or appearing as axis information.

Legend content

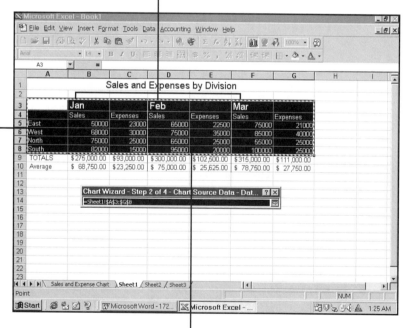

Values to be plotted in the chart

N O T E If you prefer, you can shrink the dialog box to a title bar while you select your cells. This can be easier than moving the dialog box out of the way, especially if your spreadsheet is large. After you've selected your cells, click the Expand button to reopen the dialog box to its full size.

Part

III

Ch

13

T I P When selecting a range of cells for your chart, don't include the spreadsheet title or any other extraneous text that you don't want to include in the chart.

As soon as you've selected your range of cells, click Next to move on to Step 3 of 4. You can also click the Back button to go back to Step 1 of 4.

Adding Extra Elements

After you've selected the type of chart and the cells that will be plotted in it, you can select and format the extra elements in your chart, such as titles, gridlines, and your legend. Step 3 of 4 offers a six-tab box as shown in Figure 13.6.

FIG. 13.6
Format your chart by clicking any of the six tabs displayed in Step 3 of 4.

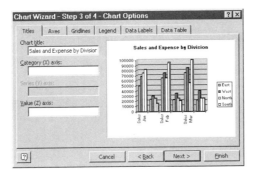

For a simple chart, you can add titles in the Titles tab (this tab should be in front when Step 3 of 4 opens), and then click Next. The remaining five tabs contain options that you can add, delete, or reformat to customize your chart. They are, however, not necessary for a basic chart or a chart that you must create quickly. The defaults for your chart's sub-type have already dictated the most universally acceptable settings for fonts, gridlines, labels, and the legend.

If you want to view or change these aspects of your chart, click the tabs and make any changes before clicking the Next button, which takes you to Step 4 of 4. Each tab represents an element of the chart and offers options for the display and/or content of that element:

- *Axes.* Choose whether to display your Value or Category axis. Choosing not to display an axis removes the text or numbers that define the data points along that axis.

- *Gridlines.* This tab allows you to turn gridlines on or off for the Value and Category axes. Your gridlines are seen as major or minor, meaning on the tick-marks (major) along the axis, or between them (minor). Figure 13.7 shows the Value axis gridlines turned on (major only).

- *Legend.* Use this tab to turn your legend off if it's redundant with chart content and therefore not necessary to understand the chart. You can also choose where the legend should be within the chart's frame. Using this placement method is easier than manually dragging the legend object with your mouse, because it not only moves it, but it simultaneously resizes it as needed to fit in its new location. Figure 13.8 shows the legend moved to the bottom, below the chart.

FIG. 13.7
Value axis gridlines enable the reader to visually follow the data points back to the axis to determine the value they represent.

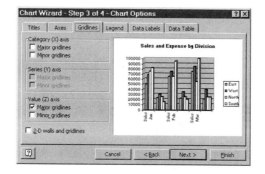

FIG. 13.8
A legend shows the reader which colored bar, line, or slice is associated with which data.

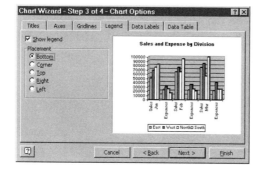

■ *Data Labels.* You can choose to display the Value and Category axis labels for each data point in this tab. For example, if you choose Show Value, the numbers represented by each bar (or pie slice) are displayed alongside the data point. Figure 13.9 shows the Data Labels tab and the Show Value option turned on.

 T I P If you find that adding the labels makes the chart look too "busy," you and your readers can point to any data point and see a ScreenTip, showing the value represented by that point.

FIG. 13.9
Although they can visually crowd the other chart elements, displaying value data labels makes it easy to see exact numerical values for each data point.

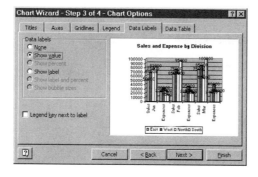

Part
III

Ch
13

■ *Data Table.* If you want to have your charted cells reiterated below your chart, click this tab and click the Show Data Table option (see Figure 13.10). An additional option (Show Legend Keys) enables you to show your legend information in the table.

T I P If you'll be using the chart in a Word document or PowerPoint slide, it can be helpful to include the data table so the cells that made up the chart data can be viewed in the target location.

N O T E If you want changes made to Excel charts and their supporting spreadsheet data to be reflected in copies that you paste into Word documents or PowerPoint slides, remember to perform a Paste Link (by choosing Edit, Paste Special) when pasting the chart into the target file.

FIG. 13.10

If knowing the exact values each data point represents is essential, an alternative to displaying data labels is to display the data in a table below the chart.

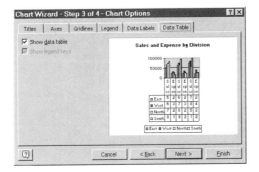

After making any changes to your chart's elements in Step 3 of 4, click Next to open Step 4 of 4—Chart Location (see Figure 13.11). Choose the As New Sheet option to display the new chart on it's own sheet (appearing as Chart1 in your workbook) or the As Object In option to place the chart on the active worksheet or any other worksheet in your workbook.

Your decision is normally based on the size requirements for the chart (placing it on its own sheet allows you to make it the size of one full page) and possible organizational issues. If your spreadsheet is large and elaborate, it can make it easier for others to find the chart if it's on its own sheet in the workbook.

FIG. 13.11

Placing a chart on its own sheet gives you a bigger chart that remains connected to your data, yet visually separate from it.

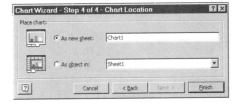

N O T E If you place your chart on its own sheet, it's a good idea to rename the Chart1 tab to something that indicates what the chart contains and/or to which data it is related. This is essential if your workbook contains more than one chart.

After selecting the manner in which your chart will be added to the workbook, click Finish. The chart appears where you designated it, and it contains the elements and formatting you established using the Chart Wizard. Figure 13.12 shows a chart added on its own sheet.

FIG. 13.12

Adding a chart on its own sheet makes it easier to find and resize, especially if it is related to data in a very large worksheet.

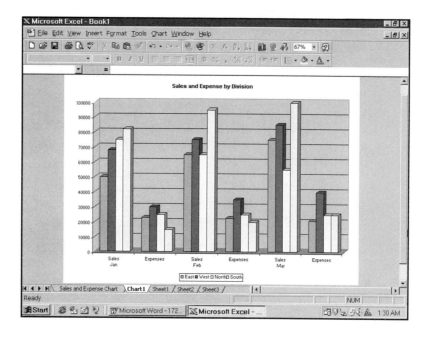

▶ **See** "Linking and Embedding Within Microsoft Office" **p. 36**

Formatting an Existing Chart

After you've created a chart, you may decide that you want to change things about the way it looks or which data is included in the chart. Excel makes it simple to make these changes.

Before making any changes to your chart, you must click it once to activate it. To activate the entire chart, click in the white area outside your chart and its titles, but within the chart's frame. You'll know the chart is active because small black box handles appear on the perimeter of the chart's frame (see Figure 13.13). If you click something within the chart—a bar or slice, for example—that element becomes active. In either case, the chart is now active and you can make the desired changes.

As soon as your chart is active, notice the Chart menu that appears on your menu bar. This menu contains commands for reformatting virtually every aspect of your chart. If you find that the changes you need to make are so extensive as to require more than one or two simple adjustments, you may find it easier to delete the chart and start over!

FIG. 13.13

By clicking somewhere on the chart itself (whether it's on a sheet by itself or on a sheet with your data), you activate the chart and Excel's chart formatting tools.

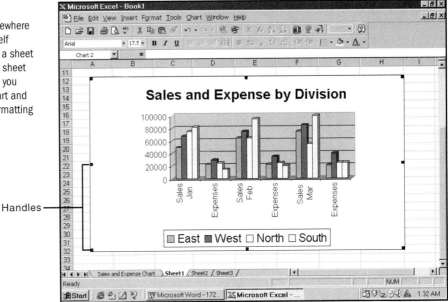

Handles

N O T E To delete your chart if it is an object within a worksheet, click once on the chart's edge to activate the entire chart, and press the Delete key. If your chart is on a sheet of its own, delete the sheet by choosing Edit, Delete Sheet.

Changing Colors

One of the most frequently changed aspects of a chart is the color. You can change the color of a data series (by choosing a new color for your bars, lines, or pie slices), or apply a colored background to your chart or the entire box in which the chart sits, also known as the Chart Area.

To change the color of any element of your chart, follow these steps:

1. With the chart active, click the element you want to re-color.

 T I P If you're re-coloring a data series, you need only click one of the bars/columns in that series and all the bars/columns in that series are selected.

2. Choose from the following methods to re-color the selected element:

- Click the Fill Color icon on the Formatting toolbar. Choose a color from the palette (see Figure 13.14).
- Choose Format, Selected *Item* (where *Item* is the name of the selected element). A dialog box opens, displaying the options available for reformatting that element (see Figure 13.15). Click the Patterns tab to view the color palette. Choose a color

from the Area section of the dialog box, and click OK to apply the color to the selected element and close the dialog box.

FIG. 13.14
Choose a color from the palette. Click the Fill Effects button to choose from pictures, textures, and other fill styles for your selected elements.

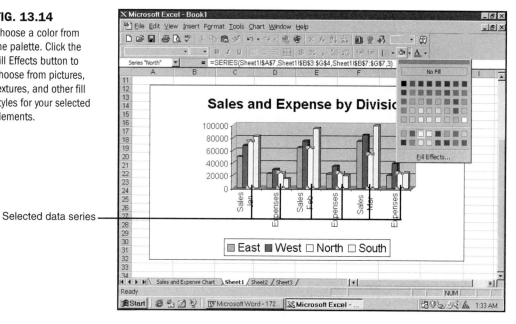

Selected data series

FIG. 13.15
The Patterns tab gives you options for changing the fill and outline colors of your selected element.

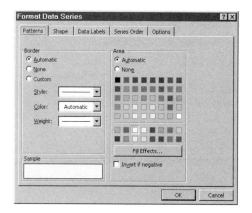

 T I P You can also open the Format Item dialog box by right-clicking the element you want to reformat.

Improving Chart Legibility

The whole point of creating a chart is to make complex numeric data easy to understand. If your chart or the fonts used within it are too small, your chart won't be easy to read, thus defeating its purpose. Other chart attributes that can contribute to its legibility are:

- *Too many colors.* Keep your colors to a minimum, and choose colors that are complementary. Don't choose a dark color to go behind dark text unless you change the text color to a light color.

- *Colors that are too similar.* If you choose red and dark pink, or navy and black for adjacent bars, lines, or slices in your chart, the audience will have problems telling them apart.

- *Too much text.* If you've added data labels, move or resize them so they don't run together or overlap the data point to which they refer. Black data label text won't be legible on top of a dark blue bar, and changing the text color to white or yellow will make it hard to read against the light chart background.

- *Too many gridlines.* If you chose to show your minor gridlines, the effect can look more like stripes than an effective tool for reading the Value axis. Unless your chart is very large, don't use the minor gridlines.

Resizing Your Chart   Resizing your chart to make it bigger can alleviate many of these problems—the more room you have, the more options you have for moving labels and legends and for increasing font size.

You can only resize a chart that is an object within a worksheet. Charts that are on their own Chart sheet are automatically sized to fit one printed page.

To resize a chart, follow these steps:

1. Click the outer edge of the chart object. Handles appear on its perimeter.
2. Point to a handle, and your mouse pointer turns into a two-headed arrow.
3. Drag outward to increase the chart size, inward to decrease it.
4. When the chart is the desired size, release the mouse button.

TIP Use a corner handle and drag diagonally to retain the chart's current horizontal and vertical proportions, also known as its *aspect ratio.*

CAUTION
Be careful when making your chart smaller or increasing font sizes without increasing overall chart size. If, for example, you increase the font size of your axis labels and don't make the chart bigger, some of your labels may not display properly or may disappear altogether.

Reformatting Chart Text   To reformat your chart's text for legibility (or for more cosmetic reasons), follow these steps:

1. In an active chart, click once on the text element you want to reformat. This can be the legend text, a title, or an axis.

2. Use the Font Size button on your Formatting toolbar. Click the drop-down list arrow, and choose a different font size.

Arial

3. As needed, change your font by clicking the Font button, also on the Formatting toolbar.

N O T E   You can also change your font and font size by right-clicking the element you want to reformat and choosing Format *Item* (*Item* being the name of the element you selected). Click the Font tab in the resulting dialog box and make your changes. Click OK to close the dialog box.

Using Interactive Charts from the Companion CD

The companion CD that accompanies this book contains a group of interactive charts. These charts contain sample data that you can replace with your own, after you've reviewed the charts and understand their functions.

To access these charts and copy them to your computer, follow these steps:

1. Insert the CD into your CD-ROM drive.
2. From within the Excel program, choose File, Open.
3. Browse to the CD-ROM drive, and open the XLCharts folder.
4. Open one of the sample charts by double-clicking it in the list of files.
5. After the chart is open, save it to your local drive or an appropriate network drive for later use.
6. Repeat steps 2–6 for any of the interactive charts that you want to view and save to your computer.

If you prefer, you can copy the files from the CD to your local or network drive by using My Computer or Windows Explorer. To copy them from the CD to your drive, follow these steps:

1. With the CD in your CD-ROM drive, start Windows Explorer.
2. Visually locate your CD-ROM drive on the left side (folder pane) of your Explorer window.
3. Click once on the XLCharts folder icon.
4. Select the chart files on the right, and then right-click them. Choose Copy from the pop-up menu.
5. Click once on the desired folder in the desired drive to which you want to copy the charts. Right-click the folder and choose Paste. ●

Part

III

Ch

13

Working with Excel Data

Setting Up an Excel Database

In addition to being an effective spreadsheet tool for manipulating numeric data and formulas, Excel is also a powerful database program. Of the entire Microsoft Office suite, including Access, Excel is the simplest and most efficient tool for storing lists of data.

Unlike Access, which gives you tools for complex reports and relationships between databases, Excel is a straightforward list database tool. Thousands of records can be stored in a single worksheet, and several separate lists can be stored in a single workbook. Although these lists cannot be related to one another as separate databases can be linked in Access, Excel's database tools make keeping lists such as names and addresses or product inventories quick and easy to manage.

N O T E An Excel list database can be used in a Word Mail Merge as the source of information for a mailing and/or labels. If you've already built a mail merge database in Word, you can paste it into an Excel worksheet and turn it into an Excel database with little or no formatting required. This is made possible by the fact that a Word mail merge document is a table, easily converted to a block of cells in a worksheet.

ON THE WEB

http://www.yahoo.com Type "`Mailing Lists`" (in quotes) in the Search box and find a list of companies that provide mailing lists for your direct mail needs. Most contact lists come in simple tabular form, which can be easily imported into Excel.

Understanding Database Structure

A database is made up of three basic components, and an Excel list database is no different. A database consists of records, each made up of one or more fields. Each field is filled with data, which the user enters (see Figure 14.1).

Although Excel is structured like any other database, there are some specific rules for successful structure and building of an Excel list database:

- *Fields are created by placing a field name at the top of a column.* A series of contiguous columns must be used, with no blank columns between fields.
- *Each row is a record.* Between the first row that contains field names and the last record in the database, there can be no blank rows.
- *Avoid using calculations within fields.* If your list is sorted or filtered, the results of any formulas may change or the formula itself may become invalid.

TIP Although not an actual rule, it's a good idea to keep your field names short. As a result, column widths can be based on the width of the data in the individual fields and not the field name.

Entering Data

After you've set up your field names, you can begin entering your records, field by field. You needn't enter them in any particular order—if you're entering names and addresses from a stack of response cards, for example, you don't have to alphabetize them first. The list can be alphabetized later, through a sort, which we'll discuss later in this chapter.

FIG. 14.1

Excel database structure creates a solid foundation on which to build your list.

Field names

Blank rows between title and field names are acceptable, but not within the list itself.

Records, one in each row

Data

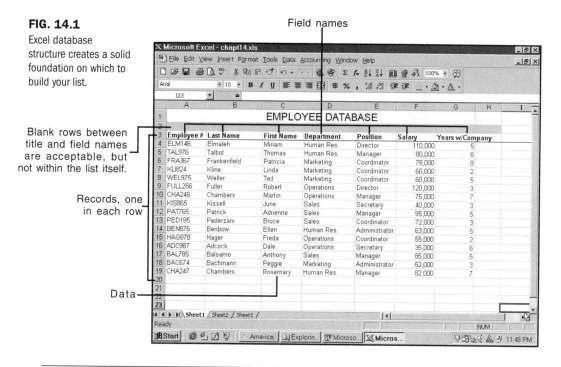

TIP As your records exceed the length of one screen (more than 25 records or so), select the row below your field names and choose <u>W</u>indow, <u>F</u>reeze Panes. This will keep your field names visible at the top of the screen as you add more records. To unfreeze, choose <u>W</u>indow, Un<u>f</u>reeze Panes.

To speed your data entry process and increase your accuracy, pay special attention to your terminology. If, for example, you're entering a list of employees, abbreviate their department or position names in a consistent way. If you use "Acctg." for the Accounting department on one record, abbreviate it the exact same way for the remaining Accounting department records. This allows you to use the AutoFill feature (which guesses your entry as you type, based on previous entries in the same column), and keeps your records consistent, which is essential for the filtering process that we'll discuss later in this chapter. Figure 14.2 shows an employee database with AutoFill assisting the user in an entry.

▶ **See** "Using AutoFill," **p. 145**

▶ **See** "Entering Content More Efficiently," **p. 138**

Part
III

Ch
14

FIG. 14.2
Consistency in your data entry makes the process of entering records go faster, and makes sorting and filtering easier.

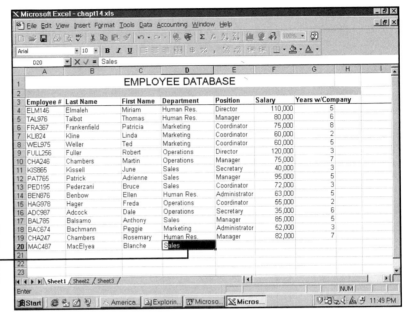

The S was typed, and then the remainder was filled in by AutoFill. Click Tab or the right arrow to accept and move on.

Sorting Lists

It's easy to enter your batches of entries in alphabetical or numerical order, but as you add records to an existing database, it's difficult to insert your new records among the existing records and maintain the order. Using the Sort command makes it unnecessary for you to worry about the order your records are entered—you can place your database in order by one, two, or three fields, at any time.

Single Level Sorts

A single level sort, or a sort on just one field within the database, is the most commonly used sort. It's also the easiest. To perform a single-level sort, follow these steps:

1. Click in any cell within your database. Do not click a cell above the field names, below your last record, or to the right of your last field in any row.

2. Choose Data, Sort. The Sort dialog box opens, as shown in Figure 14.3.

3. Click the Sort By drop-down list to see a list of your field names, and select one.

4. If necessary, change the sort order from Ascending (A-Z) to Descending (Z-A).

5. Click OK.

TIP   Select your entire database (all rows except the one that contains your field names) and click the Sort Ascending or Sort Descending buttons on the toolbar.

FIG. 14.3

Use a single-level sort to place your records in alphabetical order.

Your list automatically sorts by the field you selected. Figure 14.4 shows the employee list sorted by Last Name.

FIG. 14.4

Sorting by a text field puts your list in alphabetical order, regardless of the order in which you entered your records.

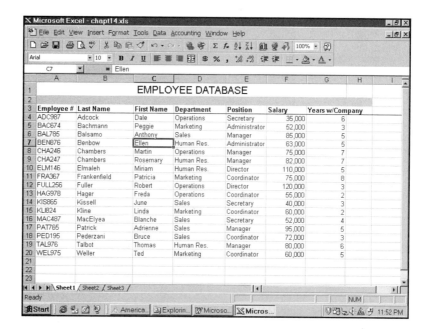

Employee #	Last Name	First Name	Department	Position	Salary	Years w/Company
ADC987	Adcock	Dale	Operations	Secretary	35,000	6
BAC674	Bachmann	Peggie	Marketing	Administrator	52,000	3
BAL785	Balsamo	Anthony	Sales	Manager	85,000	5
BEN876	Benbow	Ellen	Human Res.	Administrator	63,000	5
CHA246	Chambers	Martin	Operations	Manager	75,000	7
CHA247	Chambers	Rosemary	Human Res.	Manager	82,000	7
ELM146	Elmaleh	Miriam	Human Res.	Director	110,000	5
FRA367	Frankenfield	Patricia	Marketing	Coordinator	75,000	8
FULL256	Fuller	Robert	Operations	Director	120,000	3
HAG978	Hager	Freda	Operations	Coordinator	55,000	2
KIS865	Kissell	June	Sales	Secretary	40,000	3
KLI824	Kline	Linda	Marketing	Coordinator	60,000	2
MAC487	MacElyea	Blanche	Sales	Secretary	52,000	4
PAT765	Patrick	Adrienne	Sales	Manager	95,000	5
PED195	Pederzani	Bruce	Sales	Coordinator	72,000	3
TAL976	Talbot	Thomas	Human Res.	Manager	80,000	6
WEL975	Weller	Ted	Marketing	Coordinator	60,000	5

N O T E Excel normally sees your first row of data as field names, also known as your *header row*. If your Sort By list shows Column A, Column B, and so forth rather than your actual field names, click the My List Has Header <u>R</u>ow option at the bottom of the Sort dialog box. If your field names are not listed and you don't make this change, your field names will sort along with your data records.

After sorting by one field, you can sort by a different field, and the records will be resorted. You can sort by any field in your database.

Part

III

Ch

14

Multiple Level Sorts

Sorting on more than one field is no more complex a task to perform than a single-level sort. Multiple level sorts, however, require that some of your fields contain duplicate records. If every field's content is unique for each record, you cannot do more than a single-level sort.

When deciding on which fields to sort by, look for fields containing duplicate records, and sort first by the field with the highest number of duplicates. Your second level sort will then be by the field with the next highest number of duplicates, and then your third level sort can be on a field that need not contain duplicate records at all. For example, Figure 14.5 shows the employee database sorted first by Department, then by Position, and then by Last Name.

FIG. 14.5

Sorting by more than one field requires duplicate records in the first field by which your data is sorted.

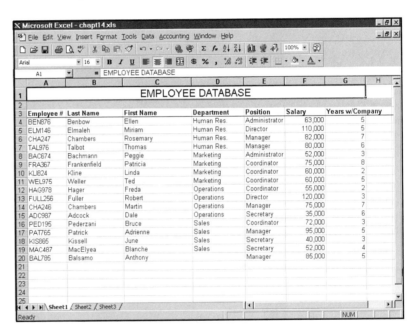

To perform a multiple-level sort, follow these steps:

1. Click a cell within your database that contains data.
2. Choose Data, Sort.
3. Click the Sort By drop-down list and select a field for the first level of your sort.
4. Click the first Then By drop-down list, and choose a second field by which to sort.
5. If you want to sort by yet a third field, click the second Then By drop-down list and choose a field from the list. Figure 14.6 shows a three-level sort of the employee database.
6. Change any of the fields' sort order from Ascending to Descending as needed.
7. Click OK.

FIG. 14.6
The lowest level field in your sort order need not contain any duplicate records.

N O T E   Click the Options button in the Sort dialog box to customize your sort. Click the Case Sensitive check box to make your alphabetical sorts place lowercase text before uppercase text. The Orientation options allow you to control the direction that Excel sorts the records. The default is Sort Top to Bottom, and for most databases, this option should not be changed.

Creating a Subtotal Report

A Subtotal report breaks your list database down into levels of detail, similar to viewing a Word document in Outline form (to see just the headings) and then in Normal view (to see the headings and the supporting text) and then in Page Layout view (to see all the graphics and page breaks). If we take our employee database as an example, a Subtotal report allows us to see just the departments, then the departments and the positions held within them, and then the complete list of employees in each department.

Before creating a Subtotal report, you must sort your list database. The number of fields on which you sorted your database dictates the number of levels to your Subtotal report. Figure 14.7 shows a Subtotal report created from the employee database.

In addition to showing levels of detail, a Subtotal report can contain calculations, such as sums, averages, and counts. These functions are applied to fields within the database. To create a Subtotal report, follow these steps:

1. Sort your database by two or more fields, choosing fields that you want to see as levels within the Subtotal report.

2. Choose Data, Subtotals. The Subtotals dialog box opens, as shown in Figure 14.8.

3. Choose a field from the At Each Change In drop-down list. A subtotal appears on your report for each different entry in this field, so you should select a field with duplicate entries, the same field you sorted on in your Sort procedure.

4. Choose a mathematical function from the Use Function drop-down list.

T I P   For fields that contain text, Count is a good choice. For numeric content, Sum or Average are frequently used.

FIG. 14.7

The fields you sort on will be the fields you can subtotal in a Subtotal report.

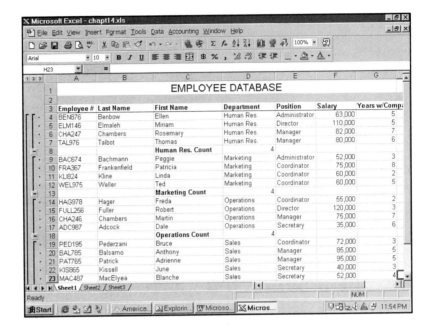

FIG. 14.8

Because the database has been sorted first, you can specify fields to subtotal when a change in content is found.

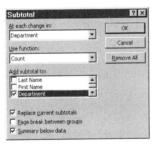

5. Choose a field under which the function's result should appear. Normally, you choose the field you're subtotaling.

6. Click OK to create the report.

N O T E The last three check boxes in the Subtotal dialog box allow you to remove previous subtotal settings, insert a page break between each subtotal, and choose whether to place the summary information below the data. The first and last options are on by default.

When your report appears onscreen, you'll notice a gray column to the left of your spreadsheet, as shown in Figure 14.9. At the top of the column you see three numbers, 1, 2, and 3, each representing a level of detail for your report.

The level 1 report shows just the grand total of whatever function totals were included in your report (see Figure 14.10). The level 2 report shows the second level field totals, and the grand total (see Figure 14.11). The level 3 report shows all the records for each subtotal, plus the second level subtotals and the grand total (see Figure 14.12).

FIG. 14.9

Applying a Subtotal report to your database is like folding a map to see only one part of it or opening it completely to see everything.

If you sorted by only two fields, you'll only see 1 and 2 at the top of the column.

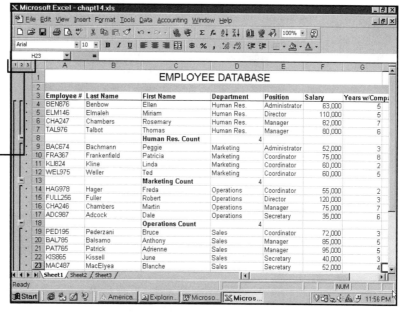

FIG. 14.10

A level 1 report shows only the "bottom line."

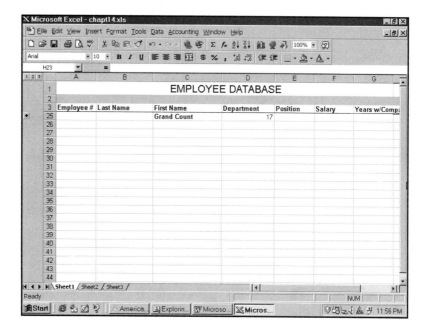

Part

III

Ch

14

FIG. 14.11
A level 2 report shows
the major groups into
which your database
was subtotaled.

Plus signs indicate
that there is support-
ing detail that is not
displayed.

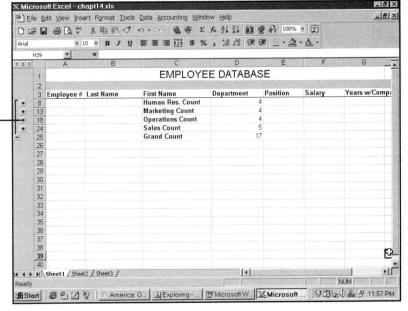

FIG. 14.12
A level 3 report shows
all the data—subtotals,
grand total, and all the
records per group.

Minus signs indicate
that all the detail is
displayed.

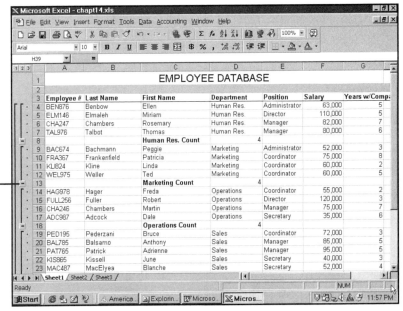

N O T E In the level 2 view, you can click the plus signs to see detail on one or more of the
subtotals that are currently hidden. When the details for a given subtotal are displayed, that
plus sign changes to a minus.

To clear the subtotal report (to go back to a straight database list or to do a new set of subtotals), choose Data, Subtotals, and click the Remove All button.

TIP Remember to redo your sort on different fields if you want to do a new Subtotal report that subtotals different fields in the database.

Filtering a List

Sorting shows all your records, but lets you choose the order in which they appear. Filtering, on the other hand, shows only those records that meet your filter criteria. Excel provides a powerful database tool called AutoFilter, which enables you to filter on one or more fields in your database, and then see only those records that pass through the filter.

Filtering a database gives you control over which records people see (you can print any set of filtered records), and allows you to search your database for records that you need to find quickly. For example, if among your 2,000 employee records, you've forgotten how long Tom Talbot has worked for the company, you can filter on Last Name for Talbot. Even if there are a few Talbots on the employee list, this narrows the list of records considerably, and you can go directly to Tom's record and see his years with the company.

To use AutoFilter, follow these steps:

1. Click any cell in your database that contains data.
2. Choose Data, Filter, AutoFilter. A down-pointing arrow appears to the right of each field name in your database, as shown in Figure 14.13.

FIG. 14.13
Choose Blanks from the list of entries to see any records that are missing data for a specific field.

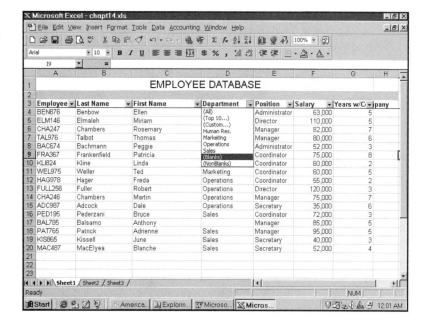

3. Click the arrow to the right of the field you want to filter. A list of all the entries in that field for the entire database appears. Click one of them to see only those records with that entry for the selected field.

You can redisplay all your records by clicking the filtered field's arrow and choosing All (see Figure 14.14) or by choosing Data, Filter, Show All.

FIG. 14.14

In case you forget which field you filtered, the arrow turns blue when you've filtered that field.

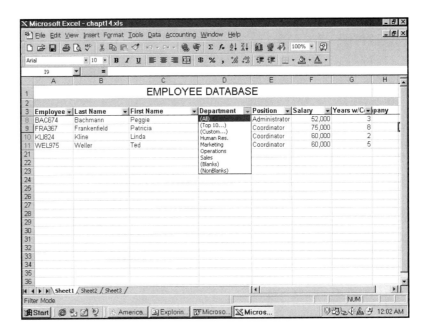

To remove the AutoFilter from your database, choose Data, Filter, AutoFilter. The arrows disappear.

Filtering on Multiple Fields

Many times, especially with fields that contain very few duplicate entries, filtering on one field gives you the results you need. If, however, your database has many duplicate entries, you may find that filtering on more than one field is necessary to narrow the list of records adequately.

To filter on more than one field, follow these steps:

1. If AutoFilter is not on, click any cell in your database that contains data, and choose Data, Filter, AutoFilter.

2. Choose the first field to filter, and click the arrow to the right of that field.

3. Choose the entry from the list. Only those records with that entry for that field will be displayed.

4. Continue to narrow your displayed group of records by clicking another field's AutoFilter arrow, and choose an entry from that list.

5. Repeat this process for as many fields as needed to narrow the list to the specific record or records you require. Figure 14.15 shows a database filtered on three fields.

FIG. 14.15

The employee database was filtered for all Coordinators in the Marketing department, making $60,000.

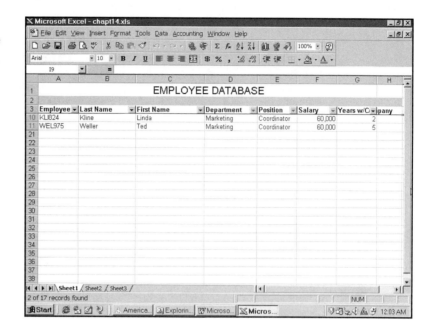

Working with Custom Filters

What if you want to know how many employees make more than $75,000 per year? And among those employees, how many have been with the company for less than 10 years? The only way to find that out with AutoFilter is to use the Custom Filter option, available in the list of entries for each field while AutoFilter is on.

Custom filters require you to choose a comparison, such as greater than, less than, or equal to. Then, enter or choose an entry to compare to all the data for that field in the database. Follow these steps to perform a Custom AutoFilter:

1. With AutoFilter on, click the arrow to the right of the field you want to filter.

2. From the list, choose Custom. The Custom AutoFilter dialog box opens, as shown in Figure 14.16.

3. The field name you selected appears in the dialog box, followed by a drop-down list containing comparisons. Select one from the list.

4. Press Tab or click inside the text box to the right of the comparison. Type a value (text or numbers) or choose one from the list.

 TIP When entering your value, use the * wildcard character for a group of characters and the ? wildcard for an individual character.

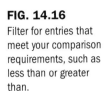

FIG. 14.16
Filter for entries that meet your comparison requirements, such as less than or greater than.

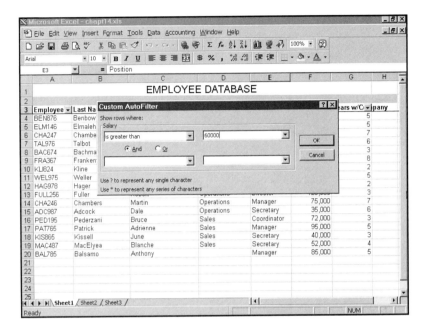

5. If you want to perform a second level filter on that same field, click the And or Or option button.

6. Enter another comparison and value for the second level of the Custom AutoFilter. Figure 14.17 shows a filter for Salaries less than $100,000 and greater than $50,000.

FIG. 14.17
Use Or if you want either of two values, and And if you want to include two different values in your result.

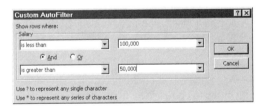

7. Click OK.

CAUTION

The most common error that occurs with a Custom AutoFilter is that no records meet the criteria. The most common cause of that is the misuse of the word And in a two-level Custom AutoFilter. Remember that And means that a field contains both values.

Making a Statement with PowerPoint

CHAPTER 15

Building a Presentation Quickly and Easily

In this chapter

Using the AutoContent Wizard

PowerPoint is a rich, yet simple program. This simplicity comes from tools such as the AutoContent Wizard—features that enable you to customize your presentation to meet your exact needs, while maintaining consistency and a streamlined look and feel.

The AutoContent Wizard is similar to the other wizards you'll find in Word and Excel—a series of dialog boxes appear, asking you to enter text and answer questions. The result is a nearly completed document, filled with formatted text and instructions for replacing it with your own content.

Where the AutoContent Wizard departs from the wizards you find in Word and Excel is in its thorough series of questions regarding the audience, duration, and goal of your presentation. You not only create a presentation through the use of the AutoContent Wizard, you learn a lot about the effective construction of a great presentation.

FIG. 15.1
PowerPoint offers three levels of assistance in starting your presentation: none (Blank Presentation), some (Template) and a lot (AutoContent Wizard).

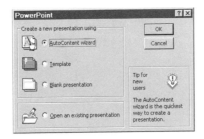

To use the AutoContent Wizard, follow these steps:

1. Start the PowerPoint program from your Start menu's Programs list. The first dialog box that appears (see Figure 15.1) gives you four options for starting your presentation.

2. Click the AutoContent Wizard option, and click OK. The wizard opens.

3. View the list of four steps (plus Finish) on the left side of the first AutoContent Wizard dialog box. This list, plus a description of the wizard, appears in Figure 15.2.

FIG. 15.2
You can click the green boxes to go to a particular step, or follow the wizard from start to finish by clicking the Next button to move to the next step.

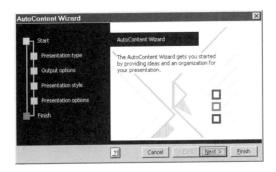

4. Click the Next button to move to the first step, Presentation Type.

5. Choose from any of the seven presentation category buttons, such as Corporate or Operations/HR. A list of presentation templates for the selected category appear on the right, as shown in Figure 15.3. Select one.

 TIP The All button can be selected to see a list of all the presentation templates regardless of category.

FIG. 15.3

Choosing the type of presentation you're giving helps the wizard compose the instructional text that will fill your AutoContent slides.

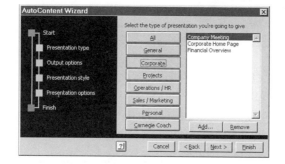

6. Click Next to move to the next step, Output Options.

7. Choose between Presentations, Informal Meetings, Handouts or Internet, Kiosk. Your selection tells the wizard how you'll be presenting your slides.

8. Click Next to move on to Presentation Style, as shown in Figure 15.4.

FIG. 15.4

Choose the type of slide output you want to use, thus helping the wizard choose backgrounds and colors for your show that match your intended medium.

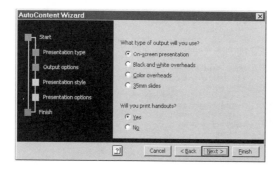

9. Choose your output options, and whether you'll be printing handouts for your presentation.

 TIP Your choices here are not carved in stone—you can choose any form of output when you print your presentation, and you can turn any presentation into 35mm slides should you decide on that output method later.

10. Click Next to proceed to Presentation Options, as shown in Figure 15.5.

FIG. 15.5
Insert the text that you want on your title slide and in any slides that refer to you or your company by name.

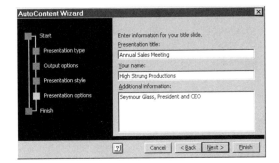

11. Click Next to go to the Finish dialog box, or click Finish to skip that step and go right to the creation of your presentation.

Based on your choices and entries throughout the wizard's steps, a presentation is created for you, and appears in Outline view, as shown in Figure 15.6.

FIG. 15.6
Read the slide titles and bullet text to see the order of subjects and how they're supported.

Instructional sample text

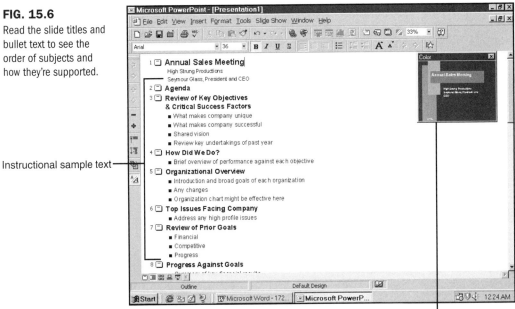

Color slide view of your presentation in a separate window

ON THE WEB

http://www.microsoft.com/powerpoint   Visit this site often for the latest information, product upgrades, and access to third-party tools to enhance your use of PowerPoint.

Replacing Instructional Text

After reading through your AutoContent Wizard presentation, you can begin to make it your own. To customize your presentation content, replace the instructional text with your text. Be sure to replace it in context, unless you want to change a slide's topic.

Notice that as you click a particular slide, the small color slide view window changes to display the selected slide. This allows you to see the graphical content of your slide, and make sure that any text you add doesn't interfere with the graphical elements. Because it's best to keep the text on each slide to a minimum, try creating an additional slide rather than trying to pack a lot of text onto one slide.

 TIP To keep your text slides from becoming wordy, use no more than five bullets per slide, and avoid using complete sentences. Use quick phrases and hit the major points. Save the details for your narration.

To replace the instructional text with your text, highlight it and type the replacement text.

Adding and Deleting Slides

Often, the AutoContent Wizard creates too many or too few slides, or some of the slides that it creates are inappropriate for your specific presentation. You may also want to add slides to accommodate extra text that won't fit on the existing slides, or to cover topics that the AutoContent Wizard didn't build into your presentation.

To delete a slide in Outline view, click the slide icon next to the title, as shown in Figure 15.7. Press the Delete key, and the slide and all of its text will disappear.

FIG. 15.7
Outline view's slide icons enable you to select the entire slide, supporting text included, for deleting, moving, or copying.

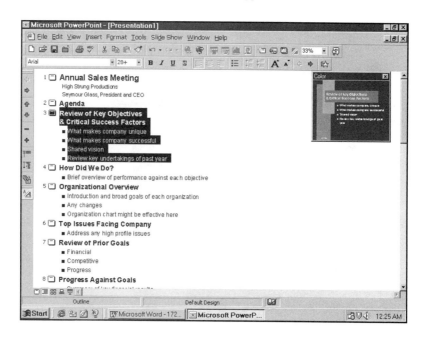

To add a slide, choose one of the following methods:

- Click the slide icon for the existing slide that will follow your new slide, and then click the Insert New Slide button on the toolbar.

- Place your cursor at the end of the text at the end of the slide that will precede your new slide. Press Enter, and then Shift+Tab to promote the new line to a slide. You may also click the Promote button.

- Click in front of the first word in the title of the slide that will follow your new slide. Press Enter. A new, blank slide appears.

N O T E   You may find that text within a slide really deserves to be the title of a new slide so that the topic can be on a slide by itself. To create a slide from your existing bullet text, click the bullet next to the text to select it, and then click the Promote button or press Shift+Tab until the text becomes a slide (you'll see a numbered slide icon appear next to the text). Conversely, slide titles and text that don't rate being a slide on their own can be demoted to bullet text by clicking the Demote button or pressing Tab with the text selected.

Quick Starts with a Presentation Design

If you've already prepared your presentation content or don't find an AutoContent Wizard presentation type that suits your needs, you can build a presentation from scratch. PowerPoint makes this relatively easy, by giving you 21 different Presentation Designs—templates for your presentation that contain background graphics, colors, and text formatting. The only thing you need to add is the content.

To start your presentation with a Presentation Design, follow these steps:

1. Start PowerPoint and choose Template from the PowerPoint dialog box (see Figure 15.8).

FIG. 15.8

Start with a template to utilize 21 different color-coordinated Presentation Designs.

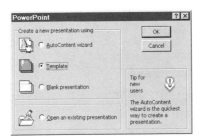

2. Click OK to open the New Presentation dialog box, containing the templates in the Presentation Designs folder (see Figure 15.9).

FIG. 15.9
Presentation Designs
make it easy for you to
create a visually
pleasing, streamlined
presentation.

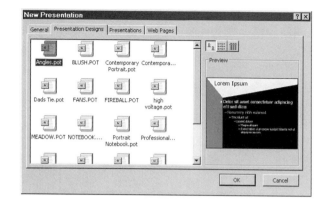

3. Preview the Presentation Design templates by clicking on them once. The preview appears on the right side of the dialog box.

4. As soon as you find one that you like, double-click it, or click it once and click the OK button.

5. The New Slide dialog box opens, offering you an array of 24 different slide layouts, as shown in Figure 15.10. Click the Title Slide (this is already highlighted), and click OK to close the dialog box and open your first slide in Slide view.

N O T E When you add your second slide, you'll notice that the New Slide dialog box has already highlighted the Bullet Text slide for you, as this layout is typically used for second and subsequent slides.

FIG. 15.10
Slide Layouts contain
placeholders for your
major slide elements.
Pick the one that's the
best match for your
needs for this particular
slide.

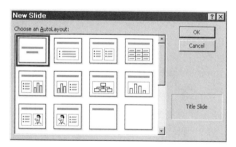

Your slide appears onscreen, with the colors and graphic background dictated by the Presentation Design you selected. In addition, the object placeholders from your selected layout are on the slide. These placeholders contain instructions such as "Click to add title" or "Double-click to add chart" (see Figure 15.11). Follow these instructions to build your slide, one element at a time.

FIG. 15.11
Click a placeholder and type your content. Your text will adhere to the template's formats for font, size, color, and alignment.

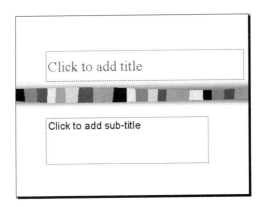

Starting with a Word Outline

For presentations that contain mostly text or that you've already created on paper, an outline can be the best way to start. If you've created an outline in Word to show the topics and supporting information that will be contained in your presentation, that outline can easily become a PowerPoint presentation.

N O T E   Whether you're building a presentation in Word or directly in PowerPoint, keep your text to a minimum. Avoid using more than five bullet points per slide, and try not to use complete sentences. Remember that your presentation will probably be accompanied by a speaker who will expand on your text.

An outline helps you organize your thoughts. You can start with your major subjects, and then develop them with supporting subtopics. As you type your outline in Word, you can use Cut and Paste (or drag and drop) to rearrange your topics as you think things through. Bringing that outline into PowerPoint or developing it from the start in PowerPoint's Outline view makes the development and rearrangement process much easier, because this view was designed for the creation of a text-based presentation.

If you have an outline that you've already created in Word, you can use it as the backbone of a PowerPoint presentation by following these steps:

1. Open your Word outline document, and save it in .rtf (Rich Text) format. Figure 15.12 shows a Word outline, and the Save As dialog box.

CAUTION
If you haven't applied the Heading 1 style to your main topics and Heading 2 and 3 to your supporting levels of text, your outline cannot be converted to slides and bullet text.

FIG. 15.12
Rich text format saves
your formatting, which
should consist of
Heading styles, applied
to your text.

Heading 1 text ──────

Heading 2 text ──────

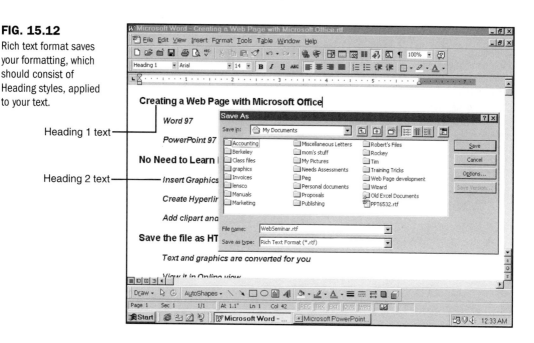

2. Close the Word file.

3. Open PowerPoint, and start your presentation from a Template or as a Blank Presentation if desired.

4. Switch to Outline view by choosing View, Outline.

5. Choose Insert, Slides from Outline. The Insert Outline dialog box opens, from which you can locate and select your Word outline in .rtf format.

6. Double-click the file or click it once and click the OK button to insert the outline into your presentation, creating slides from your Heading 1 text, and supporting text from your lower-level outline text (Headings 2, 3, and so on). Figure 15.13 shows an outline created from the Word document shown previously in Figure 15.12.

You can now add, delete, or rearrange your slides, and add, change, or delete your supporting levels of text. Switch to Slide view to see your text as slides, with your template background and formats (if any) in effect.

Working with Masters

Many presentations are based on templates, which dictate the colors, background, and text formats for the new presentation. The template is the foundation of the presentation file. After the file is created, however, it is assigned a Master—a sort of internal template, that can be altered as needed. Changes made to the Master automatically apply to all existing slides and any slides added thereafter. This process is the purpose of a Master. Rather than make a change and have to repeat it on every slide, making a change to the Master will do those repetitions for you. The result? You save time and you're assured consistency.

FIG. 15.13

Your Heading 1 text become slide titles, and your Heading 2 text becomes first-level bullet text. Lower-level Heading styles create lower-level bullet text.

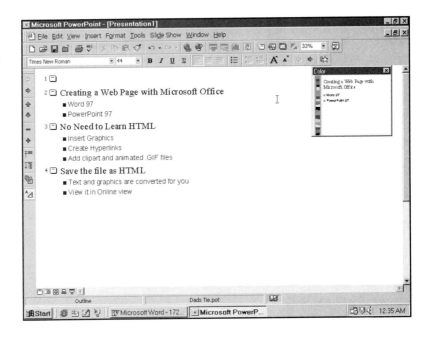

To view your presentation's Master, choose View, Master. A submenu opens, offering Masters for the major components of a presentation:

- *Slide Master.* This Master represents all the slides except the Title Slide. You can use this Master to add a graphic to every slide or reformat your text.

- *Title Master.* Because the first "page" of any document is usually a bit different from the remaining pages, a Title Slide (like a cover page) is also treated differently. By having a separate Title Master, it can be changed and formatted without affecting the remaining slides.

- *Handouts Master.* If you'll be issuing handouts to your audience, you can alter their Master by inserting text, headers and footers, or graphics on every page of the handout.

- *Notes Master.* Used as a speaker's tool or a one-slide-per-page handout, your Notes Pages output can be reformatted by altering its Master. Change the size of the text box, set default fonts for the text box text, add header and footer text, or insert your company logo on each page.

After choosing the Master you want to work with, the Master opens in Slide view, as shown in Figure 15.14.

You'll notice immediately that your text placeholders contain instructions that you "Click to edit Master styles." This is an important distinction from your Slide view of a new slide which says "Click to add text." You don't type text into the Master's text placeholders, you select the instructional text and reformat it.

You can add elements to your Master, as long as you want whatever you add to be on every Slide, Title Slide, Handout, or Notes page. A commonly added element is a graphic, usually a company logo. Insert a picture, and then move and/or resize it to be in one of the corners of the slide, out of the way of your content.

FIG. 15.14
Anything you add to, delete from, or change about the Master affects the slides or output it represents.

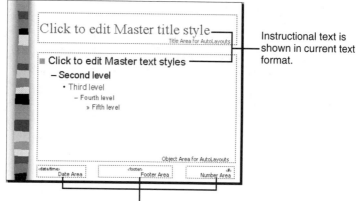

Instructional text is shown in current text format.

Format the Date, Footer, and Page Number

N O T E You can also turn your graphic into a watermark, a lightly shaded graphic behind your text. Insert a picture or shape, and then choose a light fill color for it. Place it behind the text layer by choosing Draw, Order, Send to Back from the Drawing toolbar.

You might also decide that you want your text to be white instead of yellow, or your slide titles to be bigger. Whatever text formatting you apply to the Master, applies to the slides it represents.

Regardless of the type of formatting you want to apply or elements you want to add, you'll use PowerPoint's standard tools to accomplish it:

■ *Format text.* Use the Formatting toolbar to adjust the size of your text or choose another font altogether. You can apply Bold, Italic, Underline, or Shadow to your text as well.

 N O T E If you don't care exactly what point size your text is, and you just want to make it bigger or smaller, use the Increase Font Size and Decrease Font Size buttons. Each click increases or decreases your font size by six points.

■ *Insert an extra text box.* If you want your company's slogan or the name of the event on every slide, click the Text Box tool on the Drawing toolbar. Click and drag to create a text box, and then type your text.

 T I P If you click and don't drag a box to control the shape of your text box, the text you type in it will not wrap. After typing the line of text, you can move and resize it, however, and the text will wrap within its new confines.

■ *Add a graphic.* Your company logo or some other significant image can be an effective addition to your slides. Choose Insert, Picture, From File to choose a graphic you have stored on disk. Once inserted the graphic can be moved and resized as needed. Figure 15.15 shows the Slide Master with a logo added to the lower-right corner.

FIG. 15.15

Make sure any graphics you add are on the periphery of the slide so they don't interfere visually with slide elements like clip art and charts.

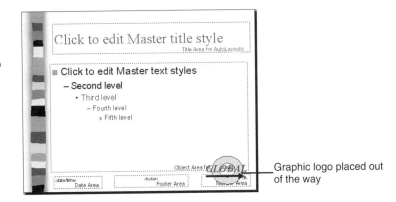

Graphic logo placed out of the way

▶ **See** "Working with Clip Art and Graphics," **p. 227**

Creating Dynamic Charts

Quick PowerPoint Charting with MSGraph

MSGraph is a program that runs within Microsoft Office, giving PowerPoint users the tools to create charts and graphs from their simple numeric data. For elaborate charts or complex information, Excel's charting tools are superior. For simple bar, pie, or line charts (the most easily displayed in a slide presentation), however, PowerPoint's MSGraph features are more than adequate.

Why do you find charting in two Office applications? Because charts are so visually effective. Charts are especially effective in PowerPoint, where clarity and simplicity are valuable to the success of your presentation. A slide presentation is no place to display lists of numbers or complex mathematical functions. For maximum effectiveness, slides need pictures, and a chart is a picture of your numbers.

T I P   If you must share those long lists of numbers or complex calculations with your audience, include them with your handout. Don't put them in your slides!

MSGraph is invoked whenever a chart is added to an existing slide. To create a chart slide, follow these steps:

1. Click the Insert New Slide button and choose the Chart AutoLayout, as shown in Figure 16.1.

FIG. 16.1

The Chart slide AutoLayout displays a column chart, although any type of chart can be created.

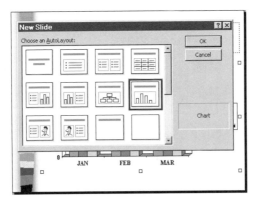

2. Double-click the chart placeholder in your new slide. This invokes the MSGraph. Your PowerPoint window changes, displaying MSGraph tools on the toolbars, and a Datasheet window is displayed (see Figure 16.2).

3. The Datasheet contains sample data that must be replaced with your data. Click the gray button in the upper-left corner of the Datasheet to select all the Datasheet's cells. Press the Delete key to remove the sample data. Your chart becomes blank, because there is no data plotted.

4. Type your data in the Datasheet. Notice that as you type your data, a chart is being reformed, this time reflecting your information (see Figure 16.3).

FIG. 16.2
Resize your Datasheet as needed to simplify data entry and editing. Drag the edges of your Datasheet outward to enlarge the sheet.

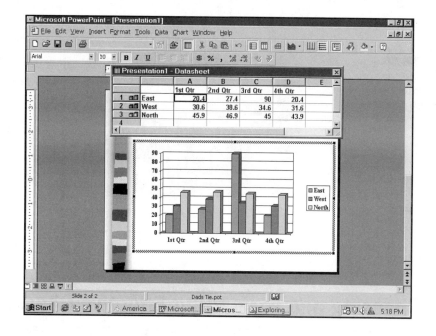

FIG. 16.3
Although you may need to change the chart type later, your column chart's creation begins as soon as you start entering your data.

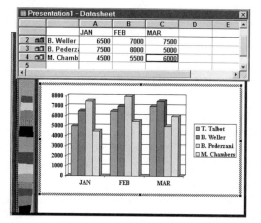

5. As soon as you've completed your data entry, close the Datasheet by clicking the Datasheet button on the toolbar. You can reopen it as needed later.

The basic column chart that is created by default can be changed to any two- or three-dimensional chart by clicking the Chart Type button on the toolbar. A palette of chart types appears, 2D on the left, 3D on the right. Select one, and your chart is automatically changed to that type.

T I P If your data consists of two or more data series (sets of data), you cannot use a pie chart. Pie charts can only show one data series at a time.

Figure 16.4 shows a completed basic chart on a PowerPoint slide.

FIG. 16.4
Your chart's default colors and text formats are dictated by your presentation's template.

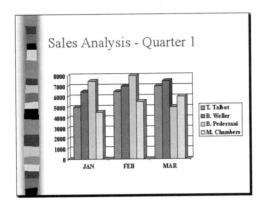

▶ **See** "Choosing a Chart Type," **p. 171**

Choosing and Formatting Effective Chart Elements

After your chart is created (and perhaps changed to another type of chart), you can begin fine-tuning it to meet your exact requirements. You can change the colors of your bars/columns, pie slices, or lines, and add text and other defining elements to the chart.

> **CAUTION**
> Be careful not to add too many extra elements to your chart. If your chart has too many features, it ceases to be simple to read, especially if your presentation is displayed onscreen in a large room. Always design your presentation elements with the worst-case viewing scenario in mind—a person in the back of a poorly lit room, straining to read your slides.

Using Titles

A title tells your audience what information to expect in the chart. You can add three titles to any PowerPoint chart—a category axis title, a value axis title, and a chart title. Add titles only when they add value to the chart. If the content of the category axis is obvious, you needn't add a title to that axis. Figure 16.5 shows a chart with a value axis title and a chart title.

To add titles to your chart, choose Chart, Chart Options. Click the Titles tab (see Figure 16.6), and type the text you want to see on one or more of your chart's titles.

Working with Data Labels

Including Data Labels in your chart is one way of showing the audience the actual number that a bar, line, or slice represents. In lieu of, or in addition to, a handout that shows the supporting data shown on your slide, you can add these labels to your chart.

FIG. 16.5

Keep your titles short and to-the-point. Don't waste precious space on your slides with information that is relayed by other slide elements or is common knowledge to your audience.

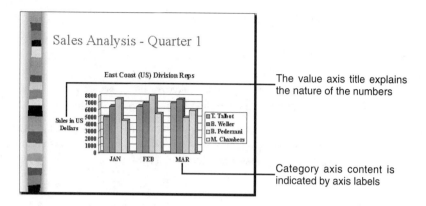

The value axis title explains the nature of the numbers

Category axis content is indicated by axis labels

FIG. 16.6

A sample chart appears in the Chart Options dialog box to show you the effect of your titles on the chart's overall layout.

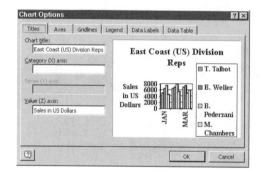

To insert Data Labels, choose Chart, Chart Options, and click the Data Labels tab (see Figure 16.7). Depending on your chart type, one or more label options will be available. For a simple bar or column chart, you can choose to show the numbers that your bars/columns represent, or to reiterate your category axis labels.

FIG. 16.7

Data Labels can be visually cluttering. Add them only if they're absolutely necessary to the understanding of your chart.

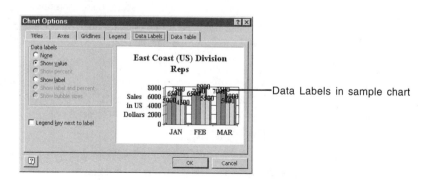

Data Labels in sample chart

If you add Data Labels, it's a good idea to move them from overlapping the bars/columns to being just above them. This saves you having to recolor the bars or the label text for legibility. To move a label, click it once. Handles appear around it. Point to the middle of the label, and drag it to its new position. You'll have to repeat this for all your labels.

▶ **See** "Adding Extra Elements," **p. 174**

Positioning Your Legend

Your legend may be one of the most important elements of your chart. Without it, your audience won't know which colored bar, slice, or line represents which data series. To change the location and appearance of your legend, try these techniques:

■ You can move the legend by clicking it once (handles appear to show it's selected), and then dragging it to a new location on the slide. You can also choose Format, Selected Legend, and choose a new location for it from the Placement area on the Legend tab (see Figure 16.8).

FIG. 16.8

Choose Bottom placement for a long, thin legend that takes up very little room on your chart.

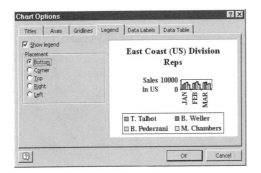

 TIP   It's often easier to adjust your legend's placement in the Chart Options dialog box or through the Format Legend dialog box, because it not only moves the legend, but it resizes it to fit its new location.

■ To resize your legend, click it once, and then point to one of the handles that appear around its perimeter. When your mouse pointer appears as a two-headed arrow, drag outward to make the legend bigger, inward to make it smaller.

■ Change the font of your legend text by clicking once on the legend and then choosing a new font from the Formatting toolbar. You can also choose Format, Selected Legend, and use the Font tab.

If you want to delete your Legend, click it once and press Delete or click the Legend button. This is a toggle switch that turns your legend on or off.

Working with Fills and Colors

If you'll be printing your presentation on color transparencies, outputting to color 35mm slides, or running your slideshow onscreen, you'll want to fine-tune your colors. You can change the color of virtually any element on your chart, from the bars/slices to the text in your chart title, to the background color of your chart area. To change an element's color, select it by clicking it once, and employ one of the following formatting methods:

■ Click the Fill Color button to change the fill of your data series, chart area, plot area, legend, or the floor of your chart (3D charts only). A palette appears, from which you can select a color for the selected object.

TIP Not sure which element you have selected? Use the Chart Objects drop-down list to see a list of all the elements in your chart. Choose one from the list, and you'll see it selected in your chart.

■ Change the color of your text by selecting the text element and choosing F_ormat, _Font. Use the Color tool in the Font dialog box to change the color of your text (see Figure 16.9).

FIG. 16.9

Change the color, font, size, and style of the selected text element.

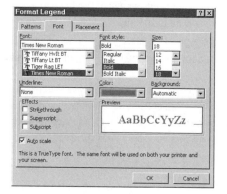

N O T E You can also apply fill effects, such as textures and patterns, by clicking Fill Effects in the Fill Color palette. Apply these fills with care—be sure the effect isn't too busy or complex to be seen at a distance (for onscreen shows) or that it will lose its impact if it's printed in black-and-white. Complex patterns and textures rarely print well on transparencies.

Using Existing Spreadsheet Data from Excel

Although PowerPoint is a program that allows you to create original text and drawings, it is also a tool designed to house existing elements from other applications, showcasing them in the form of an electronic presentation.

Just as a Word outline can be used to create a series of slides and bullet text, an Excel spreadsheet can be used to fill in a PowerPoint Datasheet, or an existing Excel chart can be added to a PowerPoint slide.

Copying Excel Data to Create a PowerPoint Chart

In a previous section of this chapter, we discussed entering your data into a PowerPoint Datasheet, simultaneously building a chart based on that data. It works well, and it's easy to do. But what if your data already exists in Excel? If, for example, you're creating a chart that shows the sales growth of your company's divisions, why retype the data into the PowerPoint Datasheet if you already have it in an Excel worksheet?

Instead of retyping, which wastes time and creates a margin for error, use the Clipboard to take your Excel data and place it in your PowerPoint Datasheet. To accomplish this, follow these steps:

1. Open the Excel worksheet that contains the data you want to copy.
2. Select the cells that contain the data, and choose Edit, Copy.
3. Open or switch to your PowerPoint presentation, and go to the slide that will contain the chart. Double-click the chart object (or insert it if necessary), and display the Datasheet.
4. Click the gray button in the upper-left corner of the Datasheet, and press Delete to remove any sample or other data in the sheet.
5. Click in the first blank cell in the Datasheet, and choose Edit, Paste from the PowerPoint menu bar. The Excel data appears in the Datasheet, and a chart is automatically built.

N O T E If you want to create an ongoing relationship between your PowerPoint chart and the Excel data, choose Paste Special instead of Paste when inserting the data into the Datasheet. Click the Paste Link option, and choose an Excel object from the list. Your PowerPoint chart will now update (when you choose to do so) whenever the Excel data is changed.

Pasting an Existing Excel Chart

If pasting Excel data into a PowerPoint Datasheet saves you work, imagine the labor savings achieved by pasting an existing chart that was already created in Excel. Not only does this save you time and effort, it allows you to include a chart that was created with more powerful and flexible charting tools (the Excel Chart Wizard).

To use an Excel chart in your PowerPoint presentation, follow these steps:

1. Open the Excel worksheet that contains the chart you want to use in your PowerPoint slide.
2. Click once on the chart to activate it. If the chart is in its own sheet, select the sheet by clicking its tab.
3. Choose Edit, Copy.
4. Switch to PowerPoint, and go to the slide (in Slide view) into which you want to place the chart.

 T I P Don't use a Chart Slide AutoLayout for the slide that will contain the Excel chart. You aren't using PowerPoint's charting tools, and won't be able to use them to edit the Excel chart once it has been pasted into the slide.

5. Choose Edit, Paste. The chart appears in the middle of the slide. Move and resize it as needed to work with the other elements on the slide.

N O T E   You can create a link between the pasted chart and the chart as it appears in the Excel
workbook. Choose Edit, Paste Special (instead of Paste), and choose the Paste Link option.
Select an Excel chart object, and click OK. The chart in your PowerPoint slide can now be updated to
match any changes to the Excel chart, whenever you choose to update links.

▶ **See** "Understanding OLE," **p. 35**

Building an Organization Chart

Part

IV

Ch

16

An organization chart is a graphic depiction of your company's structure. The boxes in an
organization chart can contain names and titles or they can contain department or division
names and short descriptions.

The level of detail you use depends on your audience and their level of interest in the details
of your organization. For in-house presentations, people generally like to see themselves and
their coworkers in the chart, as it emphasizes that they're important members of the team.

To customers, investors, or vendors, the name of the assistant to the assistant manager isn't
terribly important. The only people whose names are of interest to your customers are those
people with whom they have direct communication, such as customer service or sales repre-
sentatives, and management personnel. Seeing the chain of command in departments such as
these can be useful to your current or prospective customers.

N O T E   Creating an organization chart requires planning. You need to research the departments
and/or divisions within your organization, and find out the correct names and titles, and
understand departmental hierarchies. Errors can be embarrassing to you and upsetting to the people
incorrectly depicted.

T I P   Remember that the more boxes your chart contains, the smaller they all become, and, if your
presentation will be onscreen in a large room, the less legible they will become. Try to keep the number
of boxes to no greater than 15 per slide.

   To add an organization chart to your slide, you must choose the appropriate AutoLayout. If
your chart already exists with a different layout, click the Slide Layout button on the Standard
toolbar. Double-click the Org Chart layout (see Figure 16.10).

FIG. 16.10
Select the Org Chart
AutoLayout to change
your existing slide's
layout or set up your
new slide for an
organization chart.

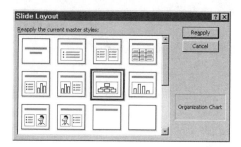

If you are adding a new slide, choose the Org Chart AutoLayout from the array that appears when you click the Insert New Slide button.

In your slide, double-click the org chart object box. This will start a program called MSOrg Chart. This is a separate program that Microsoft includes with Office.

CAUTION

If you have more than 200 fonts in your Fonts folder, PowerPoint may not let you run MSOrg Chart. The Fonts folder is a subfolder of your Windows folder. If you have more than 200 fonts, cut the excess to a folder you create for temporary storage of the fonts. When you've finished creating and editing the org chart, return the stored fonts to the Fonts folder.

Entering Names and Titles

In your MSOrg Chart window, you'll see that a four-box org chart is created for you (see Figure 16.11). The first two boxes have been completed, and the user is entering the title in the third person's box.

FIG. 16.11

When you start MSOrg Chart, you are given a four-box chart to fill in with names and titles. Add your own boxes to complete the chart.

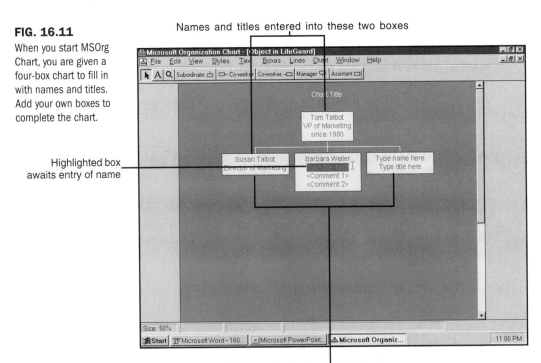

Names and titles entered into these two boxes

Highlighted box awaits entry of name

Three subordinates or first-level managers

To enter your names and titles, follow these steps:

1. If the box is already highlighted (blackened), just start typing. If the box is not yet highlighted, click once inside it, and then start typing.
2. After typing the person's name, press Enter.
3. Type the person's title. Press Enter.
4. Type any comments (location, for example) and press Enter if you have a second line of comments to type.
5. When you have finished entering the current block's text, click your next box, and repeat steps 2 through 4 for that and any subsequent boxes.

Adding People to Your Chart

After you've used the first four org chart boxes that appear by default when you start the chart, you need to add more boxes for your other personnel. Using the MSOrg Chart toolbar, click the button that best describes the rank of the next person to be added.

- Assistants are secretaries or administrative assistants, who directly support another person.
- Coworkers are people of equal rank within a department. They normally report to a manager. If you already have a subordinate, you can give him or her a coworker. Choose the coworker button that depicts the side onto which the coworker's box should be added (left or right).
- Subordinates are people who report to a manager, but are not personal assistants or secretaries. Subordinates can have and can be coworkers.
- Managers are people who have subordinates (and subordinates' coworkers) reporting to them. Managers can also have assistants.

After you've determined the rank of the next person you want to add, you can create their box.

To add Subordinates, Coworkers, Assistants, and Managers, follow these steps:

1. Click the button for the type of person you want to add. Your mouse pointer changes to signify that MSOrg Chart is waiting for you to indicate where to place this new person.
2. If adding a Subordinate or Assistant, click the existing box of the person to whom they report. If adding a coworker, click the existing subordinate with whom this new person works. If adding a manager, click the existing box of one of their subordinates.

   A box appears, with a connecting line going from the new person's box to their manager or to their coworker. The new box is highlighted, ready for your entries.
3. Type the person's name and press Enter.
4. Type their title. Normally, boxes at the Subordinate, Coworkers, and Assistant levels do not have comments.

You can continue adding personnel at all levels, until your chart is complete. Figure 16.12 shows a completed org chart with personnel in all position types.

FIG. 16.12
This org chart contains
several people, in
varying ranks within the
organization.

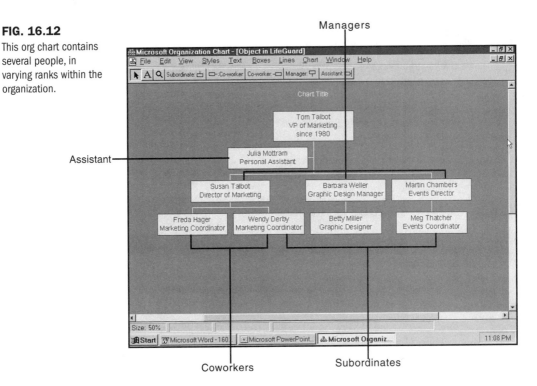

NOTE It's a good idea to save your work as soon as you have a few boxes added to your chart. A
rule of thumb for when to save (in any program) is: when you've done more work than you'd
want to or would be able to do over again, it's time to save. Choose File, Exit and Return to "presentation name." Click Yes to update your chart in the presentation.

If you then want to open Org Chart again to edit it, double-click the chart.

Moving and Deleting Boxes

After you've assigned ranks and added boxes to your chart, you may decide to change them—
perhaps someone has been transferred to another department or resigned since you made the
chart. The process of moving and deleting boxes to accommodate changes in staff is simple.

1. Click the box you want to move, and immediately drag it to its new position.

    - To reassign a subordinate to a new manager, drag the subordinate box on top of
      the new manager's box.

    - To promote a subordinate box to manager level, drag it on top of the current
      manager's manager.

2. After moving the box, retype the person's title to reflect their new position in the
   organization.

To delete a person from the staff, click once on their box, and press the Delete key or choose Edit, Clear.

Editing an Organization Chart

You can edit many aspects of your chart:

- Colors of boxes and lines
- Rank of personnel
- Font, size, and color of box text
- Background color for the chart
- Style of the chart

To edit your chart, double-click it if you have returned to your presentation, or remain in the MSOrg Chart window and use the org chart tools and menus to change the appearance of your chart.

To reformat boxes and lines, click the individual item you want to change, and then click the appropriate menu and command within it. MSOrg Chart's menus and tools are simple and direct.

 TIP To select several contiguous boxes and/or lines at once, drag a rectangle around them with your mouse. Only the items completely encompassed by the rectangle (also known as a marquee) are selected. You can now reformat the selected items as a group.

Applying Colors to Boxes

If you started your presentation from a Presentation Design template, your chart colors are decided for you. All the boxes, text, and connecting lines are color-coordinated with your template's text and background. If, however, you want to make each department a different color, or change the color of the manager boxes, for example, you can select individual boxes or groups of boxes and apply new colors to them.

- To change the color of one or more boxes, select the box or boxes, and choose Boxes, Color. Select a color from the dialog box (see Figure 16.13). Click OK.
- Apply box shadows by selecting Boxes, Shadow. Adding a shadow gives the boxes a 3D look. Choose one of the Shadow styles, which determines the angle of the shadow (see Figure 16.14).
- Give your box a border. Choose Boxes, Border Style (see Figure 16.15), and choose single, double, or artistic borders for your selected boxes. To apply a different color to the border, choose Boxes, Border Color. Your border line can also be dashed. Choose Boxes, Border Line Style and choose the style you prefer.

FIG. 16.13
Choose a color for your selected boxes by selecting Color from the Boxes menu.

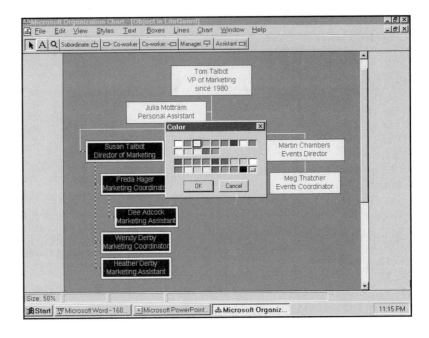

FIG. 16.14
Give your boxes a 3D look by applying a Shadow.

FIG. 16.15
Apply a border style, color, and/or border line style to your boxes. Use this effect to draw attention to specific boxes or to visually differentiate departments.

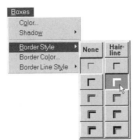

Applying Color and Style to Lines

Your lines' color and style can enhance the overall look of your chart or it can convey a message. You may choose a color that matches your boxes or that shows better against your background. You might also choose a different color or style for certain lines as a way of expressing the nature of a department's relationship to the rest of the organization. For example, a dashed line can communicate a transient relationship, although a thick line can show long-term connections.

■ To change the color of your lines, select the lines and then choose <u>L</u>ines, C<u>o</u>lor. Click OK.

■ Choose <u>L</u>ines, St<u>y</u>le to change to a dotted, dashed, or solid line.

■ To change the thickness of your lines, choose <u>L</u>ines, <u>T</u>hickness. You can choose None from this menu if you want to remove a line.

 TIP Select the entire chart, boxes, text, and lines, by pressing Ctrl+A. Then make changes to the text, boxes, and lines from their corresponding menus.

Formatting Text

Within boxes, you can apply different styles to differentiate names and titles or to improve overall legibility.

Before applying text formatting, be sure to select the box or boxes to which you want the changes to apply. If you only want to select certain text within a box, click in the box and then click the text. Your mouse turns into an I-beam, allowing you to drag through the text to select it

■ To change text color, select the box or only certain text within it. Choose <u>T</u>ext, C<u>o</u>lor, and select a color from the Color dialog box. Click OK.

■ To change the font of your text, choose <u>T</u>ext, <u>F</u>ont. The Font dialog box opens (see Figure 16.16), from which you can set the font, style, and size of the selected text.

FIG. 16.16

Use the Font dialog box to change nearly any aspect of the appearance of your selected text element.

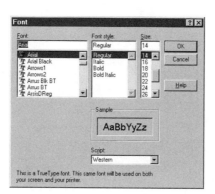

■ To change the alignment of text, choose <u>T</u>ext, <u>L</u>eft, <u>R</u>ight, or <u>C</u>enter. Most text boxes contain centered text.

Working with Clip Art and Graphics

Working with Drawn Objects: Shapes, Lines, and Text Boxes

Drawn objects that you add to a PowerPoint presentation, be they geometric shapes, straight lines and arrows, or freehand drawings, add visual interest to your slides. Shapes and lines can be added to communicate an idea or show a process through the creation of a flow chart. Drawn objects can also be added for decorative purposes. Placing a large sunburst shape behind a list of contest winners or the name of your new health insurance provider show and inspire enthusiasm and excitement.

Although not drawn objects in the truest sense, text boxes can also be added to your presentation. Text boxes are added to a slide when that slide's AutoLayout doesn't contain enough text elements for all the desired text. Figure 17.1 shows a slide that contains a variety of drawn objects, including a user-created text box.

FIG. 17.1

Add shapes, lines, and text boxes to your slides when the existing layout doesn't meet your needs for creativity and information.

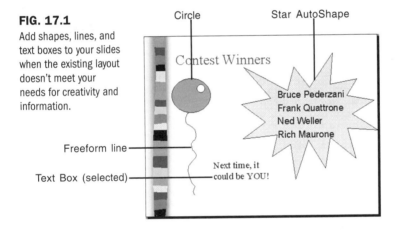

To access PowerPoint's drawing tools (which are the same as the drawing tools in Word and Excel) you must display the Drawing toolbar. Right-click any existing toolbar and choose Drawing from the list. The toolbar appears at the bottom of the screen, below the status line, as shown in Figure 17.2.

FIG. 17.2

The Drawing toolbar contains tools for creating and formatting drawn shapes, lines, arrows, and text boxes.

Drawing Shapes

Creating squares, circles, stars, and the like doesn't require great artistic ability. A little mouse control is all it takes. To create rectangles and ovals, follow these steps:

1. Click the Rectangle or Oval button on the drawing toolbar.

TIP If you want to draw several of the same shape, one after the other, double-click the button for that shape. Otherwise, the button turns off after one shape is drawn.

2. Move your mouse pointer onto the slide, and drag your mouse, starting with a click at the point where you want to begin drawing the shape.

3. Drag diagonally away from the starting point (where you clicked and began dragging) until the object is the desired size.

TIP To make a drawn rectangle into a square or an oval into a circle, press and hold the Shift key while drawing the shape. Release the mouse before you release the Shift key when you've finished creating the shape.

 To access a more extensive group of shapes, click the AutoShapes button, also on the Drawing toolbar. A menu that includes lines, arrows, flowchart symbols, and stars appears. Select the type of shape you want, and then select the specific shape from the palette, as shown in Figure 17.3.

FIG. 17.3
There are many
AutoShape buttons for
complex polygons and
lines.

After selecting a shape to draw, click and drag to draw the shape as described previously to draw rectangles and ovals. Again, press the Shift key while drawing to create objects of equal height and width.

TIP If you've drawn a shape and want to repeat it, press Ctrl+D to duplicate the shape.

Drawing Lines

  Lines are drawn by selecting the Line tool or Arrow tool if you want an arrow head on one or both ends of the line, and clicking to set the start of the line. Drag in any direction, releasing the mouse when your line is as long as you need it to be.

N O T E Holding the Shift key while drawing lines and arrows makes it easier to draw lines at 45 and 90 degree angles. The Ctrl key, pressed while drawing any shape, causes the shape to be drawn from the center out.

The Drawing toolbar contains four tools for formatting lines:

- *Line Color.* Click this tool to choose from a palette of colors.

- *Line Style.* Choose the thickness of the line, and apply double or triple line styles for more elaborate effects.

- *Dash Style.* For dotted or dashed lines, choose the type of dots, dashes, or combinations thereof.

- *Arrow Style.* Pick the arrow heads and on which end of the arrow they'll appear.

Inserting Text Boxes

Text boxes are drawn just as you would draw a rectangle—click the Text Box tool, and then click and drag to create a box. The difference between a text box and a rectangle is that the box you draw isn't the box you'll see. When a text box is drawn, as soon as you release the mouse, the box that appears onscreen is as wide as you drew it, but only tall enough for one line of text. As you type in the box, the text wraps and the length of the box increases to accommodate the amount of text you type into it. Figure 17.4 shows two text boxes drawn to the exact same size—one that already contains text, and one that doesn't.

FIG. 17.4
The vertical dimensions of your text box depend on the amount of text you type.

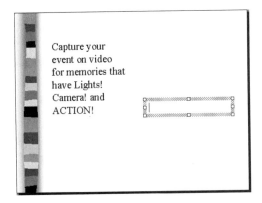

N O T E You can add text to any drawn polygon by clicking once on the shape and typing. The text you type is centered in the object. The text and the shape become one object, and they move and resize together. Choose Format, AutoShape, and click the Text Box tab to adjust the internal margins of the shape and its text, and to set either of two options: Word Wrap Text in AutoShape or Resize AutoShape to Fit Text.

Moving and Resizing Drawn Objects

After you've drawn an object, you can move it to a new spot on the same slide, or use the Clipboard to move or share it with another slide in your current presentation or another presentation altogether.

To move an object within the same slide, follow these steps:

1. Click the object once to select it (handles appear, as shown in Figure 17.5).

FIG. 17.5

Selected objects have white handles on their perimeter—one on each corner, and one in the middle of each side.

2. Point to the object itself, not to any of the handles. Your mouse pointer turns into a four-headed arrow.

3. Click and drag the object to it's new location.

To change the size of an object, follow these steps:

1. Click once on the object to select it.

2. Point to one of the object's handles. Your mouse pointer turns into a two-headed arrow.

3. Click and drag outward to make the object larger, inward to make it smaller.

 T I P Drag from a corner handle if you want to keep the object's current horizontal and vertical proportions, also known as its *aspect ratio*.

Applying Color to Drawn Objects

The colors that are applied to your drawn shapes and lines by default are dictated by your presentation's template. You can choose from a variety of other colors for your shapes and lines, and even select from a small palette of coordinated colors that are part of your presentation's template.

  To apply color to a selected shape, click the Fill Color button on the Drawing toolbar. Select a color from the palette (see Figure 17.6), or click Fill Effects to choose from a variety   of patterns and textures with which to fill the object.

FIG. 17.6
Solid color fills work well on transparencies. Fill effects (gradients, textures, patterns) work best onscreen or in 35mm slides. Use simple patterns for black-and-white presentations.

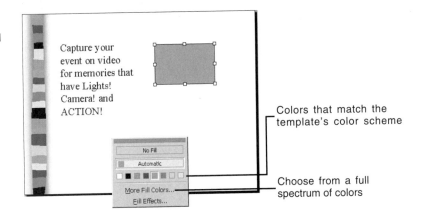

Colors that match the template's color scheme

Choose from a full spectrum of colors

The Fill Effects dialog box contains four tabs—Gradient, Texture, Pattern, and Picture—that you can use to add extra visual interest to your presentation's drawn shapes (see Figure 17.7).

FIG. 17.7
Gradient fills give the impression of three dimensions and a source of light shining on your drawn shapes.

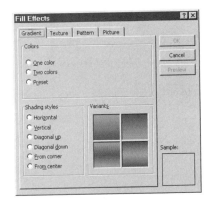

Working with Order and Alignment

The relationships between drawn objects can be important when you're trying to create a complex drawing out of several drawn elements or you're trying to create an effect by combining drawn objects and text. PowerPoint gives you the ability to create and then manipulate these relationships with simple commands and tools.

Changing the Order of Drawn Objects　The order in which objects are drawn dictates their order when stacked on a slide. If you draw a circle and then draw a square, even if you drag the circle on top of the square, when you release the mouse, the square is on top, because it was drawn last.

Because we can't always plan a drawing so thoroughly that no objects are drawn out of order, it's important to be able to change their order. To change an object's order on the slide, follow these steps:

1. Select the item that is out of desired order.

2. Choose D<u>r</u>aw, O<u>r</u>der from the Drawing toolbar. Select the action needed from the Order submenu:

   - *Bring to Fron<u>t</u> or Send to Bac<u>k</u>*. These options take the selected item and move them to the top or bottom of the stack.

   - *Bring <u>F</u>orward or Send <u>B</u>ackward*. Use these options to move the object forward or backward one layer of the stack at a time.

   - *Bring in F<u>r</u>ont of or Send Be<u>h</u>ind Text*. These options relate only to the selected object's relationship to any and all text elements on the slide.

Aligning Objects   Imagine that you're trying to create a vertical line of star shapes down the left side of your slide, as shown in Figure 17.8. You'd have to be very accurate with your mouse to place each star "just so"—spacing them equally in a vertical line, and making sure each one is the same distance from the edge of the slide. Even for the most adept mouse user, this would be a virtual impossibility. In fact, attaining perfect alignment would be impossible.

Rather than struggling with the mouse, however, you can use PowerPoint's Align or Distribute tool to position the stars exactly where you want them, in relation to each other. Figure 17.8 shows a set of shapes before alignment and after the use of PowerPoint's Align or Distribute tool.

Part

IV

Ch

17

FIG. 17.8
Create a border with a series of aligned and distributed shapes.

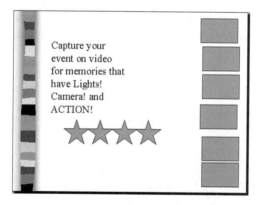

To align and/or distribute selected drawn objects, follow these steps:

1. Draw your shapes, and then select them. You can use the following methods to select your group of shapes:

   - *Marquee.* A marquee (in this context), is a rectangle drawn to encompass a group of shapes that must be selected as a group. This technique can only be used for shapes that are all in one area of the slide—if there are intervening shapes in the area, use the Shift+Click method.

   - *Shift+Click.* Click the first shape in the group, and then press and hold the Shift key. Click each of the remaining shapes until they all have handles around them.

This method is best to use when your desired shapes are scattered all over the slide or there are intervening shapes nearby that could be accidentally selected with the marquee method.

2. Choose Draw, Align or Distribute from the Drawing toolbar.

3. Select the alignment you want to apply.

4. Reselect Align or Distribute from the Draw menu, and if needed, choose a distribution command.

 TIP After you've aligned/distributed your objects, group them by choosing Draw, Group from the Drawing toolbar. This eliminates the possibility that you might drag one or more of the objects out of position.

N O T E Unless you choose Relative to Slide from the Align or Distribute menu, your objects will be aligned and/or distributed relative to each other. The last object selected in the group (with either selection method) becomes the anchor, and the other objects align or distribute relative to it.

Working with Clip Art

Microsoft Office comes with a wide selection of clip-art images, and they are all accessible from within any Office application. Stored in the Microsoft Clip Gallery, these images can be added to your presentations to break up text slides (most people prefer pictures to words), and to help make a statement by supporting your text with a related image. Figure 17.9 shows a slide that contains both text and clip art.

FIG. 17.9
Whether you choose an image that's silly or serious, pepper your presentation with clip art to keep people entertained and attentive.

 ON THE WEB

http://www.clip-art.com/ A free, categorized site that lists over 500 different clip-art images. Use them in presentations, Web pages, or any type of document. Download them from the site to your hard drive according to your browser's downloading instructions.

Inserting Clip Art

To add a clip-art image to your slide, choose Insert, Picture, Clip Art. You can also click the Insert Clip Art button. The Clip Gallery opens, displaying a list of clip-art categories. To see all the clip art, select All Categories (see Figure 17.10).

FIG. 17.10
Scroll through the list of clip-art images to find the one that matches your topic.

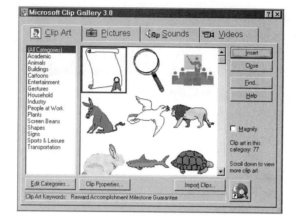

Part
IV
Ch
17

N O T E If you chose either of the Text and Clip Art AutoLayouts when you added your current slide, there is a placeholder for your clip-art image. If you're adding clip art to any other AutoLayout, the image appears in the middle of the slide when inserted.

When you've found the image that meets your needs, double-click it. It appears on your slide, where it can be moved and resized as needed. Figure 17.11 shows an inserted clip-art image.

FIG. 17.11
Clip-art images are usually too big and must be reduced to fit among the other elements on the slide.

Clip-art image is proportionately reduced by dragging inward from a corner handle

Manipulating Clip Art

After your clip-art image is inserted, you'll probably want to move it to another spot on the slide, unless you used the Text and Clip Art AutoLayout, in which case the image has been inserted in its own placeholder. You may also want to resize the image.

- ▓ To move a clip-art image, click anywhere on the image itself and drag it to the desired location.
- ▓ To resize a clip-art image, click once to select it, and then drag from any of its handles—outward to make the image larger, inward to make it smaller. Drag from a corner handle if you want to keep the object's current horizontal and vertical proportion.

If you want to reuse a clip-art image, you can save the time and effort involved in selecting and inserting the image by using the Clipboard to copy it to another slide. Follow these steps to copy a clip-art image:

1. In Slide View, click once on the clip-art image that you want to reuse.
2. Choose Edit, Copy, or press Ctrl+C.
3. Move to the slide onto which you want to place the copied image, and choose Edit, Paste, or press Ctrl+V.

To delete a clip-art image, click it once and press the Delete key. You can also choose Edit, Clear. ●

Creating Dynamic Multimedia Effects

Setting Up the Slideshow

Your slideshow is the culmination of all your time spent developing and customizing your slides. Unless you're printing your presentation on paper, transparencies, or generating 35mm slides, you'll be running a slideshow onscreen (projected onto a clean, white wall or screen or viewed on an extra large monitor) for your audience.

An onscreen slideshow can simply consist of a series of slides, shown one after the other, with nothing more than the sound of your voice to accompany them. We all know, however, what happens when we're sitting in a darkened room, reading slides, listening to a speaker. We often fall asleep, or at the very least, our minds wander. Adding the following features can keep the audience interested and awake:

- *Slide transitions.* PowerPoint offers 40 different transitions—animated effects used to create an interesting visual effect as one slide leaves the screen and the next one appears.

- *Bullet text builds.* To control the attention of your audience, you'll want to apply build effects to your bulleted text. When a bulleted list is presented, the items in the list can be shown one at a time, and previous items dimmed so they can no longer be read. This keeps your audience looking at the point about which you're speaking, not thinking about past or future topics on the current slide.

- *Text animation.* These effects apply to text as it appears onscreen for a new slide. Your text can appear one letter at a time, whole words at a time, or entire text elements can fly or crawl across the screen from any direction. Swivel effects make your presentation look very "high tech."

- *Event sounds.* You can choose to play sounds to accompany events that occur in your presentation—the transition to a new slide or the appearance of a line of text onscreen. For example, if you've chosen to have your slide title appear one letter at a time, the sound of a typewriter can accompany it.

 TIP Although it's tempting to add lots of multimedia effects to your show, be conservative in their application to avoid a circus-like atmosphere. Try to keep effects consistent throughout sections or topics within your presentation to maintain a sense of continuity.

Working with Slide Transitions

When you're ready to put your onscreen slideshow together, the first effects you need to apply are your slide transitions. You can apply one transition to an entire set of slides, or go through your presentation one slide at a time, choosing a particular transition for each one.

CAUTION

Try to avoid using too many different transition effects in one presentation. A consistent look throughout your presentation is best, as it keeps the delivery from distracting your audience from the message.

To apply a single transition to all your slides or to several slides within your presentation, follow these steps:

1. With your presentation file open, switch to Slide Sorter view, by choosing View, Slide Sorter.

2. To select all your slides (so the transition you choose applies to all of them), press Ctrl+A.

3. To select a block of contiguous slides, draw a rectangle around them by dragging your mouse, as shown in Figure 18.1.

FIG. 18.1
All the slides encompassed in your rectangular selection box are selected.

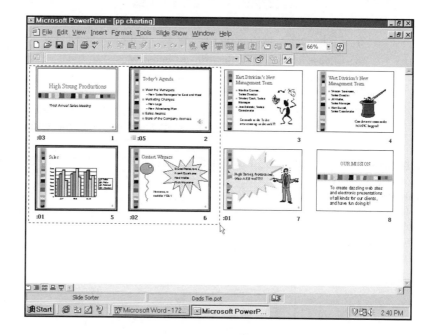

 TIP If you want to select a group of noncontiguous slides, click the first slide you want, and then press the Shift key. With the Shift key held down, click each of the other slides you want to select. When you've gathered all the desired slides, release the Shift key.

4. Click the Slide transition button to open the Slide Transition dialog box, as shown in Figure 18.2.

5. Click the Effect drop-down list (under the picture of the Bull terrier), and choose a transition. The dog turns into a key to show you how the transition will occur for the transition effect you selected.

6. Click a speed setting (Slow, Medium, or Fast).

TIP Setting some transitions to Fast makes them happen so quickly that it's as though there wasn't any transition effect at all! Set them to Medium or Slow for the most interesting animation effect.

FIG. 18.2

Choose a transition and set its speed. You can also choose a sound to go with the transition.

7. Click the Advance option you'd prefer for the selected slides.

8. Choose a Sound from the drop-down list. Most transitions do not have a sound associated with them by default, but you can choose from one of the 17 sounds listed in this box.

9. Click Apply. The dialog box closes, and you see transition icons under each of your selected slides, indicating a transition has been set for those slides (see Figure 18.3).

FIG. 18.3

Look for icons beneath your slides to indicate transitions, builds, and timings set.

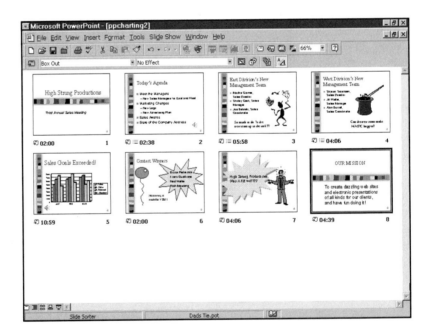

NOTE A faster, yet less dynamic method of assigning transitions to one or more slides is to click the Slide Transition Effects button on the Slide Sorter toolbar. You can choose a transition style, but you can't set the speed or choose an associated sound.

TIP Save time in applying transitions by applying one transition to all your slides. Then select individual slides and change their transition settings. This helps keep the whole presentation consistent, but with some variety as well.

Building Bulleted Text

Building your bullet text one bulleted line at a time puts you in control over what your audience sees and when they see it. If a list of five items appears when the slide opens, the audience will—regardless of your only discussing the first bullet point—be reading the second, third, fourth, and fifth items, and may not hear what you're saying about the first one.

 When your bullet points appear one at a time, however, the audience can read only the one that you're discussing as well as those that preceded it in the list. To choose a build effect for your slide's text, click the Text Preset Animation tool on the Slide Sorter toolbar. Choose an animation effect for the selected slide's text from the list.

A further control is the dimming of previous points. This keeps the audience from dwelling on a point you've already discussed.

To apply builds and set dimming options for your bullet text, follow these steps:

1. Go to a slide containing bulleted text and make sure you're in Slide view.
2. Click the bulleted text object. Click the object's border to select the entire object.
3. Choose, Slide Show, Custom Animation.
4. Click the Effects tab (see Figure 18.4).

FIG. 18.4
Customize the manner in which the selected text object appears onscreen. You can apply these setting to titles or bullet text.

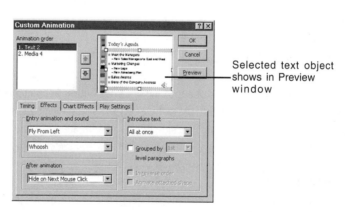

Selected text object shows in Preview window

5. Choose your Entry Animation and Sound settings by clicking the drop-down lists for each effect.
6. In the After Animation list, click the effect to be applied as soon as the text appears onscreen.

Part
IV

Ch
18

TIP Click the Preview button to see your effects applied to the sample slide in the Custom Animation dialog box.

7. Click OK to close the dialog box and apply your settings.

NOTE The Introduce Text section of the Custom Animation dialog box offers you the ability to have your text appear one letter or word at a time, or all at once. You can also choose to group text by rank within the bullets and sub-bulleted paragraphs, or to have the bulleted text appear In Reverse Order (last bullet first).

Assigning Animation and Sound to Slide Elements

Although you don't want to animate each and every slide element, creating a little movement on each slide—perhaps animating the titles of every slide—can add visual interest to your presentation and maintain audience attention.

Your animations can be accompanied by sound, and many are, by default. Of course, for sound to work, the computer you use for your presentation must have sound capability. If you'll be running your show in a large room, you'll want to amplify your computer's speakers by placing a microphone near them or by attaching your sound device to larger, more powerful speakers.

To add animation and sound to your slide elements, follow these steps:

1. In Slide view, click once to select the element you want to animate. It can be text, a chart, or a graphic.

2. Click the Animation Effects button on the Formatting toolbar. The Animation Effects floating toolbar appears, as shown in Figure 18.5.

3. Using the toolbar's buttons, choose to animate Title text or Slide text (or both) and select your animation effects.

4. After assigning an effect, the Animation Order button becomes available. If you have more than one animated item on the slide, you can choose the order of their animation.

5. Click the next item on the current slide to be animated, or proceed to another slide. The floating Animation Effects toolbar remains onscreen.

Working with Sound

Sounds are associated with various animation effects. For example, if you choose the Camera Effect for text or a graphic object on your slide, the animation is accompanied by the sound of a camera's shutter opening and closing. You can mix and match these sounds, or apply different sounds to your animation effects, perhaps using a laser sound for an object that is animated with the Flash Once effect.

Other sounds, that aren't related to animation, can be added to your slides, in the form of em-bedded icons that link the slide to a sound file stored on your computer. These sounds can be played during your show by double-clicking the icon or you can set the sounds to be triggered by the opening of the slide during the show.

FIG. 18.5

After applying your animation effects, click the Slide Show View button to see a preview of that slide and its effects. Press Esc to end the show after that slide.

Choose to animate Title text or Slide text

Animation order

Second row applies to text only

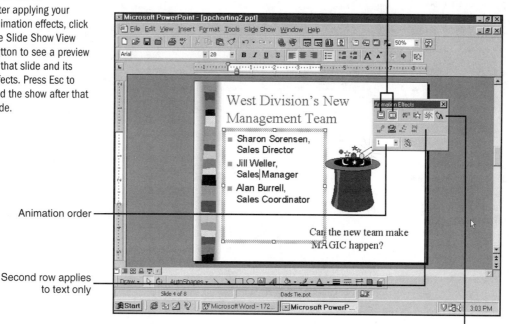

Top row of tools apply to text or graphics

To add a sound file icon to your slide, follow these steps:

1. With the slide to which you want to add a sound open in Slide view, choose Insert, Movies and Sounds, Sound from File.

 TIP You can also choose Sound from Gallery to open the Microsoft Clip Gallery. Click the Sounds tab.

2. Locate and select your sound file (normally a file with a .wav extension) in the Insert Sound dialog box (see Figure 18.6).

 TIP If you insert a sound that is stored on an external storage device, that device must be attached to your computer whenever you want to play the sound.

3. Click OK to insert the sound into your slide, as shown in Figure 18.7.

You can move or resize the icon that appears on your slide. If you'll be activating it with a double-click during your show, it's best to move it to a bottom corner and make it relatively small so the audience isn't distracted by the icon or your pointing to it.

Part
IV

Ch
18

FIG. 18.6

PowerPoint looks in the Office folder by default, but you can select any sound file stored on your local drive, a network drive, or a disk.

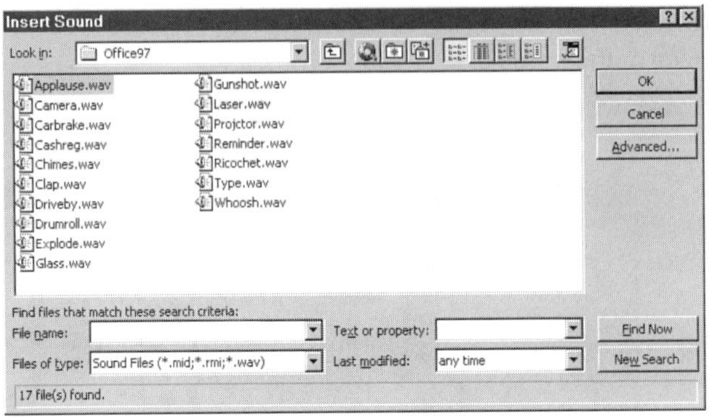

FIG. 18.7

Make your sound icon small and place it out of the way so it won't interfere visually with your other slide elements.

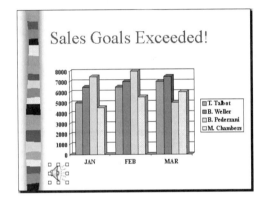

Customizing Sound Timing

Sounds can be set up to occur at specific times and to play continuously or only until another specified event occurs. Although sounds that are associated with text animation occur only while the animation is playing, sounds you add to the slide can be customized in many ways.

You can control your timings using the following steps:

1. Select the sound icon on your slide, and choose Slide Show, Custom Animation.

2. Click the Play Settings tab (see Figure 18.8).

3. Click the Play Using Animation Order option to make available the remaining options in the dialog box.

4. Choose the effect that the sound's playing will have on your slideshow, selecting either Pause Slide Show or Continue Slide Show.

5. If you choose to Continue Slide Show, the Stop Playing option becomes available, and you can choose when the sound will stop.

6. Click OK to close the dialog box and apply your settings.

FIG. 18.8
Control the beginning,
ending, and duration of
your sound as it plays
during the slideshow.

 Click the Hide While Not Playing check box to keep your sound icon out of view. If you'll be double-clicking the icon to trigger it, however, you don't want to turn this option on.

N O T E While the Custom Animation dialog box is open, you can click the More Options button to set your sound to Loop Until Stopped. If your sound is from an audio CD or you've inserted a movie clip, you can also set the options for these objects.

Applying Sounds from the CD

The CD that accompanies this book contains several sounds that will be great additions to any presentation. To preview these sounds and/or copy them to your local drive for later use in a slideshow, follow these steps:

1. Insert the companion CD into your CD-ROM drive.

2. Open the Windows Explorer.

3. Click once on the CD-ROM icon on the left side of your screen.

4. If necessary, click the plus sign next to the CD-ROM drive icon to display the CD's folders.

5. Click the Code folder's plus sign, and click once on the \Sounds folder to display its contents on the right side of the screen.

6. To preview the sounds, double-click them. This opens your computer's audio software, and the sound file plays.

7. To copy the sound file(s) to your local drive (or a network drive), select the files you want to copy.

8. Right-click the selected file(s), and choose Copy from the shortcut menu.

9. Right-click the local or network drive icon to which you want to copy the files. Choose Paste from the shortcut menu.

Part
IV

Ch
18

ON THE WEB

http://www.wavplace.com   Want more sounds? This site contains hundreds of sound files from movies, television, cartoons, and a variety of other sources. You can download all the sounds for free, and most are in .wav format, stored as single files. Follow your Web browser's instructions for copying the files to your computer.

Automating the Slideshow

Your slideshow will easily run with you at the computer, clicking the mouse or pressing the Enter key to move from slide to slide. You can even walk around during the show, wandering at least as far from the computer as your mouse cord is long, clicking the left mouse button in your hand to move to the next slide.

But what if you don't want to be tethered to the computer or have to sit by it during the whole show? What if you're not the person delivering the show, and the person who will be isn't famil-iar with PowerPoint? Automating the slideshow removes the human element from the immedi-ate running of the show, freeing you (or any other presenter) from a seat by the computer during the show.

To automate your slideshow, you must set timings for each slide and its elements. You can set your slide timings manually, or have PowerPoint record them as you rehearse the show.

To set your slide timings manually, follow these steps:

1. In Slide Sorter view, click once on the slide for which you want to set timing.

T I P   If you want to set timings for all the slides at once, press Ctrl+A to select all your slides.

2. Choose Slide Show, Slide Transition.
3. In the Advance section of the Slide Transition dialog box (see Figure 18.9), click the Automatically After option.

FIG. 18.9
Allow time for delays, and express the number of minutes as seconds, such as 240 seconds for four minutes.

4. Enter the amount of time the slide should remain onscreen before advancing to the next slide.

5. Click <u>A</u>pply to close the dialog box and apply your timing to the selected slides.

6. For PowerPoint to adhere to these settings, you must choose Sli<u>d</u>e Show, <u>S</u>et Up Show.

7. Click the <u>U</u>sing Timings, If Present option in the Advance Slides section of the Set Up Show dialog box.

> **N O T E** If your show will be running at a trade show or seminar and you want it to run over and over without any human intervention, choose Slide Show, Set Up Show, and click the <u>L</u>oop Continuously Until Esc option. You need only start the show, and then let it run until you're ready to stop it by pressing the Esc key.

Rehearsing Timings

If you'd like to set different timings for each slide based on the actual content of the slide and what you (or some other presenter) will say while the slide is onscreen, you should rehearse the show and have PowerPoint record your timings. The total time the slide is onscreen as well as the internal timings for each element on the slide are recorded.

To rehearse your timings, follow these steps:

1. With your presentation in Slide Sorter view, click the first slide in the presentation, and choose Sli<u>d</u>e Show, <u>R</u>ehearse Timings.

2. Your slideshow begins, displaying a small timer in the lower-left corner of the slide, as shown in Figure 18.10.

FIG. 18.10
Allow time for questions or other disruptions during the real show when you're doing your rehearsal.

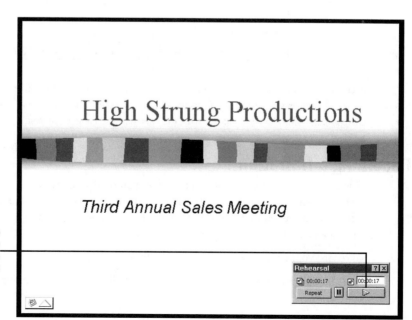

Click here to go to the next slide or the next element in the active slide

High Strung Productions

Third Annual Sales Meeting

3. Rehearse your speech for the slide that appears onscreen. Click the mouse to bring in any animated text or graphics, pausing long enough to speak about these items as well.

4. When you're ready to move to the next slide, click the mouse again. The time that the previous slide was onscreen, as well as the timings for the slide's elements, are now recorded.

5. Repeat steps 3 and 4 until your show is completed.

6. After the last slide, click Yes to record and use the timings you set.

7. Click Yes again to view the timings in Slide Sorter view, as shown in Figure 18.11.

FIG. 18.11
Total time for each slide set through rehearsal or manual settings appear in Slide Sorter view.

Total time for each slide recorded

Slides with text builds set

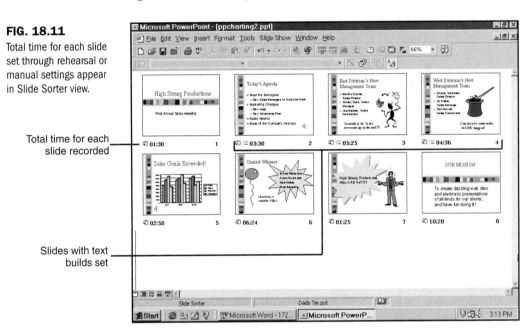

N O T E If you want to adjust the timing of an individual slide, choose Slide Show, Slide Transition and enter a new timing (in seconds) for the selected slide. If you want, however, to set new timings for the slide elements within a slide, you must repeat the entire rehearsal.

Recording a Narration

Whether you're shy about public speaking or you want your show to be run without the need for human intervention, you can record a narration to go with your slideshow. Your spoken comments are timed to match the running of your show so what you're saying matches what's onscreen at the time.

To record your slideshow narration, follow these steps:

1. In Slide Sorter view, click once on the first slide in the presentation to select it.

2. Choose Sli<u>d</u>e Show, Record <u>N</u>arration. The Record Narration dialog box opens, as shown in Figure 18.12.

FIG. 18.12

Click the <u>S</u>ettings button to adjust sound quality.

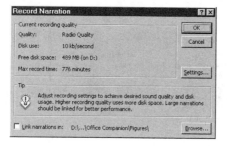

 TIP If you want your narration to be saved as a separate file, linked to the presentation, click the <u>L</u>ink Narration In option. Click the <u>B</u>rowse button to choose the folder in which the linked sound file will be saved.

3. Assuming the Current Recording Quality settings are adequate for your needs, click OK to begin the narration.

4. As soon as your slideshow begins onscreen, begin speaking. Continue to speak, using the mouse or Enter key to move between slides and slide elements.

5. At the end of the show or as soon as you press Esc, the narration process ends. Click <u>Y</u>es to save the new timings set through your narration.

6. Click <u>Y</u>es to have your new slide timings displayed in Slide Sorter view.

Your narration is now saved as part of the presentation file. Your speech is in synch with the slides and slide elements that were onscreen as your voice was recorded. As needed, your narration can be re-recorded.

Because your narration supersedes any sounds that have been added to your slides—sound objects or sounds that are associated with your animations—you may decide to delete the narration so your sounds can be used on a looping slideshow or with a live presenter.

To delete your narration, switch to Slide view, and click once on the small speaker icon (as shown in Figure 18.13) in the lower-right corner of your slides. Be careful not to confuse this icon with any sound objects you may have added to your slides. With the narration icon selected, press the Delete key. You can delete these icons from one or more of your slides.

FIG. 18.13

Narration sound icons can be seen in both Slide view and Slide Sorter view, but can only be deleted in Slide view.

Fast and Flexible Database Management with Access

Building a Database

In this chapter

Creating a New Database

Let's start off on the right foot by explaining the difference between an Excel database and an Access database. The definition of a database in Excel is closer to the true definition of the word—a table of rows and columns, each row containing a record, each column containing a field. Access has a more complex concept of what a database is, defining it as a collection of one or more tables, plus the queries, forms, and reports you create to view and use that data. This more complex view of what a database is and how data can be used makes Access a much more powerful and flexible database tool.

The core of an Access database, however, is still the table. The data table is set up similarly to an Excel list database—a set of columns, each with a heading that is also a field name, followed by a series of rows, each one containing a record in the database. After this table is built and filled with data, queries, forms, and reports can be created from it.

Access is a relational database, meaning that its databases can include several tables, and that these individual tables can be connected to each other for the purposes of elaborate queries and reports. Your tables (if you have more than one) can live independently, and never connect to any other tables, but the power to connect them through reports and queries is there.

When creating your Access database, you have two ways to start:

- *The Database Wizard.* This approach takes away all the guesswork, and builds not just your table, but the related forms (for data entry), queries (to search for specific records), and reports (to document your database). You can tweak the database to make it your own, or accept the defaults for everything.

- *Building a blank database.* This requires more work than the wizard, but gives you more freedom. If you have very specific needs that aren't covered by the wizard's offerings, you should take this approach instead. No forms, queries, or reports are made for you—you must create them all yourself, although there are other wizards available to assist you in creating these specific elements. Depending on your needs, the freedom to create just what you need may be worth the extra effort.

Using the Database Wizard

The Database Wizard gives you several databases from which to choose—they're already set up, including tables, forms, queries, and reports. All you need to do is make some minor changes so the database matches your needs, and you're ready to start entering data.

To start with the Database Wizard, follow these steps:

1. Start Access from the Programs list in the Start menu.
2. The Microsoft Access dialog box opens (see Figure 19.1). Click the Database Wizard option.
3. Click OK. The New dialog box opens, with the Databases tab in front, as shown in Figure 19.2.

FIG. 19.1

Choose the Database Wizard to take advantage of tables, forms, queries, and reports already set up for you.

FIG. 19.2

Click each icon in the New dialog box, and see either a house (for home-user databases) or a bar chart and forms for a business database.

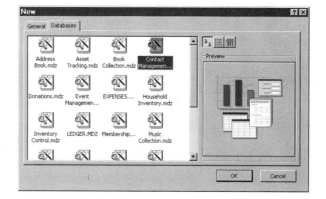

4. The Databases tab offers 22 different databases. Double-click the one that seems most appropriate for your needs.

5. The File New Database dialog box opens (see Figure 19.3), in which you must enter a File Name for your database. You can accept the default name (the database you selected, with a 1 at the end of the name), or type your own name for the database.

FIG. 19.3

When naming a database, remember that the database is not simply one table of records, but multiple tables, reports, and queries. Choose a name that expresses the purpose and use of the database, not just the name of the main table.

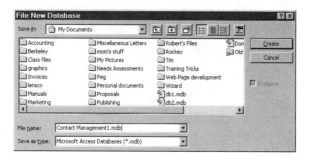

6. Choose a location to save your database from the Save In drop-down list.

7. Click Create.

Customizing Your Wizard Database   The wizard continues, allowing you to make any minor changes to the structure and appearance of your database. To finish building your database with the Database Wizard, continue with these steps:

1. The first window of the Database Wizard opens (see Figure 19.4), describing the purpose of the database you've chosen. Click Next to proceed.

FIG. 19.4

This is your last chance to Cancel if you've selected the wrong type of database. Read the description, and if it matches your needs, proceed.

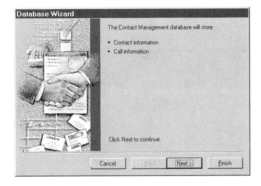

2. In the second wizard window, you'll see a list of tables in your database on the left, and a list of the fields within each table on the right. Select a table and then review its fields, clicking to add or remove check marks (see Figure 19.5). After reviewing each table, click Next.

FIG. 19.5

Scroll through the fields for each table, making sure that only the fields you want to use are checked.

The Database Wizard built three tables into this particular database.

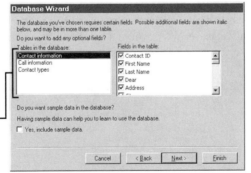

    If you're new to Access databases, you may want to click the Yes, Include Sample Data option to have your database filled with some sample data. The sample data can help you understand the nature of your fields and how your forms, queries, and reports work. You can delete the sample data when you're ready to enter your own records.

TIP For more help in seeing the potential uses and applications of Access, check out the Northwind database that is installed as a sample with Access. You'll find it in the Samples folder, a subfolder of Access in your Microsoft Office folder.

3. Choose a style for your data entry forms, selecting one of several background images (see Figure 19.6). Click Next.

FIG. 19.6
Although you may later choose to enter your records in Table view, you must choose a background for your data entry forms.

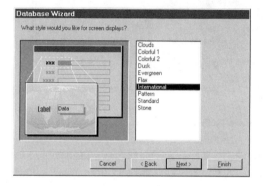

4. Choose a style for your printed reports, ranging from Corporate to Casual (see Figure 19.7). After selecting one, click Next.

FIG. 19.7
Each style uses different fonts and graphic elements. Check out the preview before making a selection.

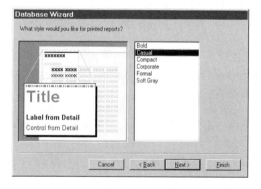

5. Type a title for your printed reports. Click Next.

6. The Database Wizard is nearly complete. Click Finish to send it off to build your database.

A variety of progress bars appear and disappear as Access builds your database. You'll see table icons appear in the Tables tab of the database dialog box on your screen as these processes continue. When the process is complete (it can take several minutes), the Main Switchboard window opens.

Using the Main Switchboard   The Main Switchboard is an interface created by the wizard to simplify your access to the components of your database. Figure 19.8 shows the Main Switchboard for a Contact Management database.

FIG. 19.8
Use the Main Switchboard as a starting point for entering your data or previewing the reports that the Database Wizard created for you.

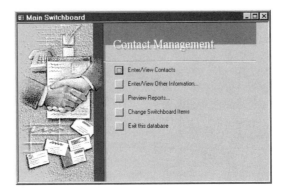

The options that appear on the Main Switchboard for your database may vary, depending on the type of database that you chose when you started the wizard. Regardless of your type of database, you'll find the following core items on your Main Switchboard:

- *Enter/View Records.* Choose this option to enter your data or look through your sample data, if you chose to have it added to your table. When you choose to enter records, the table opens in Datasheet view.

- *Enter/View Other Information.* This normally opens the second level of the switchboard, wherein you can look at the forms that were created for you by the wizard. The choices in this option vary greatly between database types.

- *Preview Reports.* Because the wizard creates queries and reports for you, these are already in the database.

- *Change Switchboard Items.* If you'd like to add or delete items from the list of switchboard actions, you can click this button and follow the instructions that appear for your type of database.

- *Exit the Database.* If you're not ready to work with the database you've just created, click this button.

If you don't want to use the Main Switchboard but do want to begin working with the database that's been created, press Ctrl+F4 to close the switchboard. Restore your database—it's minimized in the lower-left corner of the Access window. After the database window is open, you can begin entering data, using your forms, and previewing your queries and reports as they've been created by the Database Wizard.

Building a Blank Database

To start a new database from scratch (without the wizard), you first must build a table that will contain your data. Because Access is a relational database, you can have several different tables in one database, and they can be connected via common fields when you're ready to query the database or create reports.

The table (your first or only in this database) is the foundation of your database. To create it, follow these steps:

1. Choose <u>F</u>ile, <u>N</u>ew Database, or click the New Database button on the toolbar.
2. In the New dialog box (see Figure 19.9), click the General tab and choose Blank Database.

FIG. 19.9
Start with a blank slate by choosing Blank Database.

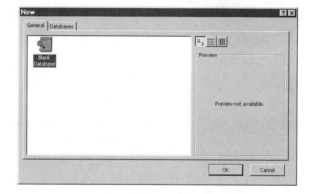

3. You must immediately save your database. In the Save <u>I</u>n drop-down list, choose a drive and folder for your database.
4. Type a File <u>N</u>ame for your database file.

T I P Don't type any extension on your filename—Access adds the .mdb extension for you.

5. Click <u>C</u>reate.

An empty database window appears, as shown in Figure 19.10. Click the Tables tab and click <u>N</u>ew to begin building a new table.

FIG. 19.10
You must build a table before you can create your other database components.

Part
V

Ch

19

To build your table, follow these steps:

1. The New table dialog box opens, from which you can select your approach to building the table. Click Design View (see Figure 19.11), and then click OK.

FIG. 19.11

Start with Design view so you can create field names and specifications for each field before you begin your data entry.

 T I P   In Design view, you can create your field names, choose the length of each field, and decide what type of data will go into it.

2. Create your field names and choose a data type for each field (see the following bulleted list for more information). Typing a Description is optional. Figure 19.12 shows the list of data types.

FIG. 19.12

Most fields, including phone numbers, are considered text fields.

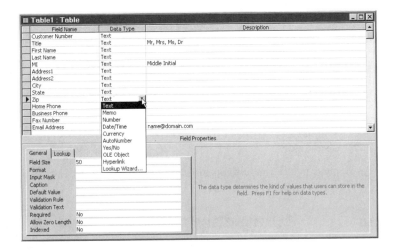

 T I P   Choose short names for your fields—this keeps your Data views from being crowded and difficult to read.

- *Text*. Allows use of up to 255 alphanumeric characters in a text field. In addition to "pure" text (words), text fields can also be used for numbers that will contain non-numeric content such as dashes, slashes, or other symbols.

- *Memo*. Type up to 65,535 alphanumeric characters in a memo field. Memo fields cannot be sorted.

- *Number.* Any numeric text, such as a quantity. For numeric content such as phone numbers and social security numbers, you'll want to use an Input Mask to set the layout for numbers entered into the field.

- *Date/Time.* Enter up to eight characters. Choose from up to seven different date and time Formats, such as short, medium, and long.

- *Currency.* Enter round numbers, up to 15 digits to the left of the decimal, and up to 6 digits to the right.

- *AutoNumber.* Use for sequential or random numbering. Access adds the number for you as each record is entered.

- *Yes/No.* Use for Yes/No, True/False, or On/Off.

- *OLE Object.* Use this field type for linked content from other applications or graphics.

- *Hyperlink.* Enter a Web address or path to a file on a local or network drive.

- *Lookup Wizard.* This data type is used primarily by developers who are creating an application in Access. Use it to set up a drop-down list of options for a data entry person to choose from when filling in this field.

3. After you've created all your fields, choose one to be your primary key. Click the field that will be your primary key, and choose Edit, Primary Key. You can also click the Primary Key button on the toolbar. A small key icon will appear next to that field, as shown in Figure 19.13.

N O T E The primary key is a unique field, required in every Access table, and used to link related tables in a single Access database. For example, in our Employee table, the Employee number is the primary key. In a second table, perhaps a table storing employee insurance data, the Employee number could be used as a field that links the two tables for reports and queries that make use fields from both tables.

Part
V

Ch
19

FIG. 19.13
Because it's unique, your primary key will be used to connect your table to other tables in the database.

Primary key ——

T I P If you don't have any unique fields in your database (such as Customer Number), create a Record Number field. This field can be set up in AutoNumber format, so Access will assign a consecutive (or random, if you prefer) number to each record.

4. Go through each of your fields and click the General tab for each one (see Figure 19.14). Check and set up your field lengths, add Input Masks and validation rules.

N O T E An *Input Mask* is a field template that controls how the content of the field is entered and stored. For example, if your field will contain a phone number, you can specify that the numbers that are entered into the field be placed as *(nnn) nnn-nnnn* and that the dashes and parentheses be stored with the record. These symbols are not entered by the person entering the record, but are added by Access, as part of the Input Mask.

FIG. 19.14

The General tab contains the tools for controlling the amount and type of data that can be entered into your fields.

Phone number Input Mask

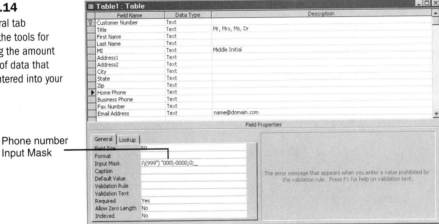

5. Choose <u>F</u>ile, <u>S</u>ave or click the Save button on the toolbar.

6. Close the table by choosing <u>F</u>ile, <u>C</u>lose or pressing Ctrl+F4.

Now that your table's fields are set up, you can begin entering your records.

Entering Your Database Records

A set of fields in a table isn't much good to anyone without the data they were built to contain. You can enter records from a variety of sources—everything from handwritten slips of paper to printed lists. You don't need to enter them in alphabetical or numerical order, and if you have missing fields in a few of the records, that's fine. You can always go back and enter the missing bits later.

Whether you created your database with a wizard or from scratch, the data entry process is the same. To enter your records, follow these steps:

1. If it's not already open, open your database by choosing <u>F</u>ile, <u>O</u>pen Database.

N O T E If you're opening a database created with an older version of Access, you may be prompted to convert the database to the new version. Don't let this concern you—each new release of the product is designed a little differently, and files created with older versions must be updated to work properly in the new release. Your tables, reports, and queries should be unaffected by the conversion process.

2. Choose your database file from the Open dialog box, as shown in Figure 19.15.

FIG. 19.15
Look for your database filename. The table you're opening is just a part of this file.

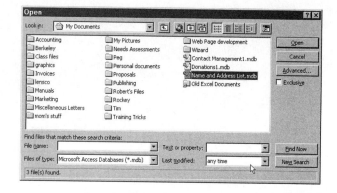

3. In the Database dialog box, select the Tables tab, and then click your table icon, as shown in Figure 19.16.

FIG. 19.16
Your database can have many tables. Double-click the desired table icon to open it quickly.

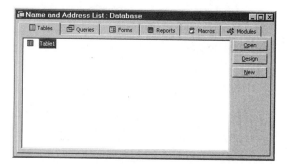

4. Click the Open button.

Your table opens in Datasheet view, as shown in Figure 19.17.

TIP You can begin entering your records in this view, or if you created your database with a wizard, switch to Form view. If you don't have any forms created, you can build them as needed.

Keyboard Shortcuts for Entering Records in Datasheet View

While in Datasheet view, you can use the keyboard shortcuts in Table 19.1 to speed up your data entry process. If you're familiar with Excel, you'll have seen some of these before.

FIG. 19.17

Datasheet view is simple to use for entry and editing of records, and is easily navigated with keyboard shortcuts.

Begin typing first record here

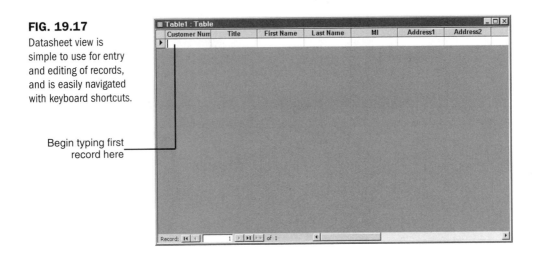

Table 19.1   Datasheet View Keyboard Shortcuts

Keyboard Shortcut	Result
Tab	Moves to the next field in the database, or the next record if you're in the last field of the current record
Shift+Tab	Moves backward one field, or to the previous record if you're in the first field of the current record
Ctrl+Enter	Creates the next blank record
Up-arrow key	Moves up to the previous record in the current field
Down-arrow key	Moves down to the next record in the current field
Right-arrow key	Moves to the next field in the record
Left-arrow key	Moves to the previous field in the record
Ctrl+Up arrow	Moves to the first record in the current field
Ctrl+Down arrow	Moves to last record in the current field

You can also navigate your records as you build them by using the record control buttons at the bottom of your datasheet. Figure 19.18 labels each of them.

Creating Forms for Data Entry

If you'd rather not work in Datasheet view or if you have people on your staff who aren't familiar with spreadsheet-like tables, you may want to create a data entry form.

FIG. 19.18

Use either the keyboard or the mouse to move from field to field, record to record, in your growing table of data.

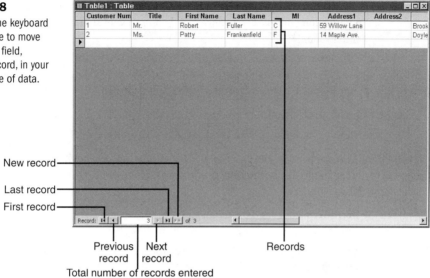

Customer Num	Title	First Name	Last Name	MI	Address1	Address2
1	Mr.	Robert	Fuller	C	59 Willow Lane	Brook
2	Ms.	Patty	Frankenfield	F	14 Maple Ave.	Doyle

New record

Last record

First record

Record: 3 of 3

Previous record   Next record

Records

Total number of records entered

T I P If you used the Database Wizard to create your database, you have a form created for each of your tables. You can have as many forms as you'd like, however, so you can use the following instructions to make forms of your own design.

Although the process of building the form is somewhat time-consuming, you'll only have to do it once for each table in your database. From that point on you'll have a user-friendly window through which to enter your records.

To create a form for your table, follow these steps:

1. Open your database, click the Forms tab, and click the New button. The New Form dialog box appears as shown in Figure 19.19.

Part

V

Ch

19

FIG. 19.19

Create a data entry form for your table, based on the fields you created in Design view.

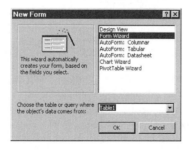

2. Choose the method you'll use to create the form. For a new user, and for most Access databases, ignore all but the following choices:

- *Form Wizard.* The wizard creates the form for you, based on your fields. Little or no effort on your part is required, and you can choose from fancy backgrounds and layouts.

- *AutoForms: Columnar, Tabular, and Datasheet.* Click each one of these once to see a description of the overall layout each one offers. The forms you build with AutoForms are very straightforward, no frills forms.

3. Click the blank drop-down list to choose the table on which your form will be based.

4. Click OK to begin building your form with the tool you selected.

If you chose an AutoForms layout, your new form appears onscreen with the default background, ready for you to use in entering your records. If you chose the Forms Wizard, you have a few choices to make:

1. In the Form Wizard dialog box, make sure the correct table is selected as the basis for your form by clicking the Tables/Queries drop-down list.

2. Select the fields for your form from the Available Fields list on the left (see Figure 19.20). Click the field and then click the single right-pointing arrow.

FIG. 19.20

Select only those fields that will be used in the database table. Having unused fields on your form risks accidental entries into those fields.

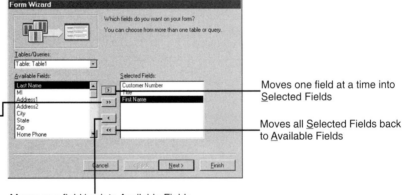

Moves all fields to Selected Fields

Moves one field at a time into Selected Fields

Moves all Selected Fields back to Available Fields

Moves one field back to Available Fields

TROUBLESHOOTING

Why wouldn't I want all my fields on the form?   Many users create different forms for different data entry personnel. If you're building an employee database, it may be that the person who's entering names and addresses isn't the same person who enters confidential salary and insurance information. Create one form for each user, omitting the unused fields when designing each form.

If you want all your fields, click the button with two right-pointing arrows. This moves all the Available Fields into the Selected Fields box.

TIP You can also pick individual fields from the Selected Fields box and remove them by clicking the left-pointing arrow. The field is put back in the Available Fields box.

3. After selecting your fields and adding them to the list of Selected Fields on the right, click Next.

4. Choose a layout for your form (see Figure 19.21), and click Next.

FIG. 19.21
Choose from four basic layouts for your fields onscreen. Click each one once to see a preview before making your final selection.

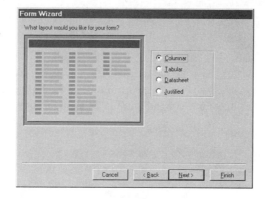

5. Select a style for your form (see Figure 19.22). The image you select will be behind your fields on the form. Click Next to proceed.

FIG. 19.22
Preview each style, choosing one that won't be too visually distracting.

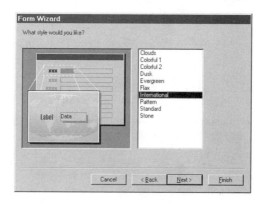

6. Type a title for your form. This is normally the name of your database or a name that indicates the type of information being entered with the form (see Figure 19.23).

TIP Before clicking Finish, you can click the Modify this Form's Design option if you want to open the form in an edit mode that allows you to move fields around on the form.

7. Click Finish.

FIG. 19.23

If you'll be designing more than one form for this table, choose names that make it simple to distinguish the forms.

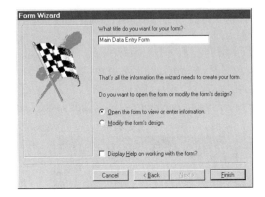

As soon as you end the wizard, your form appears onscreen, awaiting your data entry. If you're ready to do so, start entering your records. Figure 19.24 shows a completed form, with data entry already started.

FIG. 19.24

Press Tab to move through your fields as you enter your records.

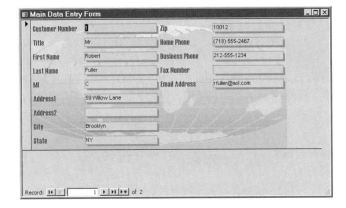

If you don't want to do any data entry now, close the form by choosing File, Close or by pressing Ctrl+F4.

ON THE WEB

http://www.microsoft.com/support   Check the Microsoft Web site and follow the Technical Support link. You can select Access as your topic, and enter any question you want. The search engine consults their online help files and brings back a relevant article for you. ●

CHAPTER 20

Editing and Reviewing Your Data

In this chapter

Sorting Records

After you've entered records into your table, you'll want to look through them, looking for errors, duplications, missing data in fields, and so forth. Also, because most people don't enter their records in any kind of order (and there's no reason to do so), most people want to shuffle their entered records so they can view their table as an alphabetical or numerical list.

Putting your list in order is called *sorting*. You can sort your data by any field in the table. You can also sort by more than one field, creating a categorized list.

Sorting by One Field

Most sorting is done on one field, to create an alphabetical list of people or objects, or numerically, to put a list in order by customer number or zip code (for a bulk mailing).

To sort your table by one field, follow these steps:

1. Open your table and click in any cell in the column (field) by which you want to sort (see Figure 20.1).

FIG. 20.1

The location of your mouse when the Sort command is issued determines the field on which your data is sorted.

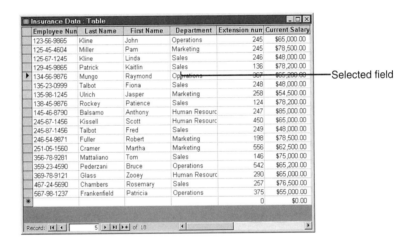

Selected field

2. Choose <u>R</u>ecords, <u>S</u>ort, and then select <u>A</u>scending or Des<u>c</u>ending from the submenu. You can also click the Sort Ascending or Sort Descending buttons on the toolbar.

3. Repeat steps 1 and 2 for as many sorts as you want to perform in this session.

Figure 20.2 shows the employee data table in Last Name order.

If you re-sort your table, each successive sort cancels out the one before it.

FIG. 20.2

This sort would be improved by a second-level sort by First Name, so duplicate last name records would be in alphabetical order. If this additional sort had been done, Fiona Talbot would precede Fred Talbot.

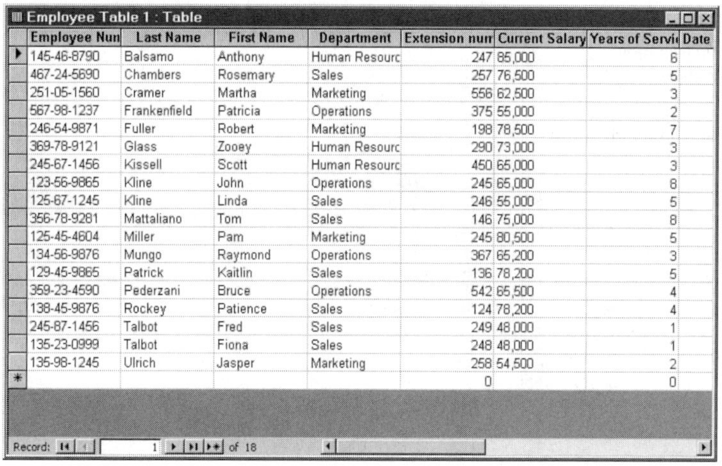

Employee Num	Last Name	First Name	Department	Extension num	Current Salary	Years of Servi	Date
145-46-8790	Balsamo	Anthony	Human Resourc	247	85,000	6	
467-24-5690	Chambers	Rosemary	Sales	257	76,500	5	
251-05-1560	Cramer	Martha	Marketing	556	62,500	3	
567-98-1237	Frankenfield	Patricia	Operations	375	55,000	2	
246-54-9871	Fuller	Robert	Marketing	198	78,500	7	
369-78-9121	Glass	Zooey	Human Resourc	290	73,000	3	
245-67-1456	Kissell	Scott	Human Resourc	450	65,000	3	
123-56-9865	Kline	John	Operations	245	65,000	8	
125-67-1245	Kline	Linda	Sales	246	55,000	5	
356-78-9281	Mattaliano	Tom	Sales	146	75,000	8	
125-45-4604	Miller	Pam	Marketing	245	80,500	5	
134-56-9876	Mungo	Raymond	Operations	367	65,200	3	
129-45-9865	Patrick	Kaitlin	Sales	136	78,200	5	
359-23-4590	Pederzani	Bruce	Operations	542	65,500	4	
138-45-9876	Rockey	Patience	Sales	124	78,200	4	
245-87-1456	Talbot	Fred	Sales	249	48,000	1	
135-23-0999	Talbot	Fiona	Sales	248	48,000	1	
135-98-1245	Ulrich	Jasper	Marketing	258	54,500	2	
					0	0	

Record: 1 of 18

Sorting by Multiple Fields

Sorting by more than one field can improve a single-level sort, or create a categorized list from your table. Figure 20.3 shows the previously performed Last Name sort with a second-level sort by First Name.

FIG. 20.3

Now all the duplicate last names are in first name order, an essential step if this list is to be used as a phone extension directory.

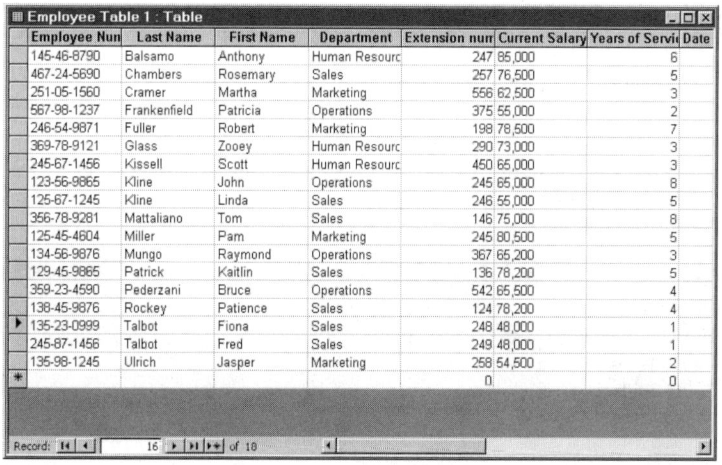

Employee Num	Last Name	First Name	Department	Extension num	Current Salary	Years of Servi	Date
145-46-8790	Balsamo	Anthony	Human Resourc	247	85,000	6	
467-24-5690	Chambers	Rosemary	Sales	257	76,500	5	
251-05-1560	Cramer	Martha	Marketing	556	62,500	3	
567-98-1237	Frankenfield	Patricia	Operations	375	55,000	2	
246-54-9871	Fuller	Robert	Marketing	198	78,500	7	
369-78-9121	Glass	Zooey	Human Resourc	290	73,000	3	
245-67-1456	Kissell	Scott	Human Resourc	450	65,000	3	
123-56-9865	Kline	John	Operations	245	65,000	8	
125-67-1245	Kline	Linda	Sales	246	55,000	5	
356-78-9281	Mattaliano	Tom	Sales	146	75,000	8	
125-45-4604	Miller	Pam	Marketing	245	80,500	5	
134-56-9876	Mungo	Raymond	Operations	367	65,200	3	
129-45-9865	Patrick	Kaitlin	Sales	136	78,200	5	
359-23-4590	Pederzani	Bruce	Operations	542	65,500	4	
138-45-9876	Rockey	Patience	Sales	124	78,200	4	
135-23-0999	Talbot	Fiona	Sales	248	48,000	1	
245-87-1456	Talbot	Fred	Sales	249	48,000	1	
135-98-1245	Ulrich	Jasper	Marketing	258	54,500	2	
					0	0	

Record: 16 of 18

Part V

Ch 20

Sorting by two or more fields can do more than improve a single-level sort, however. Sorting by several fields can break your data into categories, and within those categories place the records in order by yet another field. For example, Figure 20.4 shows an employee data table sorted by department, then by years of service, and then by last name.

FIG. 20.4

When sorting by more than one field, start with the field that has the most duplicate records.

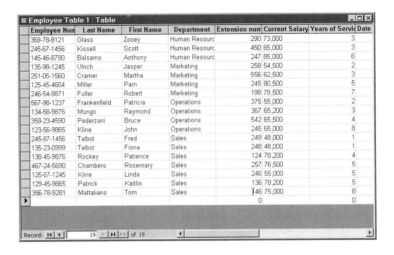

Employee Num	Last Name	First Name	Department	Extension num	Current Salary	Years of Servic	Date
369-78-9121	Glass	Zooey	Human Resourc	290	73,000	3	
245-67-1456	Kissell	Scott	Human Resourc	450	65,000	3	
145-46-8790	Balsamo	Anthony	Human Resourc	247	85,000	6	
135-98-1245	Ulrich	Jasper	Marketing	258	54,500	2	
251-05-1560	Cramer	Martha	Marketing	556	62,500	3	
125-45-4604	Miller	Pam	Marketing	245	80,500	5	
246-54-9871	Fuller	Robert	Marketing	198	78,500	7	
567-98-1237	Frankenfield	Patricia	Operations	375	55,000	2	
134-56-9876	Mungo	Raymond	Operations	367	65,200	3	
359-23-4590	Pederzani	Bruce	Operations	542	65,500	4	
123-56-9865	Kline	John	Operations	245	65,000	8	
245-87-1456	Talbot	Fred	Sales	249	48,000	1	
135-23-0999	Talbot	Fiona	Sales	248	48,000	1	
138-45-9876	Rockey	Patience	Sales	124	78,200	4	
467-24-5690	Chambers	Rosemary	Sales	257	76,500	5	
125-67-1245	Kline	Linda	Sales	246	55,000	5	
129-45-9865	Patrick	Kaitlin	Sales	136	78,200	5	
356-78-9281	Mattaliano	Tom	Sales	146	75,000	8	
				0		0	

Record: 19 of 19

Because the Department field has many duplicates, it's a natural first-level sort. Within each department, there are people with the same number of years of service. Last of all, sorting by Last Name makes it easy to find someone within the groupings created by the first two sorted fields.

 T I P When sorting by a single field, you needn't worry about the number of duplicates in the field on which you're sorting.

To perform a multiple-level sort, follow these steps:

1. With your table open, choose Records, Filter, Advanced Filter/Sort.

2. A filter window opens, as shown in Figure 20.5. Click in the first Field cell and click the arrow to see a list of your fields.

FIG. 20.5

You can ignore the Criteria and Or cells for each field when you're not filtering the data.

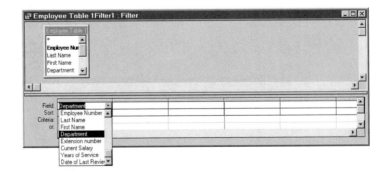

3. Select the first field on which you'll sort.

4. Click the Sort cell directly under the Field cell, and click the arrow to choose Ascending or Descending (see Figure 20.6).

FIG. 20.6

Choosing (Not Sorted) from this list defeats the purpose of the sort. This option is only used when filtering.

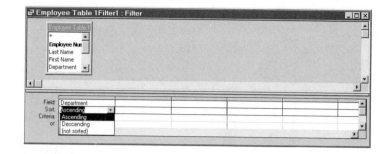

5. Click the next Field cell and choose your second-level sort field.

6. Choose a sort order for the second field.

7. Continue to move from left to right, selecting fields and a sort order for each one. Figure 20.7 shows the setup for a three-level sort.

FIG. 20.7

Before applying your sort, check to make sure you've selected the correct fields and sort orders for each.

Click inside the table window when you're ready to apply the sort.

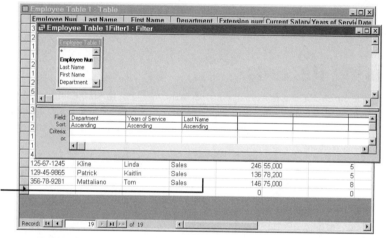

8. To apply this sort to your table, click back inside your table window, and choose Records, Apply Filter/Sort.

TIP If you'll be performing this multiple-level sort again in the future, save yourself the setup time by saving the sort. Choose File, Save As Query. Name the sort, and click OK. The sort will be available from your Table window's Query tab.

Figure 20.8 shows the employee table sorted by Department, then by Salary, and finally by Last Name.

TIP You can't sort by fields that are designated memo, hyperlink, or OLE object fields.

Part
V

Ch
20

FIG. 20.8

Your last sort field should be the one with the least amount of duplicates.

Employee Num	Last Name	First Name	Department	Extension num	Current Salary	Years of Servi	Date
369-78-9121	Glass	Zooey	Human Resourc	290	65,000	3	
245-67-1456	Kissell	Scott	Human Resourc	450	65,000	3	
145-46-8790	Balsamo	Anthony	Human Resourc	247	85,000	6	
135-98-1245	Ulrich	Jasper	Marketing	258	54,500	2	
251-05-1560	Cramer	Martha	Marketing	556	62,500	3	
246-54-9871	Fuller	Robert	Marketing	198	78,500	7	
125-45-4604	Miller	Pam	Marketing	245	78,500	5	
567-98-1237	Frankenfield	Patricia	Operations	375	55,000	2	
123-56-9865	Kline	John	Operations	245	65,000	8	
134-56-9876	Mungo	Raymond	Operations	367	65,200	3	
359-23-4590	Pederzani	Bruce	Operations	542	65,500	4	
245-87-1456	Talbot	Fred	Sales	249	48,000	1	
135-23-0999	Talbot	Fiona	Sales	248	48,000	1	
125-67-1245	Kline	Linda	Sales	246	55,000	5	
356-78-9281	Mattaliano	Tom	Sales	146	75,000	8	
467-24-5690	Chambers	Rosemary	Sales	257	76,500	5	
129-45-9865	Patrick	Kaitlin	Sales	136	78,200	5	
138-45-9876	Rockey	Patience	Sales	124	78,200	4	
					0	0	

Record: 19 of 19

To remove this sort and revert your data back to the previous order, choose Records, Remove Filter/Sort.

Filtering Records

Although sorting leaves all your records visible in the table and merely changes the order in which they appear, filtering applies a set of criteria to your table and hides all records not meeting that criteria. The hidden records aren't removed or deleted, and they can be brought back to view easily.

You'll find filtering to be a powerful tool in searching for certain records. Using the employee table as an example, if you want to know how many people make more than $75,000 per year in salary, filtering the Salary field for numbers greater than $75,000 would give you your answer.

Like sorting, filtering can be performed on more than one field. For example, Figure 20.9 shows the employee table filtered for people in the Marketing department who have been with the company for more than two years.

Filtering by Selection

Filtering by Selection means that you select a cell in your table that contains the data you want to use as filter criteria. For example, Figure 20.10 shows the table prepared to filter for employees who work in the Sales department.

To perform a Filter by Selection, follow these steps:

1. With your table open, click in the cell that contains the data for which you want to filter.

2. Choose Records, Filter, Filter by Selection, or click the Filter by Selection button on the toolbar.

FIG. 20.9

The more fields you filter, the more refined the list of displayed records you'll see.

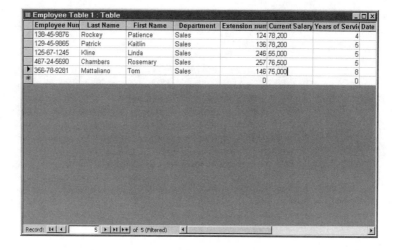

You can continue to filter the records that met your selection criteria by clicking yet another cell to refine the filter. Figure 20.11 shows members of the Sales staff (our first selection-based filter) who make $48,000 per year.

FIG. 20.10

Click the cell that contains your filter criteria. This sorts one field only, for the criteria contained in the selected cell.

Filter for Sales in Department field

Filtering by Form

Another way to filter your data on more than one field is to perform a Filter by Form. Filtering by Form enables you to choose the criteria for one or more fields, progressively shrinking the number of displayed records as you click field after field.

To apply a Filter by Form, follow these steps:

1. With your table open and all your records displayed, choose Records, Filter by Form. You can also click the Filter by Form button on the toolbar.

FIG. 20.11

As you continue to make selections, your list of records shrinks.

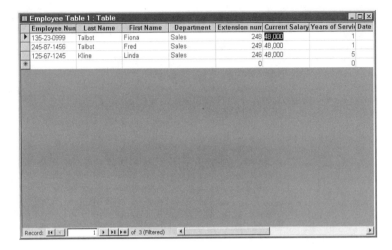

2. Your records are hidden, and only your field names and a blank row appear (see Figure 20.12). Click the fields on which you want to filter. Select your criteria from the list.

FIG. 20.12

Click the empty cell beneath your field name to see a list of entries for that field.

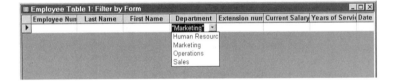

3. When you've selected criteria for all the desired fields, choose Filter, Apply Filter/Sort.

Your list now includes only the records that met the criteria you set in your fields. If none of your records meet the criteria, zeros appear in the row under your field names.

To remove your filter (successful or not), choose Records, Remove Filter/Sort.

N O T E   If you want to find just one record in a large database, click the Find button on the toolbar. Enter the text or numbers you're looking for, and click Find First. If no records are found, be sure the Find dialog box is set to search all fields (turn off Search Only Current Field). If the first record isn't the one you want, click Find Next until you come to the desired record. Click Cancel to close the dialog box.

Advanced Filtering

Filtering by Selection and Filtering by Form allow you to look only for records that are an exact match for the content of your records. For example, you can only search for employees who make a salary that exists in one of the employee records, such as $75,000. If you want to search for all the employees making less than or greater than $75,000, you need to use Access' advanced filtering tools.

To perform an advanced filter on your data, remove all previous filters, and follow these steps:

1. Choose Records, Filter, Advanced Filter/Sort.

2. Select your first Field cell (as shown in Figure 20.13).

FIG. 20.13

Choose a field from the list or drag your field by name from the floating list box.

Field names in floating list box

Field being dragged into grid

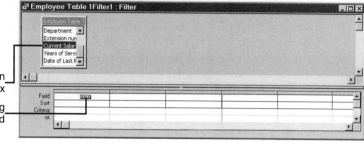

3. In the first Sort field, click to choose Ascending, Descending, or (Not sorted).

4. In the Criteria cell, type your filter criteria, such as >5 (greater than five) and/or <75,000 (less than 75,000), as shown in Figure 20.14.

FIG. 20.14

Use the word "and" to set up two sets of criteria for one field.

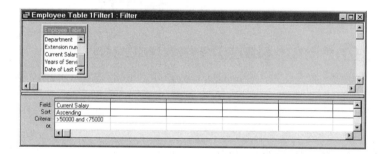

5. Move to the next set of Field, Sort, and Criteria cells, and set any second-level filters.

 TIP Use the Or cell to choose alternate data for your first criteria. For example, you can search for "Sales" or "Marketing" by placing Sales in the first Criteria cell, and Marketing in the Or cell.

Figure 20.15 shows the setup for a filter that results in all members of the Marketing and Sales departments who earn between $50,000 and $80,000 in salary.

Figure 20.16 shows the results of the department and salary advanced search.

 TIP Use the asterisk wildcard to search for words that contain a certain letter or group of letters. For example, to find all employees whose names start with F, the criteria cell would contain F*.

Part

V

Ch

20

FIG. 20.15

Be sure to type carefully and use spaces between the parts of your criteria statement.

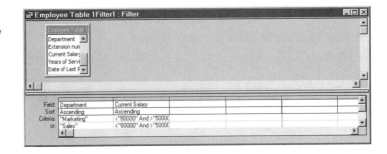

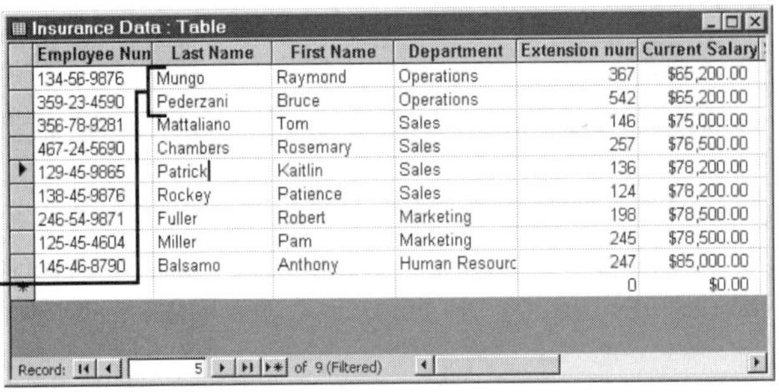

FIG. 20.16

In addition to filtering, an alphabetical sort was added to keep the records in last name order.

Duplicate salary records are in last name order.

Changing Your Database Content

Nobody's perfect, and your records won't be, either. Typos, missing data, mixed up data, and forgotten fields are common database problems. Access makes it relatively simple to correct your mistakes:

- Delete outdated and duplicate records with one click of a button.
- Add fields to an existing table, no questions asked. Insert the field and set it up. Your data won't be adversely affected.
- Delete fields. Although there will be a few questions asked, the fields and the data in them are easy to get rid of when the need arises.
- Change your forms to accommodate your table setup changes. Add a field to the form, or take one away.

Deleting Records

Old records, duplicates, or records that you entered into the wrong table are all candidates for removal. To delete a record, follow these simple steps:

1. Open the table that contains the records you want to delete.
2. Click the gray button to the left of the first field in the record, as shown in Figure 20.17.

FIG. 20.17

Don't click a cell in the record; select the entire record before attempting to delete it.

Employee Num	Last Name	First Name	Department	Extension num	Current Salary	Years of Servic	Date
123-56-9865	Kline	John	Operations	245	65,000	8	
125-45-4604	Miller	Pam	Marketing	245	78,500	5	
125-67-1245	Kline	Linda	Sales	246	48,000	5	
129-45-9865	Patrick	Kaitlin	Sales	136	78,200	5	
134-56-9876	Mungo	Raymond	Operations	367	65,200	3	
135-23-0999	Talbot	Fiona	Sales	248	48,000	1	
135-98-1245	Ulrich	Jasper	Marketing	258	54,500	2	
138-45-9876	Rockey	Patience	Sales	124	78,200	4	
145-46-8790	Balsamo	Anthony	Human Resourc	247	85,000	6	
245-67-1456	Kissell	Scott	Human Resourc	450	65,000	3	
245-87-1456	Talbot	Fred	Sales	249	48,000	1	
246-54-9871	Fuller	Robert	Marketing	198	78,500	7	
251-05-1560	Cramer	Martha	Marketing	556	62,500	3	
356-78-9281	Mattaliano	Tom	Sales	146	75,000	8	
359-23-4590	Pederzani	Bruce	Operations	542	65,200	4	
369-78-9121	Glass	Zooey	Human Resourc	290	65,000	3	
467-24-5690	Chambers	Rosemary	Sales	257	76,500	5	
567-98-1237	Frankenfield	Patricia	Operations	375	55,000	2	
				0		0	

Record: 8 of 18

3. Press Delete. The record disappears.
4. Click Yes to permanently delete the record.

To delete more than one record at a time, click and drag through the gray buttons to the left of the series of records, and then press Delete. The same prompt appears, and you can click Yes to delete the records.

TIP You can also use the Shift key to select a series of records. Click the first record in your intended series, and then press the Shift key. With the Shift key pressed, click the last record in the series, selecting the entire series.

If the records you want to delete are not consecutive and cannot be made so by sorting your table, you must delete them one at a time.

Cutting and Copying Records Between Tables

Just as the Clipboard allows you to cut and copy text between documents or spreadsheets, you can use it to cut and copy records between tables and databases.

To cut records from one table to another, follow these steps:

1. Select the records and then choose Edit, Cut.
2. Confirm that you want to delete the selected records, as shown in Figure 20.18.

Part
V

Ch
20

FIG. 20.18

Be sure you've selected only the records you want to cut before confirming their deletion.

3. Open the target table (in Datasheet view), and click the empty row below your last record. Choose <u>E</u>dit, <u>P</u>aste.

Copying records is performed in the same way, although there is no need to confirm the copy, as it doesn't delete the selected records.

TIP If your records can be used in several different tables, you can <u>P</u>aste them repeatedly after they've been cut or copied.

Adding and Deleting Fields

Planning is the key to successful table design. With that in mind, know that you will probably forget a field when you're designing your table, or you'll decide to remove one after you've set up the table and entered some or all of your records. No amount of planning can eliminate last-minute great ideas or finding out that a good idea wasn't so good.

Deleting One or More Fields Knowing that you'll have the need to add and delete fields from your database, Access makes the process simple. To add a field, follow these steps:

1. Open your table in Datasheet view.
2. Click the field name that you want to delete, as shown in Figure 20.19.

FIG. 20.19

Like selecting a column's letter in Excel, click the field name to select the entire field and all the data in it.

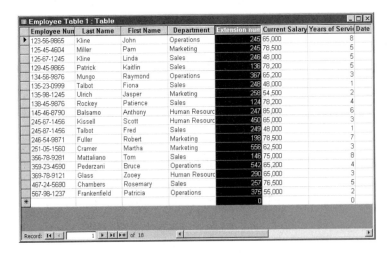

Employee Num	Last Name	First Name	Department	Extension num	Current Salary	Years of Servic	Date
123-56-9865	Kline	John	Operations	245	65,000	8	
125-45-4604	Miller	Pam	Marketing	245	78,500	5	
125-67-1245	Kline	Linda	Sales	246	48,000	5	
129-45-9865	Patrick	Kaitlin	Sales	136	78,200	5	
134-56-9876	Mungo	Raymond	Operations	367	65,200	3	
135-23-0999	Talbot	Fiona	Sales	248	48,000	1	
135-98-1245	Ulrich	Jasper	Marketing	258	54,500	2	
138-45-9876	Rockey	Patience	Sales	124	78,200	4	
145-46-8790	Balsamo	Anthony	Human Resourc	247	85,000	6	
245-67-1456	Kissell	Scott	Human Resourc	450	65,000	3	
245-87-1456	Talbot	Fred	Sales	249	48,000	1	
246-54-9871	Fuller	Robert	Marketing	198	78,500	7	
251-05-1560	Cramer	Martha	Marketing	556	62,500	3	
356-78-9281	Mattaliano	Tom	Sales	146	75,000	8	
359-23-4590	Pederzani	Bruce	Operations	542	65,200	4	
369-78-9121	Glass	Zooey	Human Resourc	290	65,000	3	
467-24-5690	Chambers	Rosemary	Sales	257	76,500	5	
567-98-1237	Frankenfield	Patricia	Operations	375	55,000	2	
*				0		0	

Record: 1 of 18

3. Choose <u>E</u>dit, Delete Colu<u>m</u>n.

TIP To delete several contiguous fields at the same time, select them by dragging through their field names.

4. When prompted, click <u>Y</u>es to permanently delete the field and the data in it.

You can also delete one or more columns by opening the Design view of your table. Select the row for your field (see Figure 20.20) and press the Delete key.

FIG. 20.20

Click the gray button to the left of the field name to select the entire field.

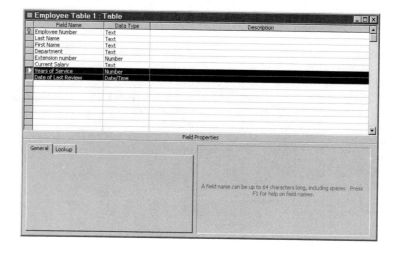

Adding Fields to a Table Forgetting that your table needs to include a particular piece of information is a common mistake. Thinking of a way to break down an existing field into two fields is also a common afterthought in database development. The more separate fields you create to house your data, the more control you have over it and how it's used.

To insert a field, follow these steps:

1. Open your table in Design view.
2. Select the field below where you want to insert your new field.
3. Choose Insert, Rows. A single row is inserted above the selected row.

 To insert more than one field at a time, select the number of existing fields that you want to add, and then choose Insert, Rows. Your new blank rows will appear above the selected group of fields.

4. Type a name for the new field and proceed to build the field's settings for Data Type, Field Size, and so forth.
5. Choose File, Save or press Ctrl+S to save your table with the additional field.

Editing Forms

If your database includes forms, you'll want to update them whenever you make changes to the tables to which they're related. Adding or deleting fields can render a form less than useful, as new fields will be missed and deleted fields will still appear on the form. If someone other than you is using the forms for data entry, he or she may not be aware of the changes you've made to the table and won't be able to use the form properly.

Use the following steps to change your table's form:

1. Open the database that contains your table.
2. Click the Forms tab, and click once on the icon for the form related to your table.

Part

V

Ch

20

3. Click the Design button to open the form in Design view, as shown in Figure 20.21.

FIG. 20.21

Your form consists of field boxes that can be deleted to reflect field deletions in your table. Boxes can also be added to match new fields.

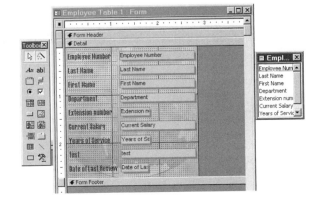

4. To delete a field box from the form, click it once. The box and the field name to its left become selected.

5. Press the Delete key. The field box and name disappear.

If your form needs a new field added to it, follow these steps:

1. Open your form in Design view.

2. Resize your form as necessary to accommodate the added field (see Figure 20.22).

FIG. 20.22

Drag your form footer down to make the form longer, or grab the left side and drag out to make the form wider.

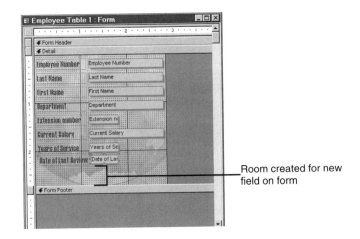

Room created for new field on form

TIP After resizing your form, move some of your existing field boxes (drag them with your mouse) to make room for the new field in a logical position.

3. From the floating Field List, drag the new field onto your form. Figure 20.23 shows a new field being added to the form.

FIG. 20.23

Drop your new field into a clear spot on the form.

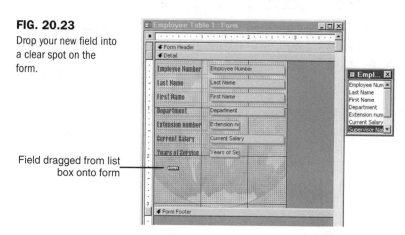

Field dragged from list box onto form

4. Choose File, Save or Press Ctrl+S.

If you need to reposition your new field or the surrounding fields to accommodate your form's new content, drag the fields with your mouse. Your mouse pointer turns into a hand, as shown in Figure 20.24.

FIG. 20.24

Click to select the field name and field box and then drag them to their new location on the form.

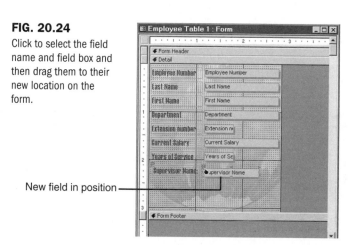

New field in position

Part
V

Ch
20

 A hand with a single pointing finger moves either the name or the field box. A hand moves them together.

TIP Point to the handles around the selected field name or field box, and when your mouse turns into a two-headed arrow, click and drag to resize the object.

If you have added more than one or two new fields, it might be easier to delete the form and create a new one, using the Form Wizard. The wizard lists the new fields and allows you to add them to the new form. ●

Querying a Database

Using Data with Queries

Conceptually, it's very easy to confuse filtering (as described in Chapter 20, "Editing and Reviewing Your Data") with querying. Both functions ask your table to show only records that meet some sort of criteria, such as all the customers in a particular state, or how many cars were rented to people named Smith who live in Missouri. Just as a filter can be applied to several fields, so can a query. Where queries have more power is in their capability to apply their criteria to fields in more than one table. For example, if you have a customer information table (names and addresses) and a credit history table (customers and their credit status/limit), you can query both tables in one query process, resulting in a dynaset table that shows data from both tables.

N O T E   A *dynaset* is the table that displays the results of a filter or query. It is often confused with the data table, but it is merely a transient container for a set of dynamic (changing) data, thus the name dynaset.

The easiest way to query your table or tables is to run the Query Wizard. There are actually several types of Query Wizards, and the most useful ones are documented in this chapter.

Designing a Query

Access is an object-oriented database, a concept that doesn't have too much meaning to the casual user until the topic of queries comes up. This is because the act of designing a query requires that you select and drag data objects into your query, as though you were placing clip art or AutoShapes on a document. This concept makes designing a query simple.

Many queries involve two or more tables. Querying a single table can be overkill (a saved filter or sort may be sufficient) unless you need to create a query to be used by other users (and you don't know if they know how to sort or filter) or if your query will be added to another file or a Web site. When two or more tables are involved, however, a query allows you to select the tables and draw fields from each or all of them, deciding which fields to merely display and which ones to filter for specified criteria.

Figure 21.1 shows the setup for a query that draws from an employee database and a database of employee review ratings. Only those employees rating below a five appear in the query results dynaset. After setting up the query, the query results appear as shown in Figure 21.2.

To design your own query, follow these steps:

1. Open your database, and click the Query tab.
2. Click the New button, and choose Design View, as shown in Figure 21.3. Click OK.
3. The Show Table dialog box opens, offering you a list of all the tables in your database. To select your tables, click them and then click the Add button (see Figure 21.4).
4. Close the Show Tables dialog box.

FIG. 21.1

Drag the field names from either database into the grid, setting criteria for one or more of the fields.

A common field connects the two tables.

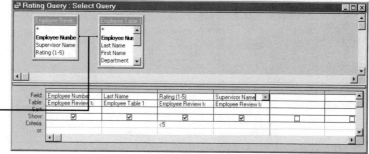

FIG. 21.2

The dynaset is not a table, but the results of a query. The query can be saved to be run again in the future, creating a new dynaset.

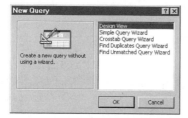

FIG. 21.3

Choose to design your query from scratch. It's faster than the Query Wizard.

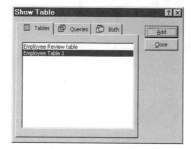

FIG. 21.4

Add only the tables that contain fields you'll be using in your query.

5. For each table added, a floating field list appears in the query design window. Drag fields from each of the table boxes down onto the query design grid (much like setting up a filter). Figure 21.5 shows fields being placed in the grid.

FIG. 21.5

A small box follows your mouse pointer as you drag fields from the floating boxes down to the query design grid.

Selected field ⎯

Drag into position on grid

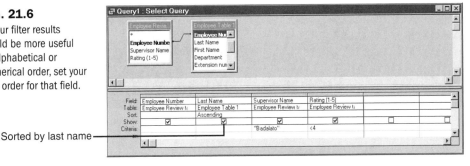

6. Set criteria for any fields on which you want to filter.

7. Choose your sort orders for any fields you want to sort. Figure 21.6 shows both filter and sort settings in place.

FIG. 21.6

If your filter results would be more useful in alphabetical or numerical order, set your sort order for that field.

Sorted by last name ⎯

8. When your query is set up, choose <u>F</u>ile, <u>S</u>ave or click the Save button.

9. Click the Run button or choose <u>Q</u>uery, <u>R</u>un. Your query is performed, creating a dynaset in its own window, as shown in Figure 21.7.

FIG. 21.7

Your results appear in their own table. As your data changes over time, your results will change each time you run the query.

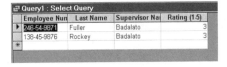

Queries you've created appear in the Query tab for your database. If a query doesn't work or becomes obsolete, click once on the query icon and press Delete.

N O T E   Your queries (as well as your tables and reports) can be saved as HTML, and then published to the World Wide Web. Choose <u>F</u>ile, Save as <u>H</u>TML, and follow the steps in the Publish to the Web Wizard. This powerful, yet simple tool enables you to publish certain parts of your database or all of them—your tables, queries, and reports. You can also apply templates from the installed Access Web templates, choose the type of HTML file and the resultant flexibility (to publish reports and queries as well as tables) and even opt to build a home page based on your data.

Running the Simple Query Wizard

The Query Wizard achieves the same goal as a query designed from scratch—combining fields from two or more databases and sorting/filtering fields within them. The Query Wizard takes you through the query-building process with a series of dialog boxes.

Follow these steps to run the Query Wizard:

1. Open your database, and click the Query tab.
2. Click New, and select Simple Query Wizard from the list.

 TIP If you have a large database that was built by several people or by one person over a long period of time, run the Find Duplicates Query Wizard. When a database has a lot of hands in its creation or is built slowly, the chance that the same records were entered two or more times increases.

3. Choose the tables you want to use from the Tables/Queries drop-down list (see Figure 21.8). Select them one at a time.

FIG. 21.8
Choose only the tables from which you'll be selecting fields for your query.

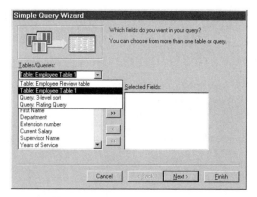

4. For each table selected, choose fields from the Available Fields drop-down list and add them to the Selected Fields drop-down list. Use the right-pointing arrow to select them individually (see Figure 21.9).
5. After you've selected fields from all the desired tables, click Next.
6. Choose a Detail or Summary query.
7. Choose how to group your records.
8. Type a name for your query, and click Finish.

FIG. 21.9

Click a field and then add it to the Selected Fields box. Don't add them all at once unless you mean to use every field in the selected table.

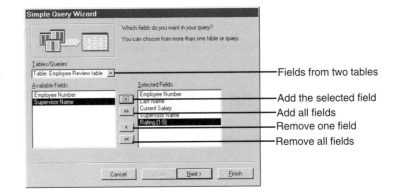

Fields from two tables
Add the selected field
Add all fields
Remove one field
Remove all fields

N O T E   After you've completed the query (through your own design process or the wizard), you can filter and sort your dynaset before closing it.

Documenting Your Data with Reports

Although you can print a query or any view of your table, designing an actual report gives you the ability to create a professional-looking document that shows only the data you need, in a format that's effective for your audience.

You can create reports from scratch using Access' design tools, or run a wizard to select your databases, fields, and layout through a series of dialog boxes. Access also gives you AutoReports that output all your fields in either a columnar or tabular format.

Designing a Report

If you decide to forgo the wizard and design a report on your own, do a little planning ahead of time. Jot down your basic layout on paper, and decide which data you want to see on the report.

To put your plan into action, follow these steps:

1. Open your database and click the Reports tab.
2. Click New, and select Design View from the list.
3. Before exiting this dialog box, choose the table or query from which you want to select your report's content (see Figure 21.10).
4. Click OK.
5. The Report window opens, displaying a detailed grid, a floating toolbar, and a floating field list (see Figure 21.11).
6. Drag the fields from the field list onto the grid, placing them where you want to see them on the report. Figure 21.12 shows a field being placed on the grid.

T I P   Use the grid to place your field objects neatly—align their edges along the same vertical lines in the grid to give your report a crisp, professional layout.

FIG. 21.10

Save yourself some work—if an existing query contains all the fields you want for your report, choose it from the list.

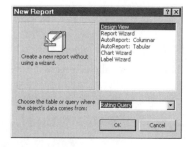

FIG. 21.11

The grid represents your paper, onto which you'll place the fields you want to see on your report.

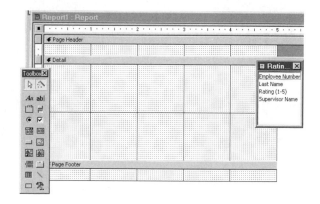

FIG. 21.12

Your mouse pointer turns into a small box as you drag a field from the floating field list to the grid.

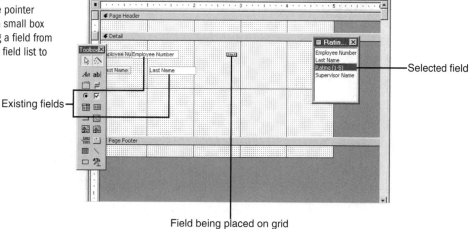

Existing fields

Selected field

Field being placed on grid

7. Move and resize the field objects as needed.

TIP Remember that you need to watch for a variety of mouse pointers when moving field objects. A pointing hand moves the field name or field box individually, a hand moves them in tandem. A two-headed arrow resizes the selected object.

8. When your report is set up as desired, choose File, Save or press Ctrl+S. Give your report a name, and click OK.

9. Choose File, Close or press Ctrl+F4 to close the report design window.

10. In the Reports tab of your database window, click Preview to see how your report will look (see Figure 21.13).

FIG. 21.13

Using Preview is environmentally sound— if you don't like the report, you haven't wasted paper finding out.

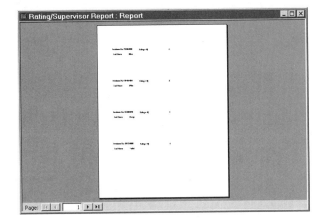

If you don't like the preview, you can edit your report by opening it in Design view, or you can delete it and start again.

Running the Report Wizard

The Report Wizard takes the designer role from you, allowing you to choose your tables and fields and choose from some predesigned layouts for your report. For this reason, many people prefer to use the wizard.

To run the Report Wizard, follow these steps:

1. Click the Reports tab in your database window.

2. Click the New button, and choose Report Wizard.

3. Select a table or query on which to base your report, and click OK to start the wizard.

4. In the first wizard dialog box, select your fields for the report. Click Next to proceed.

5. Choose the grouping order and placement of your fields, as shown in Figure 21.14.

6. Click Next to move on to the next step.

7. Choose the sort order for your report (see Figure 21.15). You can sort as many of your report's fields as you want.

8. Click Next.

9. Choose a Layout and an Orientation for your report (see Figure 21.16), and then click Next.

FIG. 21.14

Select your fields and then change their order within the report by clicking the Priority arrows.

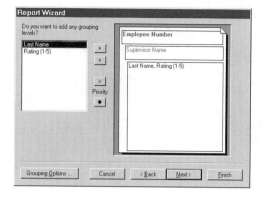

FIG. 21.15

Click to choose ascending (A-Z) or descending (Z-A) order for each sorted field. When sorting numbers, ascending places lowest numbers first, descending places highest numbers first.

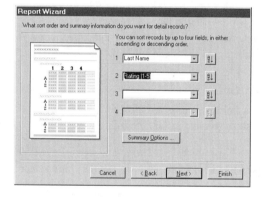

FIG. 21.16

As you make selections, the preview box changes to show you how your choice will look on paper.

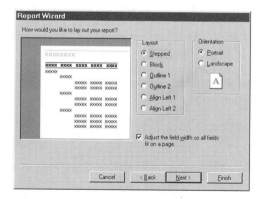

 TIP By default, your report is set to size all your fields so that they fit on one page.

10. Choose a style for your report, and click Next.

11. Give your report a name (see Figure 21.17) and click Finish.

FIG. 21.17
If your database will
have several reports in
it, give them easily
distinguishable names.

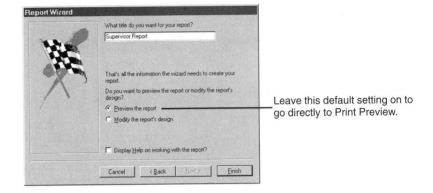

Leave this default setting on to
go directly to Print Preview.

If you've left the Preview default on, as soon as you click the Finish button, the report appears in a large Print Preview window. If you like the report, you can print it (choose File, Print), or you can close the preview window (press Ctrl+F4) and print it later. Your report will be available from the Reports tab in your database window.

Working with AutoReports

AutoReports use all your fields in a selected table and place them in columnar or tabular format. Use the following steps to create a fast, no-frills AutoReport:

1. Click the Reports tab in your database window, and click New.
2. Select the AutoReport format (columnar or tabular), and select a table or query on which to base the report.

 The only way to run an AutoReport on two or more tables is to base it on a query that reflects data from two or more tables.

3. Click OK.

Your report is created instantly, and appears in Print Preview (see Figure 21.18). You can print it, or close the Preview window and run it later from the Reports tab.

FIG. 21.18
This columnar AutoReport isn't fancy, but it was created quickly and easily.

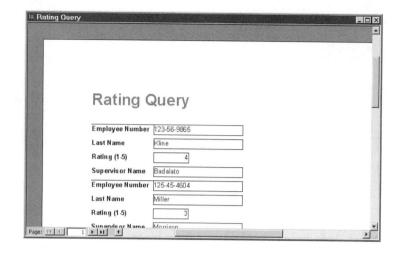

Printing Your Data

You can print any view of your data, from a table in Datasheet view to a report you designed from scratch. The key to printing in Access is to have the desired content displayed in the active window onscreen:

- To print your data table, select it from the Tables tab and click Open. While the table is open, choose File, Print or press Ctrl+P. Your table prints in Datasheet view, the printout looking much like a spreadsheet.

- To print a query, make sure the query's dynaset is the active window, and select the File, Print command. Like a data table, the query table prints in a spreadsheet format.

- To print a report, click once on the desired report icon in your reports tab, and click Preview. While the report is showing in the Print Preview window, choose File, Print or click the Print button on the toolbar.

Just like any Microsoft Office application, the Access Print dialog box (see Figure 21.19) enables you to choose which printer to send the print job to, which pages to print, and how many copies.

FIG. 21.19
You can choose your print setup options from this dialog box.

Part
V

Ch
21

Appendixes

Mouse Power

In this chapter

Understanding the Many Faces of Your Mouse

The mouse is your primary tool for communicating with Microsoft Office, as well as all your other Windows-based applications. Whether a standard serial mouse, a trackball, or a pointing device embedded in your notebook computer's keyboard, your mouse has three main uses, and has different faces for each of them. Many seasoned Windows users may have not noticed them all:

■ *Pointing.* Your mouse normally looks like a left-pointing arrow when you're pointing to icons, toolbars, or dialog box options. Figure A.1 shows your pointing mouse.

CAUTION

If your mouse is moving and pointing, but nothing happens when you double-click, perhaps your program is "hung up," to use a not-too-technical description. Try pressing Ctrl+Alt+Delete once to see the Close Program dialog box (if you have Windows NT, the Task Manager dialog box opens). If your program is listed as not responding, click the End Task button. You'll lose all unsaved work in all open files in the non-responsive application.

FIG. A.1

Pointing is like shopping without buying—not until you double-click (or single-click if you're using Internet Explorer 4) will you select the item.

Pause on a toolbar button when pointing, and you see a ScreenTip.

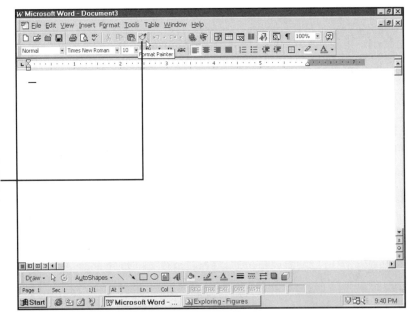

■ *Selecting.* Whether with a double-click or a single-click, the mouse, after you've pointed to something you want, can be used to invoke a program or open a file. In addition, the mouse can be used to select text or cells within a spreadsheet. Figure A.2 shows an I-beam mouse pointer, prepared to select text in a Word document.

FIG. A.2

Click and drag through
your text to select with
an I-beam.

```
*** Insert Figure A.2 here (Use file AFIG02.PCX) ***
Click and drag through your text to select with an I-beam. I
*** Begin Note ***
```

N O T E   In Word, if you point to the outer left margin, your mouse pointer will turn to a right-pointing
arrow, which you can use to select the entire line next to the arrow, or by double-clicking,
the entire paragraph next to the arrow.

◼ *Moving and resizing.* Graphics, chart elements, cell contents, and selected text can all be
moved from place to place within or between documents. When you're moving a graphic
element, your mouse pointer turns into a four-headed arrow, as shown in Figure A.3.
When you're resizing, your mouse pointer turns into a two-headed arrow, as shown in
Figure A.4.

FIG. A.3

Point to the graphic
object (not to a handle)
and drag to move the
object.

A dashed border
follows your mouse
while you drag.

The object in its original
position, with handles

The Picture toolbar appears whenever
an inserted picture is selected.

FIG. A.4

Any graphic object in
an Office document
resides in an invisible
box—you can make the
box bigger, allowing the
object to grow.

N O T E If you're using the drawing tools to create a rectangle, circle, AutoShape, or line, your mouse pointer turns into a cross. Click and drag the mouse away from your starting point to create the image. When you release the mouse, your pointer turns back into a pointing arrow.

When your computer is busy, it shows you one of two mouse pointers. One is an hourglass, which indicates that the computer is busy and should not be disturbed until the process is complete and the mouse pointer returns to normal (for whatever you're doing at the time).

CAUTION

One of the most common causes (aside from low-system memory) of an application seeming to freeze, causing you to shut the application (and perhaps Windows) down, is the impatient user. If your mouse pointer is an hourglass, don't click incessantly or rap the mouse on the desk. Wait for your computer to finish what it's doing, and then ask for your next action.

If your computer is busy for too long or your hard drive light goes out for a long time, press Ctrl+Alt+ Delete to open the Close Program dialog box (in Windows NT, this is called the Task Manager). Chances are, the program will be listed as not responding, in which case you should click the End Task button and start over.

If your computer is busy but able to take other requests, it appears as an hourglass and a pointer arrow at the same time.

Use Windows' Control Panel (double-click the Mouse icon) to change your mouse pointers as desired, and fine-tune your mouse to meet your needs.

N O T E If you've installed Microsoft Plus (a companion product for Windows 95 and 98), you can choose from a variety of other mouse pointers. You can select them a la carte or apply schemes that set up new theme-based pointers for all the different faces your mouse has. You may find that the use of these pointers slows down your computer, however.

Opening Shortcut Menus

Prior to Windows 95, the right mouse button didn't have a lot to do, unless you were left-handed (and had switched your main mouse button) or unless you were using a software program that had uses for the right mouse button (usually graphics and illustration software).

In Windows 95 and 98, however, the right-mouse button has many jobs, the most dynamic of which is to bring up shortcut menus for just about any object onscreen, from text in a document to icons on the desktop.

To open a shortcut menu, right-click any of the following items:

- Your Windows desktop
- Any desktop icon
- Your taskbar
- Any Office toolbar
- Selected text in a Word document
- Selected cells in an Excel spreadsheet
- Any slide element in PowerPoint

Each item you right-click produces a shortcut menu, the contents of which varies by item.

Accessing Properties Information

When right-clicking anything on your Windows Desktop or a file in the Windows Explorer (or My Computer), one of the shortcut menu items will be Properties. Figure A.5 shows the taskbar shortcut menu.

FIG. A.5

Properties are stored information about many Windows elements. Transient elements (such as text) don't have viewable properties.

Properties refers to extra information, ranging from statistics (dates that a file was changed or last printed) to how much memory your system has available. Some properties can be changed, others are there merely to be viewed for information purposes (see Figure A.6).

FIG. A.6

Some Properties boxes contain advanced system settings that you shouldn't change unless you're completely familiar with the settings and the ramifications of changing them.

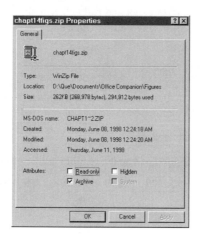

T I P When you're in any Office application's Open dialog box (reached by choosing <u>F</u>ile, <u>O</u>pen), you can right-click any file listed in the selected folder, and choose to view its <u>P</u>roperties.

Viewing Toolbars and Screen Elements

To switch to another toolbar in any Microsoft Office application, right-click your mouse on any displayed toolbar. A list of available toolbars, plus a Customize command, appears. The toolbars currently displayed in the active application have a check mark next to them, as shown in Figure A.7.

FIG. A.7

Turn off a toolbar that's already displayed by clicking its check mark.

▷ **See** "Customizing Toolbars," **p. 122**

Activating the Clipboard

Any selected Word text, Excel data, PowerPoint slide element, or Access data can be cut or copied to the Clipboard by clicking the right mouse button.

To move or share your Office document content within the same or another document, select the content, and right-click it. Choose Cut or <u>C</u>opy from the shortcut menu. To place it in its new desired location, right-click the target spot and right-click again—choose <u>P</u>aste from the shortcut menu. Figure A.8 shows selected Word text and a shortcut menu.

Applying Formats

 Word, Excel, and PowerPoint all contain a button on their Standard toolbar called the Format Painter. This tool is used to copy formatting from one set of selected content to another.

To use the Format Painter, follow these steps:

1. Select the content that is formatted as you'd like other content to be.
2. Click the Format Painter button. Your mouse pointer now has a paintbrush on it, as shown in Figure A.9.

Part

VI

App

A

FIG. A.8
Many users become so accustomed to using the right mouse button for Cut and Copy that they rarely use the Edit menu anymore.

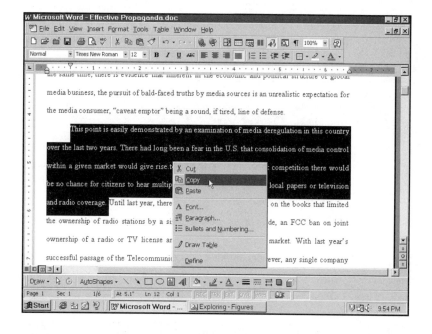

FIG. A.9
Save a lot of repetitive steps and retain formatting consistency by using the Format Painter to format text or cells in a large document.

Format painter pointer————

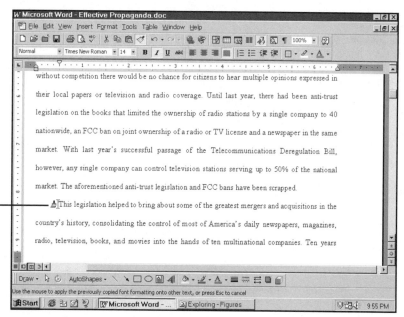

TIP With a single click, the Format Painter allows you to "paint" the selected format once. If you double-click it, however, you can paint the formats many times—click the Format Painter again or press Esc to turn the tool off.

3. Click and drag through the content that you want to format with the Format Painter.

TIP Select any Word text and right-click it. Within the shortcut menu, you'll see a Font command. Select it to open the Font dialog box.

Working with Drag and Drop

Unlike many Windows and Office tools that can be invoked by using a toolbar button, menu command, keyboard shortcut, or the mouse, drag and drop is a feature that can only be used with the mouse. Drag and drop is used to move (cut) or copy content from one place to another, without using the Clipboard:

- Rearrange words in a sentence, sentences within a paragraph, or two contiguous paragraphs.

- Move or copy cell content from cell to cell in an Excel worksheet or a Word table.

- Move or copy content between two tiled document windows or two tiled application windows, as shown in Figure A.10.

FIG. A.10
Right-click the taskbar and choose Tile Windows Vertically (or Horizontally) to make it possible to drag and drop between applications.

Selected Excel content

Small box accompanies mouse pointer to target spot

Although even this short list of uses opens up many possibilities, drag and drop has some limitations:

- When rearranging content in a Word document or Excel worksheet, you cannot drag content outside the currently displayed portion of the document page.

- To copy selected content, you must press and hold the Ctrl key while dragging content. Release the key after you release the mouse.
- When dragging between applications, formatting may not come with the content.

Part

VI

App

A

Keyboard Shortcuts

Many users prefer to use the keyboard to issue frequently used commands. Although not all commands that can be issued from the menu and/or toolbars have a keyboard equivalent, many of them do. Keyboard shortcuts can be especially useful if you're a fast typist or are in the middle of a typing-intensive process—having to take your hand off the keys to move the mouse can slow you down.

The following table contains a list of keyboard shortcuts that can be used in all the Microsoft Office applications.

Table B.1 Microsoft Office Keyboard Shortcuts

Keyboard Shortcut	Command Issued
Ctrl+N	Create a new file
Ctrl+O	Open a new file
Ctrl+P	Print the active document
Ctrl+S	Save the active document
Ctrl+Z	Undo the last action
Ctrl+C	Copy selected content to the Clipboard
Ctrl+X	Cut selected content to the Clipboard
Ctrl+V	Paste the Clipboard's contents

continues

Table B.1 Continued

Keyboard Shortcut	Command Issued
Ctrl+K	Insert a hyperlink
Ctrl+B	Apply Bold formatting to selected content
Ctrl+I	Apply Italic formatting to selected content
Ctrl+U	Apply Underline formatting to selected content
Ctrl+L	Left justification
Ctrl+E	Center justification
Ctrl+R	Right justification
Ctrl+F4	Close the active document
Alt+F4	Close the active application
F1	Open the Help window
Shift+F1	What's This? Help (use the mouse to click the object for which you need help)

TIP To open any menu, press the Alt key plus the underlined letter in the menu name (for example, press Alt+F to open the File menu). To access commands within a menu, press the underlined letter by itself.

To view all the keyboard shortcuts for application-specific commands, choose Tools, Customize. Click the Keyboard button and then select a Category and one of the Commands (see Figure B.1). The currently assigned keyboard shortcuts will be displayed in the Current Keys list.

FIG. B.1
Keyboard shortcuts for every command available in the active application can be viewed, including any user-created commands and macros.

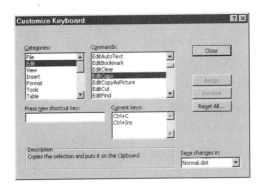

Getting the Help You Need

Understanding Your Help Options

One of the first things you'll notice about Microsoft Office Help (both in this appendix and through your hands-on use of Help) is that there is a lot of help, and a lot of ways to access it. Normally, something that can be done in many ways becomes confusing, as we feel compelled to learn all the ways to do it.

In the case of Microsoft's Help, however, the variety of methods of accessing Help exists to accommodate the different ways people think and how much information on the given topic they already have.

First, let's take the Help menu. The choices you'll find in any Microsoft Office application's Help menu are

■ *Microsoft* Application Name *Help*. This opens the Office Assistant (see Figure C.1); you must type a question for the Assistant.

FIG. C.1
The Office Assistant pops up on its own as you work or when you ask for it by choosing *Application Name* Help from the Help menu.

■ *Contents and Index.* This opens a three-tab dialog box, each tab offering a different way to access the main application help files (see Figure C.2).

FIG. C.2

If you're looking for general help on a topic and you're not sure what terminology to use, click the Contents tab.

■ *What's This?* A mouse-oriented Help tool, this feature enables you to click something in a dialog box, a tool on a toolbar, or virtually any screen element, and you get a pop-up box containing help text (see Figure C.3).

FIG. C.3

Your mouse pointer sports a large question mark (?) when you invoke What's This? Help.

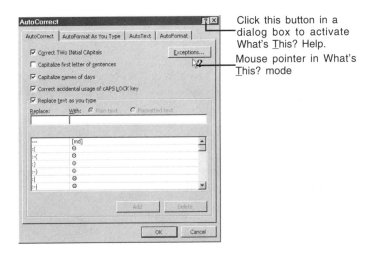

Click this button in a dialog box to activate What's This? Help.

Mouse pointer in What's This? mode

 TIP   You can also open What's This? Help in any dialog box that has a question mark button in its upper-right corner. Click the button and then click the dialog box feature with which you need help.

■ *Microsoft on the Web.* This opens a submenu of topics that can be found on the Microsoft Web site, as shown in Figure C.4.

FIG. C.4

Choose a subject or area of the Microsoft Web site from this submenu. If your Web connection is set up properly, the site opens onscreen.

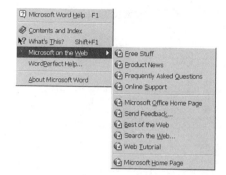

- *About <Application Name>*. Select this command to see an informative dialog box that contains the version number and copyright date of the application, as well as the name of the person who installed it (see Figure C.5). Click System Info to see a Readme file about the application's configuration.

Part

VI

App

C

FIG. C.5

Check to see if you're running the latest version of the software, by checking the software version number and copyright date.

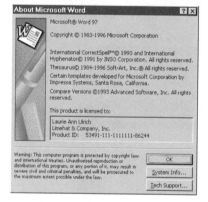

Searching Help Contents

When you choose Help, Contents and Index, a three-tab dialog box opens. The Contents tab contains general topics, each accompanied by a purple book icon (see Figure C.6). To see what more detailed topics can be found in each general area, double-click a book icon. More books and/or page icons appear. When you've found the topic you need (accompanied by a page icon), double-click it, and read the Help file for that topic.

Using the Help Index

The Index tab is the most expeditious route to Microsoft Office's Help files. Its proficient use, however, requires that you know the correct name of the feature or term for the situation with which you need help. Many users think there isn't help for a topic merely because the words they're using don't match any of the indexed words in the Help files.

FIG. C.6

Searching for help in the Contents tab is like reading a table of contents in a book—you look for the closest topic match, and then turn to the indicated page.

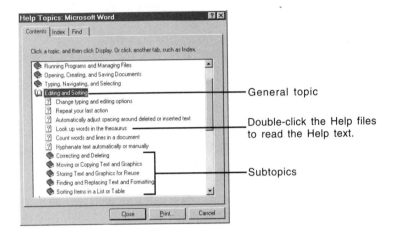

General topic

Double-click the Help files to read the Help text.

Subtopics

To search for help using the Index tab, type a word (or just a portion of it) in the step 1 box. The list below the step 1 text box moves alphabetically to the closest matching word (see Figure C.7). Scroll through the list until you find the word you're looking for, and double-click it.

FIG. C.7

To find help on Printing, you need only type "Pri" in the text box.

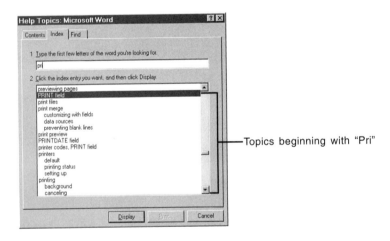

Topics beginning with "Pri"

If a variety of related topics exist, they'll appear in the Topics Found dialog box (see Figure C.8). Double-click the topic you're looking for, and the related Help file displays in its own window.

After you've read the Help file, you can go back to the three-tabbed Help window by clicking the Help Topics button.

TIP   You can print the displayed Help file by clicking the Options button. Choose Print Topic.

FIG. C.8

The wording of some topics may be confusing or misleading. Check them all if you're in doubt.

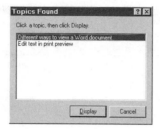

Asking Questions with Help Find

The third of the three tabs in the Help Topics dialog box is Find. This tool for retrieving Help files requires that you type a word or phrase, which is compared to an internal list of words that are referenced in the Help files (see Figure C.9). This works similarly to the Index tab, although it's more confusing and often takes you to inappropriate topics, completely unrelated to what you asked for. I suggest you avoid this Help feature!

Part
VI

App
C

FIG. C.9

Find works from a list of hundreds of words, and searches for help based on a question you type. It doesn't work too well.

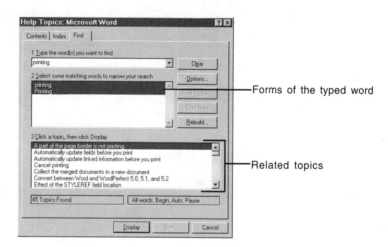

Forms of the typed word

Related topics

Working with the Office Assistant

The Office Assistant is an animated character that appears spontaneously when you're working or when you choose Help, Microsoft *Application Name* Help from the menu bar.

When the Office Assistant appears spontaneously, it asks you if you need help with a specific task, one that it has determined you're attempting to perform, such as writing a letter. This "spontaneity" is the result of programming that tells the Office Assistant to appear whenever a specific set of conditions exist, such as when you're typing the word "Dear" at the beginning of a short sentence that ends in a colon or comma. You can accept its offer of help, or you can tell it to go away by clicking either the Cancel button or the Just Type the Letter Without Help option (the text of this option varies by task). Figure C.10 shows the Office Assistant offering help with a letter.

FIG. C.10
Scribble the Cat is just one of several characters you can choose from for the Office Assistant. An animated paper clip is the default character.

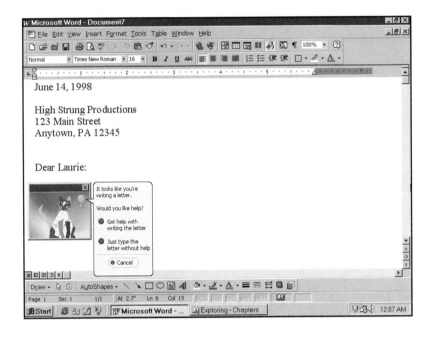

ON THE WEB

http://www.microsoft.com   Check the Microsoft Web site for more Office Assistant characters to download.

Posing Questions to the Assistant

If you need the Office Assistant, press F1. It appears and asks you what sort of help you need, which you can type in the form of a question or short phrase into the text box as shown in Figure C.11.

FIG. C.11
Click Search to send the Office Assistant off in pursuit of the appropriate Help file.

Customizing the Office Assistant

Whenever the Office Assistant is onscreen, click the Options button to see the Office Assistant options dialog box (see Figure C.12). You can choose from some of these useful options:

FIG. C.12

Choose when and how the Office Assistant works for you.

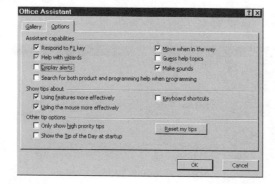

- To keep the Office Assistant from appearing spontaneously, turn off the Display Alerts and Guess Help Topics options.

- Click the Gallery tab to choose the Office Assistant character you want to use (see Figure C.13).

FIG. C.13

You can change Office Assistant characters to suit your mood.

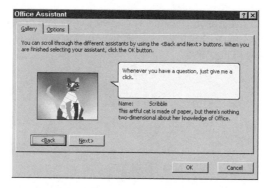

Online Help from Microsoft

Microsoft's Web site contains a great deal of helpful information, as well as technical support. The site's layout changes periodically, but for the most part, you'll be able to find help in one of the following ways:

- From the Microsoft home page, click Support (see Figure C.14).

NOTE Can't find the help you need online? Call for support by dialing Microsoft's main number: (800)936-5700. If you aren't a registered user or your free support time has run out, you can get help at $35 per question by dialing their 900 number: (900)555-2000. You can call as many times as you need to on a particular question—until it's resolved—for the one flat fee of $35.

- Go directly to the Web page for the application you're working with, such as:

   www.microsoft.com/powerpoint

FIG. C.14

Support online is often faster than telephone support, because you're never on hold.

Click this button on the Microsoft home page, and the displayed page appears.

Click this link to search for a specific topic.

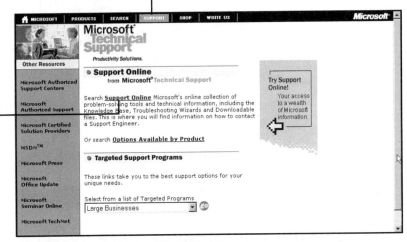

▓ Click the MSDN (Microsoft Developers Network) link and follow the process of registering for access to the network's documentation and daily emails on topics from software releases to bug fixes.

What's on the CD

The companion CD is an essential partner to the topics covered in this book because many of the Office features that the book shows you how to use are enhanced by files found on the CD. You'll also find several programs on the CD that can enhance not just your use of Office but your productivity in the workplace and at home.

You'll find the following categories of files and software on the companion CD:

- Word Templates from KMT Software, Ghostware, Eon Solutions Ltd., and WriteExpress Corporation. Look for templates for business forms, stationery, awards and certificates, fax cover sheets, marketing materials, resumes, and cover letters. You'll find them in the **\Templates** folder on the companion CD.

- HTML Templates from Tela Communications. This is a demo version of the Ant HTML program that turns Word documents, including tables and WYSIWYG text, into HTML code for your Web page. Look in the **\Templates** folder for these, too.

- Excel Templates from KMT Software. Exceptional tools for business and home use, from cash flow and balance sheets to a travel itinerary. Create spreadsheets to analyze your sales and marketing efforts, and amortize a loan. These templates will simplify your creative use of Excel. Browse the **\Templates** folder to find these.

- Interactive Excel Charts. Found in the **\XLCharts** folder, these charts do two jobs: They show you how great charts look and what components they contain, and they show you how to integrate your data into preformatted worksheets so that your data can be viewed in the charts. Learn from them to improve your own charting skills, or simply use them for creating complex charts quickly.

- Access Applications. Look for great applications from Microsoft, BeCubed, Cowlitz River Software, Pragmatic Software, Alma Internet Publishing, and Transcan. Use these applications for everything from printing labels to creating Access reports. You'll find all these (plus a lot of other great software) in the **\3rdparty** folder on the CD.

- Sound Files. Enhance your PowerPoint presentations and Web sites created through Word with .WAV format sound files. You'll find them in the **\Sounds** folder on the CD.

- Animated GIFs. Add motion to your Web site or any document. Check the **\Animgifs** folder for these files.

- Clip Art. From Little Men Studios and MDP, find a vast array of images to complement your letters, reports, and presentations. Look in the **\Clipart** folder on the CD.

- Photographs. Add real photographs to your documents, Web pages, and presentations. Use our large selection of public domain images, found in the **\Photos** folder.

- Video Clips. Enjoy Net Toob from Duplexx, and add video to your PowerPoint presentations. Find this in the **\3rdparty** folder.

- Shareware. Many companies design programs that will enhance your use of Office—among them, Office Toys 98, CD Player for Word 97, Visual Fonts, Adarus Business Plan, FontFinder, and Font F/X. You'll find these and more in the **\3rdparty** folder.

- Utilities. Protect your computer from macro viruses, compress your files for easier and faster storage and Internet transmission, create passwords for your programs, and have fun with a psychedelic screen saver collection. These tools and more can be found in the **\3rdparty** folder on the CD.

How to Find What You Need on the CD

Your companion CD contains seven directories, each for a specific category. Most of these folders are broken into subfolders for further categorization of files, mostly by software manufacturer or file creator.

To browse the CD, insert it into your CD-ROM drive and click the plus sign that appears next to the CD-ROM icon in Explorer, or double-click the CD-ROM drive icon in your My Computer window. Either method will display the folders on the companion CD and enable you to explore the individual folders and their subfolders.

To activate a program, double-click the application icon in the software folder. For sounds, clip art, photographs, and video clips, double-click the file and Windows will open the program it associates with that type of file.

Copying CD Files and Installing Programs

Most of the files on the CD can be merely copied to your computer, while others require installation. In general, templates and graphic files (clip art, animated gifs, video clips, and sound files) can be copied to your computer using Explorer or My Computer to display the CD drive and your target folder on your computer.

You may also decide to add these files to the Microsoft Clip Gallery. The Clip Gallery is accessible from Word, Excel, and PowerPoint through the Insert menu. For example, to add clip art to the Gallery, choose Insert, Picture, Clip Art. Click the Import Clips button in the Gallery window, and browse the CD for the images you want to add to the Gallery. You can do this from within Word for clip art, video clips, photographs, and sound files, and they'll be accessible from any Office application.

Some of the programs on the CD, such as Antivirus for Macros, the PowerPoint Player, and Internet Explorer, must be installed. Double-click their program file on the CD to begin the installation process. During installation, you'll be able to choose the folder on your computer into which the software will be installed.

Part
VI

App
D

Index

Special Rebate Offer
$ 5.00 US

Highlighted Features

1 Real time macro virus protection

2 Cleaning (Automatic)

3 Scan documents & files on opening

4 Scan documents & files by association

5 Scan documents & files on demand

6 Scan Network drives

7 Generate Log Reports

8 Embedded in Microsoft Word

9 Heuristic Scanning (unknown macro viruses)

10 FREE signature file updates for registered users

LOOK Software Systems Inc.
http://www.look.com
sales@look.com

Virus ALERT for Macros
(Microsoft Office97 Edition)

What is a Macro Virus?

A macro virus is a type of destructive 'program' that infects Microsoft® Word® documents and templates. Their effects vary from minor inconvenience to major system damage and data loss. Macro viruses are very difficult to detect and safely remove. Competitive anti virus software's are designed to use standard virus detection and removal techniques which are not effective against non-standard viruses like the macro virus family - their unique nature demands a unique solution.

The _first_ Word in Macro Virus Detection

VIRUS ALERT _for_ Macros™ has been designed to address the unique nature of Microsoft Word macro viruses in an innovative way which allows it to achieve levels of detection accuracy, cleaning and user friendliness that cannot be matched by standard anti-virus utilities.

The Key - Integration

VIRUS ALERT _for_ Macros™ achieves its' superior results by installing completely and seamlessly _into_ Microsoft® Word 97. _Effectively_ VIRUS ALERT _for_ Macros™ becomes part of Microsoft® Word®. This results in truly accurate macro virus protection during normal Word operation.

Documents and templates are automatically scanned when opened. No manual commands are required - _it protects as you use_ Microsoft® Word®.

Remove the Virus Keep the Document

VIRUS ALERT _for_ Macros™ uses a _safe macro virus cleaning_ technique which removes only the viral macros from an infected file, without corrupting the file or removing legitimate macros. VIRUS ALERT _for_ Macros™ leaves the document, text and all other contents fully intact - as if they were never infected.

FREE Signature Upgrades and Technical Support

All registered users of VIRUS ALERT™ products receive _FREE_ virus signature updates, down-loadable from our World Wide Web site at 'www.look.com', as well as _FREE_ technical support via our toll free number, email and website. * _some restrictions may apply._

Pricing

Single User	$ 29.95 US
Corp 5 Pack	$ 89.00 US
Corp10 Pack	$189.00 US
Corp25 Pack	$297.50 US

Special Template Offers from KMT Software

KMT Software, is a world leader in the developer of "application content" or templates for the leading software programs including Microsoft Office, Lotus SmartSuite, and Corel Office. The twenty templates included with this book are a mere sample of the hundreds of templates you can purchase in our value-packed collections. We have assembled some very specially priced collections for Macmillan book readers

Office In Color – Platinum Template Collection

The Office In Color - Platinum Template Collection contains over 650 templates for Microsoft Excel, Microsoft Word and Microsoft PowerPoint. The Office In Color Platinum Collection combines three popular collections of Office templates (Word Gold Collection, Excel Gold Collection and PowerPoint Gold Collection) into an economical collection of productivity tools. With Office in Color, you can produce persuasive, business and personal documents that look as if they were professionally designed and printed. Good looking, intelligently designed documents get results. They improve professionally productivity, foster efficiency, bolster your company's image and in the end even help to win new clients. Yet, in the real world, how many people have the time it takes to create these documents? Fortunately, with Office in Color, there is a better way.

- The Excel categories include: **Company Finance, Sales and Marketing, Personal Finance, Business Forms, Personal Planning & Real Estate. Over 180 templates**
- The Word Template categories include: **Basic Business Forms, Stationery Sets, Meeting Materials, Reports, Awards and Certificates, Fax Cover Sheets, Resume and Job Builder Templates, & Marketing Materials.. Over 350 templates**
- Over 100 **PowerPoint** templates especially designed for color printing are also included.

This platinum collection is available for just $49.95 to Macmillan book readers users, a considerable savings over the individual purchase price of these three template collections. The regular list price of the platinum collection is $99.95.

Winning Business Plans In Color

Turn your copy of Microsoft Office into a complete Business Planning System. Winning Business Plans In Color is a comprehensive product designed for Microsoft Office that provides a complete approach to developing a successful business plan. If you want to LOOK GREAT and get terrific results for a new business or an established company, act now on this offer. This product has been especially designed for users with color printers, but it will also provide spectacular results for black and white printer owners.

Winning Business Plans In Color guides you every step of the way:
- An integrated Excel workbook that speeds the development of your detailed financial analysis
- An integrated Word document has prompting text and embedded links to the financial workbook
- A PowerPoint presentation template provides a stunning presentation based on your plan
- Winning Business Plans In Color comes with five completed sample plans (Service, Retail, Manufacturing, Mail Order/Wholesaler, Large Company Spin-off)

Winning Business Plans In Color is the most comprehensive business planning product available:
- The Excel workbook contains detailed financial analysis on Profit and Loss, Cash Flow, Market and Sales Forecasting, Break-even analysis, Income Statement, Balance Sheet and Financial ratios
- The Microsoft Word business plan template contains a complete business plan outline with a table of contents and example prompting text for each section of the plan. The Excel financials are linked to the template and color charts and tables are automatically positioned in the document
- The PowerPoint presentation example provides you with a persuasive presentation tool
- A complete on-help system is provided. The product even comes with supplemental files that make your life easier, like a non-disclosure agreement, and financial tools like an Average Selling Price and Sales Seasonality Analyses

Winning Business Plans In Color supports both Office 95 & Office 97.Winning Business Plans In Color, normally priced at $129.95 value, is available to Macmillan readers for just $79.95 Check out the KMT bonus pack for even greater savings!

The Ultimate Financial Calculator

HIRE an MBA!

With the Ultimate Financial Calculator, you will be able to solve the financial problems most commonly encountered on a daily basis. In one integrated Excel workbook, the user can easily select over 40 worksheets from a main menu to solve the following financial calculations:

Determine the value of a bond; determine the annual yield for a bond if held to maturity	Establish book and liquidity values
Quickly determine liquidity and activity ratios	Calculate debt and profitability ratios
Determine the present value of a single amount, a mixed stream of cash flows or annuity	Understand the future value of a single amount or an annuity
Calculate the net present value of an investment with up to 15 years of cash flow;	Compute the annual rate of return needed to meet a financial goal
Determine the real rate of return and the after tax return;	Calculate a monthly lease payment for a car
Determine loan pay-off amount	Assess a consolidation loan to pay off debt

Use the refinancing calculator to see if refinancing makes sense	Compute monthly payments and final payment for balloon mortgage
Amortize a loan; calculate a biweekly mortgage; determine housing affordability	Understand your personal safety debt ratio

The Ultimate Financial Calculator is $59.95 and is available for both Excel 95 and Excel 97. As a Macmillan reader the product is available for $49.95. Check out the KMT bonus pack for even greater savings!.

Personal Financial Primer

Use the power of Microsoft Excel to better maximize your personal financial goals. The Personal Financial Primer guides you each step of the way. Select a topic like Personal Net Worth, Retirement Planning, 401 K Planning, or College Savings, and the Primer defines each topic for you clearly -- you just enter the data in the predefined area. The Personal Financial Primer prepares summary worksheets based on your data entry and charts your financial progress. With the primer, you will be able to plan your financial future by better understanding the following:

- Personal Data and Goals
- Personal Financial Statements
- Cash Flow Plan

- Retirement Plan
- 401 K Analysis
- Invested Asset Allocation

- Life Insurance Needs
- Disability Insurance Needs
- College Funding Needs

Valued at $39.95 . . . . . Special Price for Macmillan readers $29.95. Check out the KMT bonus pack for even greater savings!

Special Order Form for Additional KMT Products

To order additional KMT products directly from KMT Software, Inc., print out this form, fill it in and:

Fax it to 978-287-0132
Mail it to KMT Software, Inc., 71 Lee Dr., Concord, MA 01742.
E-mail to sales@kmt.com
To order by phone call 1-800-KMT-CALC (568-2252) (Orders only). International call 1-978-287-4125

Name _____

Address _____

City, State, Zip _____

Telephone _____

Email _____

Office 97 ☐   Office 2000 ☐   Other _____
Credit Card ☐   Visa ☐   MasterCard ☐   Check Enclosed ☐
Credit Card # _____   Expiration Date _____

Product Name and Description	Regular List	Book Special	Quantity	Total
Special Office in Color Template Collections				
Office in Color Platinum Edition (Over 650 templates)	$99.95	$49.95		
Task Based Applications				
Winning Business Plans in Color	$129.95	$79.95		
Ultimate Financial Calculator	$59.95	$49.95		
Personal Financial Primer	$39.95	$29.95		
KMT Bonus Pack: special price on the 3 above products	$229.95	$99.95		
Microsoft Excel 97 Template Master Toolkit (call for info)	$149.95	$129.95		

Mail in Your Order: **KMT Software, Inc.**

71 Lee Drive,

Concord, MA 01742

Fax in Your Order: 978-287-0132

Call in Your Order: **800-568-2252.**
978-371-2052, Outside USA

KMT on the Web: http://www.kmt.com

Subtotal . . . .

5% Sales tax (MA only) . . . .

Add an additional $5.00 for FedEx shipping

Shipping ($12 outside USA) . . . . | $7.00

TOTAL in $US . . . .

Unconditional Money back guarantee

Don't forget to ask about how our expert consulting on Microsoft Office can help your organization!

SOFTWARE END USER LICENSE AGREEMENT AND DISCLAIMER

PRODUCT NAME: dbQuickPage   **VERSION NO:** 1.1.8

TERMINOLOGY. Term USER identifies any individual person, commercial institution, non-commercial institution and any other group or organization, or an individual person acting on behalf of a single entity installing and/or using a copy of this software product (THE SOFTWARE) on a computer system accessed by the USER. THE SOFT-WARE is identified by all binary and non-binary computer files, and may include associated media, printed materials, and "online" or electronic documentation.

NOTICE TO USERS: CAREFULLY READ THE FOLLOWING LEGAL AGREEMENT. THE USE OF THIS SOFT-WARE IS CONDITIONED UPON COMPLIANCE BY USERS WITH THE TERMS OF THIS AGREEMENT. BY IN-STALLING, COPYING, OR OTHERWISE USING THE SOFTWARE YOU ARE AGREEING TO BE BOUND BY THE TERMS OF THIS EULA. IF YOU DO NOT WISH TO BE BOUND BY THE TERMS OF THIS AGREEMENT OR DO NOT AGREE WITH THE TERMS OF THIS EULA, DO NOT INSTALL OR USE THE SOFTWARE PRODUCT.

THE SOFTWARE MAY BE EVALUATED FOR A PERIOD OF FORTY-FIVE (45) DAYS ON A ROYALTY FREE BASIS. AFTER EXPIRATION OF THE EVALUATION PERIOD THE USER IS OBLIGED TO PURCHASE THEIR COPY OF THE SOFTWARE OR REMOVE EVALUATION COPY FROM THE USER'S COMPUTER SYSTEM.

COPYRIGHT. THE SOFTWARE is protected by United States copyright laws and international treaty provisions. User acknowledges that no title to the intellectual property of the SOFTWARE is transferred to User. User further acknowledges that full ownership rights to THE SOFTWARE will remain the exclusive property of TRACSCAN, and the USER will not acquire any rights to THE SOFTWARE except as expressly set forth in this license. User agrees that any copies of THE SOFTWARE made by USER will contain the same proprietary notices, which appear on and in THE SOFTWARE.

REVERSE ENGINEERING. USER agrees that he or she will not attempt, and will use its best efforts to prevent its employees from attempting to reverse compile, modify, translate or disassemble this SOFTWARE in whole or in part.

LIMITED WARRANTY. It is hereby warranted that this software will perform substantially in accordance with the accompanying documentation for a period of ninety (90) days from the date payment is received.

NO OTHER WARRANTIES. TRACSCAN does not warrant that THE SOFTWARE is error free, except for the expressed limited warranty above. TRACSCAN disclaims all other warranties with respect to this SOFTWARE, either expressed or implied, including but not limited to implied warranties of merchantability, fitness for a particular purpose and noninfridgement of third party rights.

NO LIABILITY FOR CONSEQUENTIAL DAMAGES. In no event shall TRACSCAN or its third party distribu-tors and/or suppliers be liable for any special, consequential, incidental, or indirect damages of any kind arising out of the delivery, performance or use of this SOFTWARE, even if TRACSCAN has been advised of the possibility of such damages. In no event will TRACSCAN's liability for any claim, whether in contract, tort or any other theory of liability exceed the license fee paid by the user.

GOVERNING LAW. This Agreement will be governed by the laws of the State of New Jersey as they are applied to agreements to be entered into and to be performed entirely within New Jersey. The United Nations Convention on Contracts for the International Sale of Goods is specifically disclaimed.

Office Productivity Pack License Agreement

This package contains one CD-ROM that includes software described in this book. See Appendix D for a description of these programs and instructions for their use.

By opening this package you are agreeing to be bound by the following: